DATE DUE

13|10			
io|3|11			
04|08|11			

Cognitive Behaviour Therapy for Acute Inpatient Mental Health Units

Cognitive Behaviour Therapy for Acute Inpatient Mental Health Units presents innovative ways of delivering CBT within the inpatient setting and applying CBT principles to inform and enhance inpatient care.

Maintaining staff morale and creating a culture of therapy in the acute inpatient unit is essential for a well-functioning institution. This book shows how this challenge can be addressed, along with introducing and evaluating an important advance in the practice of individual CBT for working with crisis, suited to inpatient work and crisis teams.

The book covers a brief cross-diagnosis adaptation of CBT, employing arousal management and mindfulness, developed and evaluated by the editors. It features ways of supporting and developing the therapeutic role of inpatient staff through consultation and reflective practice. Chapters focus on topics such as:

- providing staff training
- working within psychiatric intensive care
- innovative psychological group work

Cognitive Behaviour Therapy for Acute Inpatient Mental Health Units will be essential reading for those trained, or those undergoing training, in CBT as well as being of interest to a wider public of nurses, health care support workers, occupational therapists, medical staff and managers.

Isabel Clarke and **Hannah Wilson** are working together to develop an innovative psychological therapies service at Woodhaven, an acute mental health inpatient unit, serving West Southampton and the New Forest. They are both clinical psychologists working for the Hampshire Partnership NHS Trust.

Cognitive Behaviour Therapy for Acute Inpatient Mental Health Units

Working with Clients, Staff and the Milieu

Edited by Isabel Clarke &
Hannah Wilson

Routledge
Taylor & Francis Group

LONDON AND NEW YORK

First published 2009 by Routledge
27 Church Road, Hove, East Sussex BN3 2FA

Simultaneously published in the USA and Canada
by Routledge
270 Madison Avenue, New York, NY10016

Routledge is an imprint of the Taylor & Francis Group, an Informa business

Typeset in Times by Garfield Morgan, Swansea, West Glamorgan
Printed and bound in Great Britain by TJ International Ltd, Padstow, Cornwall
Paperback cover design by Sandra Heath

This publication has been produced with paper manufactured to strict
environmental standards and with pulp derived from sustainable forests.

British Library Cataloguing in Publication Data
A catalogue record for this book is available from the British Library

Library of Congress Cataloging-in-Publication Data
Cognitive behaviour therapy for acute inpatient mental health units : working
with clients, staff, and the milieu / edited by Isabel Clarke & Hannah Wilson.
    p. ; cm.
  Includes bibliographical references.
  ISBN 978-0-415-42211-6 (hardback) – ISBN 978-0-415-42212-3 (pbk.) 1.
Cognitive therapy. 2. Psychiatric hospital patients. I. Clarke, Isabel. II.
Wilson, Hannah, 1971–
  [DNLM: 1. Cognitive Therapy–methods. 2. Crisis Intervention–methods.
3. Hospitals, Psychiatric. 4. Psychiatric Department, Hospital. 5.
Psychotherapy, Group–methods. WM 425.5.C6 C67662 2008]
  RC489.C63C6428 2008
  616.89'1425–dc22

                                                           2007052007

ISBN 978-0-415-42211-6 (hbk)
ISBN 978-0-415-42212-3 (pbk)

Contents

Figures

Tables

Contributors

Isabel Clarke is a consultant clinical psychologist, currently working for the Hampshire Partnership NHS Trust as lead for Psychological Services at Woodhaven, an acute psychiatric inpatient unit, serving West Southampton and the New Forest. She has previously worked for 12 years in psychiatric rehabilitation and outpatient psychological services in Southampton, where she developed an Interacting Cognitive Subsystems (ICS) based approach to severe mental health problems (Clarke 1999), and to psychosis (Clarke 2002a). She has wider interests in understanding the relationship between psychosis and spirituality; she edited a book on the subject (Clarke 2001), and organized two conferences on this theme, both held in or near Winchester, in 2000 and 2001. Details of her publications in this and other areas can be found on her website: www.scispirit. com/Psychology/.

Dr Vivia Cowdrill, is a consultant clinical psychologist working in the inpatient service at the Department of Psychiatry, Royal South Hants Hospital, Southampton. She is an accredited cognitive behaviour therapist and has obtained further specialist training in dialectical behaviour therapy. She is a tutor and supervisor on the diploma course in CBT at the University of Southampton. Her clinical and research interests are in post-traumatic effects of childhood abuse, dissociation, and personality disorders, particularly borderline personality disorder. She is currently interested in working with mental health staff to change negative attitudes of working with people with personality disorders.

Dr Laura Dannahy is a clinical psychologist working at the Department of Psychiatry, Royal South Hants Hospital. She has a half-time post working on the inpatient wards, and a half-time post working within the rehabilitation service. Her main areas of clinical interest and research include adapting traditional therapeutic approaches to inpatient settings (including CBT and dialectical behaviour therapy, DBT approaches), and facilitation of reflective practice groups across staff teams.

Caroline Durrant is a psychology graduate, currently working as an assistant psychologist, and about to become a clinical psychology trainee on the Southampton University doctoral course in clinical psychology. From October 2004 until March 2005, she worked as an assistant psychologist with Isabel Clarke and Hannah Wilson where she designed and set up an audit project assessing outcomes for brief psychological interventions in the hospital and was the first author in the publication of the results.

Bernadette Freemantle is a staff nurse, currently working on the acute ward at Woodhaven Mental Health Unit. She has training in DBT, and is part of the Woodhaven DBT Consult Group. She previously worked on the psychiatric intensive care ward at Woodhaven.

Dr Chris Hall is a chartered clinical psychologist with the South West London & St George's Mental Health NHS Trust. He works within a community mental health team and as part of this role, he provides input to an acute inpatient ward (christopher.hall@swlstg-tr.nhs.uk).

Dr John Hanna is a consultant clinical psychologist who heads the Acute Inpatient Clinical Psychology Service at the Highgate Mental Health Centre in Islington, north London. He has worked in the National Health Service since qualifying, having trained in the United States at the University of Pennsylvania (Philadelphia, Pennsylvania) and the Wright Institute (Berkeley, California). Dr Hanna is co-chair of the Inpatient Psychological Practitioner Network and serves on the national committee of the Psychosis and Complex Mental Health Faculty within the Division of Clinical Psychology, British Psychological Society.

Graham Hill is a trainee mental health practitioner currently working on the psychiatric intensive care ward at Woodhaven. He completed a Combined Honours Degree in Psychology with Applied Biology at University East London in 2003 and just finished a postgraduate Diploma in Mental Health Studies at the University of Southampton (2007). He has training in DBT, and is part of the Woodhaven DBT Consult Group.

Dr Fiona Kennedy was, before her recent retirement, professional adviser for psychology services on the Isle of Wight with 23 years experience of working in the NHS. Her present clinical work is carried out in the inpatient wards and PICU of the general hospital and in learning disability services. She uses CBT, DBT and systems approaches. She is particularly interested in complex post-traumatic reactions and their influence on psychopathology and has developed and researched a new CBT model of dissociative reactions. She has published widely in these areas. She is interested in empowering other professions and clients themselves to become proficient users of psychological knowledge and interventions.

Professor Peter Kinderman is professor of clinical psychology at the University of Liverpool, and has an honorary appointment as consultant clinical psychologist with Merseycare NHS Trust. His research activity and clinical work concentrate on serious and enduring mental disorders such as schizophrenia, bipolar disorder and personality disorder. He has trained and supervises the research activity and clinical work of psychologists, psychiatrists and other professionals. He is the author of numerous scientific journal articles and contributions to edited works, has presented to national and international conferences and scientific meetings, and has been awarded (with colleagues) research grants from the Medical Research Council, the Wellcome Trust, the NHS Forensic Mental Health Research and Development Programme, the European Commission, and others. He chairs the British Psychological Society Standing Committee for Psychologists in Health and Social Care, and sits on the Mental Health Task Force.

Dr John McGowan completed a PhD at the University of Wales, Cardiff looking at attention and failures in skilled activity. Following this he spent two years at Sussex University researching the effects of hormone replacement therapy on cognitive performance. He qualified as a clinical psychologist on the South East Thames course in 2000 and has subsequently worked in acute psychiatric units in Kent and Sussex. His recent publications include investigations of outcome factors in CBT for psychosis.

Marie is a service user with experience of inpatient services and receiving CBT and DBT who agreed to share her story for the information of professionals working in this field.

Dr Anthony Morrison is reader in clinical psychology at the University of Manchester and a consultant clinical psychologist. He is well known as an authority on CBT for psychosis, having published widely both research results and books, and is involved in developing innovative services for psychosis.

Amanda Rendle is a specialist occupational therapist working in adult mental health services. She graduated from Brunel University in 2004 and completed her DBT training in 2006. She worked at Woodhaven inpatient unit for three years and is currently employed by Cygnet Hospital Kewstoke, a 57-bedded low secure psychiatric facility, near Bristol.

Dr Ché Rosebert is a chartered clinical psychologist with South West London & St. George's Mental Health NHS Trust. Her role is to coordinate psychology services for the adult inpatients of two of the five London boroughs that the Trust serves. This work includes providing clinical interventions to five acute wards and one psychiatric intensive care unit (che.rosebert@swlstg-tr.nhs.uk).

Dr Suzanne Sambrook is a consultant clinical psychologist who is taking up a post as lead clinician in a new low secure unit, having spent a number of years as lead for personality disorders and with the psychiatric intensive care unit at the Department of Psychiatry of the Royal South Hants Hospital, Southampton. She has also spent a year as lead for psychological input to the acute wards at the Royal South Hants. She has published an evaluation of her work introducing DBT to that hospital.

Abigail Tolland is currently a trainee clinical psychologist on the Southampton University Doctoral Program for Clinical Psychology. She worked as an honorary assistant with Isabel Clarke and Hannah Wilson where she helped set up an audit project assessing outcomes for brief psychological interventions in the hospital.

Dr Hannah Wilson is a chartered clinical psychologist, currently working for Hampshire Partnership NHS Trust Psychological Services at Woodhaven, an acute psychiatric inpatient unit, serving West Southampton and the New Forest. In this role, she leads the inpatient DBT team. She has a particular interest in mindfulness approaches to mental health. She has previously worked for two years in a child and adolescent community mental health team and completed a PhD in social identity development.

Foreword

Anthony Morrison

In recent years, cognitive behaviour therapy has made significant advances in our ability to both understand and intervene with many different types of mental health problems, in many different settings. As a result, service users and their carers have experienced improvements in their quality of life and reduced distress and disability, and have been able to look forward to brighter futures with hope that not only have their difficulties alleviated, but that these gains may be maintained in the longer term too, by the ongoing application of skills that have been developed throughout therapy. This collaborative, enabling approach that relies upon the scientific method and uses guided discovery to help people reach their own conclusions about what has caused and maintained their problems, and translates this into change strategies to help achieve valued goals, should be ideally suited to helping people in acute distress and present on psychiatric wards.

However, there are clearly many barriers to the effective implementation of cognitive behavioural approaches in such a setting and with such a population of service users. The culture clash between an optimistic and normalizing cognitive behavioural conceptualization of mental distress and the prevalent medical model, which is often experienced as pessimistic and stigmatizing, is probably most evident on an acute psychiatric ward. The flawed assumption that the physical model of health care, where what is required is a combination of beds, physical interventions, doctors and nurses, is equally applicable to mental health is at its most obvious in psychiatric hospital settings. Service user accounts, including those present in this book, regularly demonstrate the assumption that hospital wards are seen as places in which people have to wait until the physical interventions provided (usually medication, sometimes ECT) begin to take effect. Attempts to access evidence-based psychosocial interventions are usually prevented, either by a lack of provision within such settings, or by active blocking by mental health professionals who believe that such approaches will be ineffective at best or dangerous or counterproductive at worst. While the evidence base for providing CBT within such settings is limited, and much more research is required, there is certainly enough to suggest that it may speed up recovery and is usually welcomed as an acceptable and desirable treatment option.

On a personal note, I have a very vivid memory from about ten years ago of requesting that a young man with psychosis, who had been an inpatient on an acute psychiatric ward for at least six months, be referred to me to see if CBT might be of help. Once everyone in the room stopped laughing (the young man had already left the room following an angry outburst on hearing that his medication was being increased again), the consultant psychiatrist suggested that they try clozapine first, and then see how things were, forbidding me from seeing the person. Thankfully, ward rounds and attitudes appear to be changing (albeit rather too slowly), and there is now an evidence base to suggest that CBT for psychosis has roughly equivalent effect sizes to clozapine for 'treatment-resistant schizophrenia', and that providing CBT to people in acute phases of psychosis whilst in hospital is achievable, acceptable and speeds up recovery. However, there is clearly a long way to go before such treatments are routinely offered to people in such settings.

Therefore, the authors of this book are to be thanked for providing examples of how to deliver cognitive behavioural therapies within psychiatric hospital environments. This offers hope that the culture clash can be reconciled, and that we can provide an optimistic and normalizing alternative to traditional inpatient care. This book provides many practical suggestions along with a theoretical justification for how CBT can be implemented with this deserving population. It highlights the opportunities that are afforded by an inpatient admission, and describes how formulation-driven care can be utilized to improve outcomes and help service users achieve their goals, both directly, using groups and individual CBT, as well as indirectly by working with ward staff and changing attitudes. This book will be an invaluable tool for mental health professionals working in inpatient settings, and will hopefully inspire people to increase access to such approaches and conduct the research required to firmly establish the evidence base. A combination of increased evidence, increased pressure from users, carers and commissioners, and developments such as advance directives or statements and direct payments will hopefully provide the impetus for widespread availability of CBT as a treatment option for people in psychiatric hospitals. This book helps to provide the answers as to how we can do this in practice.

Anthony Morrison

Preface

This book is written both for and by those people who find themselves in acute mental health inpatient units in the UK, whether as members of staff, of different professions, or as service users. The aim of the book is to show how therapy can be used in this setting, in practical ways, to promote recovery for service users and to improve the overall atmosphere and experience for both staff and service users. The case examples are therefore a crucial part of the book. Wherever possible, the person whose case is presented has given explicit permission for this. They have chosen whether they wish their own first name, or a pseudonym, to be used. Where this was not possible, names and details have been changed to protect anonymity.

Abbreviations

ACT	Acceptance and Commitment Therapy
AIMS	Accreditation for Acute Inpatient Mental Health Services
APA	American Psychiatric Association
BABCP	British Association of Behavioural and Cognitive Psychotherapists
BPD	Borderline Personality Disorder
BPRS	Brief Psychiatric Rating Scale
BPS	British Psychological Society
CAT	Cognitive Analytic Therapy
CBT	Cognitive Behaviour Therapy
CMHT	Community Mental Health Team
CMT	Compassionate Mind Training
CORE	Clinical Outcomes in Routine Evaluation
CPA	Care Programme Approach
CPD	Continuous Professional Development
CPN	Community Psychiatric Nurse
CSIP	Care Services Improvement Partnership
DBT	Dialectical Behaviour Therapy
DCP	Division of Clinical Psychology
DSM-IV	*Diagnostic and Statistical Manual of Mental Disorders IV*
ECS	Emotional Coping Skills
ECT	Electro Convulsive Therapy
EMDR	Eye Movement Desensitization Reprogramming
GMC	General Medical Council
GP	General Practitioner
HCC	Healthcare Commission
HONOS	Health of the Nation Outcome Scales
IAPT	Improving Access to Psychological Therapies
ICD-10	*International Classification of Mental and Behavioral Disorders – 10*
ICS	Interacting Cognitive Subsystems
IPPN	Inpatient Psychological Practitioner Network

IT	Information Technology
LCB	Locus of Control of Behaviour
LSE	Low Self-Esteem
LWE	Living with Emotions
MAS	Manpower Advisory Service
MDT	Multidisciplinary Team
MHCS	Mental Health Confidence Scale
MHPIG	Mental Health Policy Implementation Guide
NAPICU	National Association of Psychiatric Intensive Care Units
NHS	National Health Service
NICE	National Institute for Clinical Excellence
NIMHE	National Institute for Mental Health, England
NSF	National Service Framework
OT	Occupational Therapy
OU	Open University
PICU	Psychiatric Intensive Care Unit
PRN	Prescription Required as Needed
PTSD	Post Traumatic Stress Disorder
RCT	Randomized Control Trial
RMO	Responsible Medical Officer
RP	Reflective Practice
SMART	Specific, Measurable, Achievable, Realistic and Time-limited
SEMI	Severe and Enduring Mental Illness
WHO	World Health Organization

Chapter 1

Introduction

Isabel Clarke

The case for optimism

Therapy, and indeed any service provision, is about offering hope. There is a problem; but something can be done about it. Hope is one of those powerful but hard to pin down non-specific factors that so complicate the search for the 'active ingredients' in the evaluation of particular therapies. Hope is first on the list of factors promoting recovery that came out of the studies of Ohio and Maine service users that have been the foundation of the Recovery movement in mental health (Ralph *et al.* 1996, quoted in Allot *et al.* 2002).

This book is about hope for the role of psychological therapy in general, and cognitive behaviour therapy (CBT) in particular, in the acute mental health inpatient unit. It is about challenges and difficulties, but with the emphasis on how these can be overcome; how creative innovation, and sound multidisciplinary co-operation can meet the challenges. The greatest challenge to the provision of psychological therapy in the inpatient environment is the sense that it cannot be done, or that it is somehow not worth it. Marie, who has experienced the services first hand over many years, explains eloquently in Chapter 4 why it is worth it and why it must be done. Other chapters in the book look at the way in which the culture of service provision is changing to make putting psychological therapy at the heart of inpatient provision possible and achievable (Chapter 2, John Hanna, and Chapter 3, Peter Kinderman). The rest of the book essentially demonstrates how this can be done, whether through direct provision of therapy, or working through and developing the therapeutic skills of the staff group.

A clash of cultures

The encounter between cognitive behaviour therapy and the acute inpatient unit inevitably entails a clash of cultures. Therapy is about introducing order into the chaos of human emotions and human relationships. All therapies stress orderly induction into therapy and progress through it.

Providing space for cool reflection is of the essence. CBT adds to this the discipline imposed by science. Predictable conditions are a prerequisite for repeatability. The acute psychiatric hospital by contrast must contain crisis and unpredictability. There is no filtering of admissions by diagnostic group or anticipated length of intervention. The service is needs led, and at the sharp end of need.

Then there is the matter of fundamental philosophy. The inpatient unit is the last bastion of the medical model in its pure form. Community teams, rehabilitation units and forensic services might offer multidisciplinary services with a plethora of therapeutic approaches, but the hospital has traditionally been seen as somewhere for the person at risk and in acute crisis to receive medication, be stabilized, and return to the care of the community services.

Why CBT?

Why then should the CBT therapist wish to venture into this potentially unpromising and even hostile territory? There are several reasons. The first is to do with the people the hospital serves. Mental breakdown is not such an uncommon event in people's lives. The lifetime prevalence of admission is high. Few people will not know someone who has been admitted to a psychiatric hospital. As human beings, all these people will have a need to make sense of an experience which has probably seen the planned course of their life come to a shuddering halt. Indeed, surveys of patient opinion about mental health services in general and hospital services in particular regularly and loudly make the plea for more talking therapies.

This is true of many but not all hospital admissions. For others, they have accepted the explanation of their problems offered and are content with it. They have an illness with an impressive sounding name, and the medication (or electro convulsive therapy, ECT) offered by the doctor will cure it. This can work well for the first few admissions, but for repeat users of the service, this conceptualization can be a barrier to adaptation, and the CBT therapist has a role in persuading the, possibly reluctant, individual that they have a vital role to play in the process. There is a parallel here with the Recovery notion of 'The Turning Point' (see Allott et al. 2002; Repper and Perkins 2003) which will be covered in Chapter 6.

These reasons for CBT in the inpatient setting focus on the needs of the individual. What about the needs of the institution itself? If hospital admission represents a crisis in someone's life that requires reflection and reappraisal, it could also be argued that the institution itself is in crisis, and could similarly use reflection and reappraisal. This is not a new idea. Bob Hinshelwood (Hinshelwood and Chiesa 2001) argued that institutions, left to themselves, operated in an anti-therapeutic way as a defence against anxiety, and he was influential in the therapeutic community movement as a result. Considerable though the achievements of this movement have been, it has not made a major impact on the average inpatient hospital. This book will argue that the CBT therapist is in perhaps the best position to make that impact.

The acute inpatient problem

The account that follows describes UK health services as that is the location of the contributors to this volume, but it is likely that there will be parallels with the situation in other countries. Acute psychiatric inpatient units in Britain have not been receiving a good press. The 1998 Sainsbury Centre report (SCMH 1998), and the Department of Health sponsored document that followed it (DH 2002b), spell out the familiar criticisms, of lack of privacy and dignity, lack of safety, and lack of therapeutic input. Service user forums such as Asylum and Mind reiterate these complaints, and demonstrate time and again that people in crisis want someone to talk to: someone to take their predicament seriously and help them to make sense of it. There are, of course, exceptions and developing good practice. The various chapters of this book illustrate this, and John Hanna's Chapter 2 outlines the initiatives to raise standards. Unsurprisingly, staff morale in the acute inpatient sector mirrors user dissatisfaction, as evidenced by the crisis in nurse recruitment. The exceptions, and developing good practice, cannot alter the high probability that someone accessing such a service at a time of personal crisis, at an arbitrary location in Britain, will find it a less than truly therapeutic experience.

There is a context to this depressing picture. More widely, mental health services have seen dramatic development over the last ten years. First came the establishment of community mental health teams; then the assertive outreach teams were set up, and most recently, crisis resolution and home treatment teams. At the same time, much thought has been put into secure services, with the development of new medium and low secure units. Apart from the addition of psychiatric intensive care units (PICUs), all these developments have tended to impact negatively on the traditional acute psychiatric inpatient unit by concentrating within its walls those whom nobody can manage outside, and by poaching some of the more adventurous staff.

However, most people who experience acute breakdown, or ongoing major psychiatric problems, tend to end up in hospital at some time or another, and many are repeat users of this service. The 2004 Mind survey estimated 37,996 people at one time in this position. Their experience and the support they receive at this time can be crucial in terms of the impact that their breakdown has on the course of their life, and unfortunately there is much evidence to suggest that this impact can be negative. Trends in the wider society have not helped, with increased alcohol and drug use leading to disinhibited behaviour, and the prevalence of family and relationship breakdown eroding natural social supports for those who are struggling.

The development of CBT approaches to severe mental health problems

Over the same period, cognitive behaviour therapy has seen dramatic spread and development. The approach allies itself naturally with a scientific, experimental stance, and has benefited from a strong research base. The therapy has therefore been perfectly placed to take advantage of the move towards evidence-based practice in the UK. The National Institute for Clinical Excellence (NICE) guidelines recognize CBT as a treatment of choice for a wide variety of conditions, ranging from depression, through post traumatic stress disorder (PTSD) to schizophrenia. Community mental health teams and the newer teams listed above routinely employ CBT therapists, or clinical psychologists with a CBT background. It is becoming accepted that this therapy should be available to clients of these services, and that the staff team should have access to the specialized assessment and formulation skills offered by the clinical psychologist.

At the same time as CBT was becoming more widespread, major developments have taken place over the last 15 or so years to develop the approach for application to more serious disorders, such as personality disorders and psychosis. Partly this has been achieved by elaborating the model, as with the development of schema focused cognitive therapy (Young 1994) and partly by looking beyond CBT, and adopting or partially adopting approaches from humanistic and psychodynamic therapies, such as emphasis on the therapeutic relationship, transference and counter-transference, and a recognition of the importance of past history to present pathology. Recent developments have seen a more dramatic departure in the model, characterized by one of its exponents (Steve Hayes) as 'Third Wave CBT'. The first wave was traditional Beck and Ellis, and the second, the schema-focused approach.

In the third wave paradigm the route to change lies not so much in altering thought to alter feeling, but in altering the person's relationship to both thought and feeling. Mindfulness is the key means, common to these therapies, to effect this. Prominent examples of these new therapeutic approaches are: mindfulness-based cognitive therapy for preventing relapse in depression (Segal et al. 2000); Linehan's (1993a, 1993b) dialectical behaviour therapy (DBT) for borderline personality disorder, with a particular emphasis on the control of self-harm; and Steve Hayes' acceptance and commitment therapy (Hayes et al. 1999). Paul Chadwick and others have developed and researched mindfulness groups for voice hearers (Chadwick et al. 2005), so applying it to psychosis. Other applications continue to be tried out, researched and published all the time.

As well as introducing the emphasis on mindfulness, the third wave approaches also soften the boundaries between CBT and other therapeutic approaches. In a similar spirit, while primarily focused on CBT, this book does not leave out of consideration other modalities that have much to offer in this field. Specifically, systemic thinking has contributed greatly to our understanding of institutions and team working, and a number of contributors reference this contribution. Cognitive analytic therapy (CAT) ways of using the reciprocal role to understand the transferability of patterns of relating, when working with staff teams in formulating individuals who represent a challenge to the team (Ryle 1995, 1997), fit well with the CBT model. John McGowan in Chapter 9, for instance, includes CAT in his examples of practice.

Innovation in CBT and inpatient services

From this account it would appear that the groundwork is laid for a CBT-led therapeutic revolution in inpatient services. Effective approaches are being developed and researched for the major diagnostic groups represented in the inpatient population: severe recurrent depression; psychosis; self-harm and personality disorder. However, this development is not necessarily taking place. DBT is being widely applied in inpatient settings, but for the most part these are specialist units for people in need of secure accommodation, or for specific problems such as eating disorders. The Thorn initiative which trains nurses in psychosocial, family and some CBT for psychosis has had as much or more impact on community services as in the acute hospital.

There are reasons for this, and they are to be found in the particular challenges faced by the therapist working in the general acute inpatient setting. These challenges are examined below, and creative ways of meeting them form the main subject matter of the book. However, on a more optimistic note, change is in the air. CBT therapist and clinical psychologist posts are being created specifically for inpatient units. In the part of the UK with which I am familiar, Hampshire, this has been a rapid development taking place over the last two or three years. The Workforce Development Consortium has identified acute hospitals as an area for the expansion of clinical psychology services. Thorn-trained nurses are having their impact in the sector, and the development of the new post of trainee mental health practitioner, specifically in order to marry the number of psychology and social science graduates wanting to work therapeutically in the health sector with the unmet demand for more therapy from service users, is having its effect. Peter Kinderman covers these developments in Chapter 3.

Even in the area of management of aggression and risk, where hard-line attitudes have traditionally prevailed, the latest message from government advisors is in line with the approach that CBT has to offer. The NICE guidelines (2005c) on the management of risk and aggression state:

> The primary focus when dealing with aggressive behaviour should be that of recognition, prevention and de-escalation in a culture that seeks to minimize the risk of its occurrence through effective systems of organizational, environmental and clinical risk assessment and management. This approach should also promote therapeutic engagement, collaboration with service users and the use of advanced directives.

The same guidelines identify the issues that influence the development of violent incidents as 'lack of opportunity to participate in therapy' and 'poor staff attitudes'. Suzanne Sambrook says more about this in Chapter 11.

So the need for a CBT-based philosophy throughout the operation of the institution has been recognized, but institutions are notoriously resistant to change. One or two individuals with extra training in the middle of a team working with a different ethos and a different model cannot be expected to make an automatic impact. All too often, what results is rapid disillusionment and demoralization as specialist skills are not utilized, possibly devalued, and they are expected to fulfil the same role as the rest of the team. Changing the culture so that it is supportive of therapeutic approaches and providing the necessary supervision and development opportunities for practitioners with some CBT skills is another element to the challenge for CBT in the acute hospital.

Facing the challenge

The challenge referred to by the section title can be broken down into: the challenge for individual therapy work; the challenge for effective evaluation of this work, and the wider challenge of having a real impact on the culture of the unit, and on the morale of the multidisciplinary staff group in general. Understanding the nature of these difficulties goes a long way to explaining why CBT, with its runaway success in other areas, has so far failed to have a comparable impact in this sector. This understanding is also the first step to pointing the way towards effective CBT service delivery for inpatients, and arising out of that a more therapeutically oriented acute hospital. It is the aim of this book to assist in laying the foundations for these developments.

The acute hospital setting undermines the attempt to deliver traditional CBT therapy in a number of ways. There is the unpredictability of length of stay, which can be very short. People characteristically arrive at the hospital in a state of crisis, which is in itself a therapeutic challenge, and once the crisis has abated are discharged to make room for the constant pressure of new admissions. There is the complete mixture of diagnostic groups, with frequent uncertainty about diagnosis. Where CBT protocols are linked to particular diagnoses, this presents a problem. The potential for a clash of philosophy where the medical model reigns supreme has already been referred to, as the CBT therapist attempts to formulate the problem from a different angle. This volume will expound new developments of the CBT model, arising naturally from the current 'third wave' climate as outlined above, to meet these challenges, as well as demonstrating how CBT can be introduced acceptably to influence the whole ward culture through the judicious use of reflective practice groups (Chapter 10), training (Chapter 12) and supervision initiatives.

Part I

Setting the scene

Chapter 2

CBT on the wards

Standards and aspirations

John Hanna

Introduction

I have been working with acute inpatients, full or part time, quite regularly since my first clinical training placement. A few years ago I became a consultant clinical psychologist and head of a small service covering five acute wards in north London. I have all along, and especially since obtaining my current post with its full focus on inpatients, argued for greater access to psychological therapies and clinical psychology services for acute inpatient wards, as I believe that inpatients are, undeservingly, among those service users least likely to receive psychological interventions. The overall treatment options for acute mental health inpatients in the UK today are regularly described in pejorative terms by organizations representing service users (cf. Mind and the Sainsbury Centre). I often find myself placed in a position to defend or apologize for the NHS for the lack, in particular, of psychologically therapeutic engagement and the ongoing dominance of a traditional medical model. The 'diagnose-prescribe-administer, then watch-wait-manage-untoward-behaviour until it feels safe to discharge' approach is endemic to wards across the nation, peppered, if one is lucky, with a little occupational therapy and, occasionally, a clinical psychologist on the ward for an afternoon a week. Doctors, nurses and support workers, who by statutory regulations must be present, often do have training in some or other form of psychological therapy or approach, but just as often have no suitable supervision for its delivery, and therefore do not deliver it, or deliver it unsupervised and against best practice guidelines. Without more training, supervision and specialist input, the status quo remains.

What therapeutic intervention is available is not usually cognitive behavioural therapy. Behavioural management plans abound and are a necessary component of ward life, but too often those who develop them neglect to obtain possible collaboration and rarely include any cognitive components; such plans cannot usually be considered to be CBT. Occupational therapists and nurses sometimes lead anxiety management or coping with depression psycho education groups which are based on CBT techniques. Although these groups have great value and represent a promising start to the introduction of CBT, in themselves they lack the individual psychological formulation and plan of intervention to be considered CBT in its fuller sense. Evidence-based family work, again a necessary and highly valuable part of ward life, employs elements of psycho education derived from CBT theory and research, but like psycho education groups cannot be considered 'pure' or gold-standard CBT as defined by the British Association of Behavioural and Cognitive Psychotherapists (BABCP), by the National Institute for Clinical Excellence (NICE) and by other eminent sources. CBT requires formulation, the application of that formulation to a collaborative treatment schedule, an emphasis on changing thought as well as behaviour patterns, goal setting and homework between sessions, and consensus on generally focused problem areas identified, clarified and optimally resolved in a time-limited frame. Sounds simple, in a way – but according to the Sainsbury Centre (2005), less than 20 per cent of ward managers surveyed could report that their ward's inpatients have access to CBT (and let us remember that this statistic counts access to, not universal delivery of, CBT – those who actually get CBT is a fraction of this 20 per cent).

What would it take to provide access to evidence-based, NICE- and Department of Health-ordered, service user-demanded CBT to every inpatient service user who needed it? Is CBT what inpatients need and what inpatient ward staff members need to be trained and supervised to deliver? Will the training up and supervising of multidisciplinary staff, without the ongoing direct clinical input of highly trained and experienced specialists, be enough to ensure good enough delivery of CBT? Will the introduction of CBT help resolve the much-reported service user perspective of not being heard, emotionally cared for, appreciated and respected? Will CBT make the ward a more therapeutic environment? If CBT is the solution, how do we proceed to a desired outcome? I hope to answer these questions in the next few pages.

The case for national standards

As I write in 2007, there exist no mandatory minimum standards for the delivery of CBT to inpatients in the UK. This is not likely to surprise many readers, who will know that inpatients are often the least well-represented service user population, often because they are of course most of the time outpatients, using a variety of community-based services where they might hope to be better represented, or are individuals who do not receive mental health service follow-up for reasons legitimate or otherwise and might be inclined to put any difficult inpatient experience behind them. Individuals are inpatients for as brief a time as possible, when they are most acutely distressed, and then they are no longer inpatients and are getting on with their lives. It is challenging, therefore, to draw together advocates for inpatients. However, a growing number of committed service users around the country, as well as service user representative organizations like Mind and the Sainsbury Centre, remain focused on the wards and their inhabitants, and increasingly psychological therapists drawn together into professional bodies like the Inpatient Psychological Practitioner Network (IPPN) are stepping up to lobby government to set national standards.

Accreditation for Acute Inpatient Mental Health Services (AIMS) has set reasonably rigorous standards for psychological therapies and clinical psychology, with an emphasis on NICE guidance around CBT. The British Psychological Society's Division of Clinical Psychology (BPS, DCP) has recently responded to the Healthcare Commission's (HCC) consultation on acute inpatient care, arguing for basic national standards for psychological therapy, with an emphasis on CBT. So we are making a start. Here is the case as I make it:

The Department of Health National Service Framework (NSF, DH 1999a) states that service development for people with severe and enduring mental illness (SEMI) is first priority. The conclusion I draw from this is that government ought to be providing evidence-based CBT to all inpatients who need it before considering the provision of CBT to other individuals. The NSF further states that core functions are to be provided by multi-professional teams who assess, plan and offer early, effective interventions for those with SEMI. I would argue that these teams be mandated to include qualified cognitive behaviour therapists under supervision capable of providing CBT to inpatients, especially as the NSF also states that service performance will be assessed at a national level by access to psychological therapies. Let us remember that the NSF is the contract between government, professionals, service users, carers and the local community that effective mental health services will be delivered, and as such is arguably the most important document in mental health service delivery.

NICE has recommended the delivery of CBT for individuals diagnosed with schizophrenia (2002), bipolar disorder (2006), depression (2004b), eating disorders (2004c), post traumatic stress disorder (2005a) and self-harm (2004d). These descriptors are dominant in any ward's list of reasons for admission, yet actual delivery is very much behind schedule as compared to other Department of Health-ordered NICE policy implementation projects. NICE has also recommended the delivery of CBT for anxiety (2004a) and for obsessive compulsive disorder (2005b), which are usually not primary reasons for admission, but are often secondary features of an inpatient episode. Another major driver of government policy, the National Institute for Mental Health, England states in *Personality Disorder: No Longer a Diagnosis of Exclusion* (2003a) that individuals diagnosed with personality disorder should be able to access cognitive therapy among a variety of other psychological therapies. As a nation, we expect that the Health Service follows NICE and NIMHE guidance. This guidance needs to be implemented in accordance with NSF, which in my view should place inpatients first in the queue. This can only be achieved through setting fair but rigorous HCC-regulated national standards.

Who should lead on policy implementation?

I will argue throughout this chapter that the only successful implementation of service provision of evidence-based psychological therapies will require the direct involvement of clinical psychologists, or the very near equivalent professionals. Although clinical psychology and CBT do not automatically equate, CBT is an increasingly dominant influence within the profession. Clinical psychologists, at least in working with individuals with severe, enduring and/or complex difficulties, are ordinarily expected to use CBT even if, like myself, they can and do practise integratively. Due to the short episode of care and the need to quickly and effectively alleviate acute distress, I would argue that CBT (individual and group where appropriate) is more often than not the inpatient ward psychologist's prime objective in selecting a course of treatment (although I would not, personally, go without my training in individual psychodynamic, systemic, experiential group and existential approaches, which are useful to me when or if I reach an impasse in providing CBT).

It is hard to find anyone to argue against my stance that a clinical psychologist is an essential component of training and supervising multidisciplinary staff and of care provision, especially in the context of risky and complex presentations, although this may change as CBT training outside of clinical psychology expands to more challenging areas of work. Some counselling psychologists, advanced cognitive behavioural therapists and lead nurses registered as CBT specialists may also be suitable to hold roles perhaps more often held by clinical psychologists, as long as their competencies fit the requirements to train, supervise and directly intervene with the more challenging presentations. All clinical ward staff should, ideally, be included to receive training of CBT as well as ongoing support and supervision to practise CBT to the full extent of their level of competency. All staff must intervene psychologically, and as such provide basic CBT, if we are to meet Department of Health and NICE guidance. Indeed, the recent Chief Nursing Officer's review of mental health nursing (DH 2006a) stated that mental health nurses need to widen their skills to provide more evidence-based psychological therapies.

The BPS, DCP presses for greater access to psychological therapies and clinical psychology for people with severe and complex mental health difficulties, including inpatients, and greater access to training and supervision from colleagues in allied professions. Its publications *Recent Advances in Understanding Mental Illness and Psychotic Experiences* (BPS 2000) and *Clinical Psychology in Services for People with Severe and Enduring Mental*

Illness (BPS 2002) remind us of the skills of clinical psychologists in respect to individual case formulations to assist in the development of multidisciplinary care plans. Psychological formulations sum and integrate the information acquired through the assessment process and are hypotheses about the nature and origin of problems, which are tested out over time. Psychological case formulations are complex and may commonly incorporate several hypotheses, based on a variety of psychological theories, each drawing on scientific research. Kinderman (2005b) argues that psychological formulation can form a basis for an inpatient treatment service, co-ordinated by an experienced clinical psychologist and delivered mainly by assistant psychologists.

According to the Department of Health, clinical psychologists will be required, at least, to train and supervise staff. Ideally they would deliver direct patient care as well, to allow the most challenging presentations to be passed on by multidisciplinary staff to a specialist. The Department of Health has regularly indicated the need for clinical psychologists on wards. Its *Mental Health Policy Implementation Guide: Adult Acute Inpatient Care Provision* (2002b) states that 'clinical psychology input needs to be increased to assist ward staff with the acquisition and practice of the necessary skills and to input into group and individual treatment and care arrangements'. In its *Community Mental Health Teams Mental Health Policy Implementation Guide* (2002a), the Department of Health notes that a CMHT should include a clinical psychologist as part of its multidisciplinary team, and that this psychologist's practice should include input into the relevant acute inpatient ward linked to catchment area and/or service specification. Without regulation of standards based on these orders of government, we are left with a situation where few clinical psychologists are employed for dedicated work on wards or with ward-based staff, and where those attached to CMHTs generally offer only limited and oftentimes no input to their link ward.

Other national documents relate in principle to the provision of CBT for inpatients and the involvement of clinical psychologists in developing service delivery. The Manpower Advisory Service (MAS 1989), many years ago now, argued that all service users should have access to three levels of psychological therapy: (a) basic interventions provided by all service providers; (b) focal interventions provided by trained service providers; (c) complex interventions provided by highly trained service providers. MAS states that clinical psychology is ideally equipped to implement training requirements for multidisciplinary staff. NIMHE (2004a) asserts that workforces must be planned by competencies and led by all professions, and that training is required to adapt psychological interventions, including CBT, to the acute ward context. NIMHE recognizes CBT skills as a key training need for ward staff, further recommending that opportunity to practise such skills once taught is equally important to successful service delivery. Other reports are even more specific in their recommendations. The Sainsbury Centre (2005) asks for a 1:20 full-time clinical psychologist to inpatient ratio by 2010. The BPS, DCP Workforce Planning Advisers (2004) similarly estimate that four full-time psychologists and two full-time assistant or associate psychologists would be required for an 80-bed acute mental health unit (1:20 and 1:40 respectively). Marion Janner from Bright (Bright 2006), in her rather masterful work *Star Wards*, sets what for me is the ultimate national standard in her call for access to psychological therapies for anyone admitted to an inpatient ward who needs it.

Although I mention the demand of service users for CBT last, it is by no means the least reason why we need the regulation of national standards. The Sainsbury Centre for Mental Health (1998, 2001, 2002), the Mental Health Foundation (2006) and Mind (2004) all condemn the practice revealed in accumulating reports they have collected of boredom, disrespectful conduct and lack of therapeutic input to wards. All further call for CBT, as it is proven effective for so many service users, as they call for a change in therapeutic stance, from custodial to collaborative, from observational to engaging and encouraging – all principles of CBT alongside many other psychological therapies. Service users regularly demand parity between the delivery of psychiatric and the delivery of psychological care and, as major stakeholders in mental health service development, their voice must be answered.

Is there a case against CBT on the wards?

My reassuringly quick answer to this question is no, at least not an overpowering one, but let me explain why by presenting my collection of nay-sayers' protests, and my respective replies:

> 'CBT is a bit complicated for ward staff; we need to focus on the shift toward straightforward therapeutic engagement without any intent to take on the task of psychological therapy.'

I think this comment undersells the abilities of ward staff and also overcomplicates the sort of CBT we would sensibly be asking ward staff to undertake. Again, the guidance is there to be implemented.

> 'There is not enough time in a given admission to complete a course of CBT as guided by NICE; six months required for a diagnosis of schizophrenia, more for a diagnosis of bipolar disorder.'

This is true in a strict sense, but work can commence and be handed over, or might be able to continue under certain service provision arrangements (such as a CMHT psychologist working into wards). It is also important to stress that good and basic yet essential CBT work can be done in a few sessions.

> 'The evidence base for NICE was gathered from outpatient studies. Acute inpatients are too unwell to engage effectively in psychological therapies.'

My experience tells me otherwise. Yes, there are a few studies which do indicate that CBT for psychosis is more effective in post-episode rather than acute episode treatment; inpatients are likely to be acute episode. But many post-episode patients remain on the wards for some time. This is the recommended time to engage in CBT – if there is no one providing CBT, this opportunity will be missed.

Regardless of these studies, however, NICE guides us to intervene with CBT for those most at risk of relapse and/or those with the most persistent experience of distress. It is important to consider that ward admissions are usually driven by episodes of not only psychosis but also suicidality, often resultant from depression, personality difficulties and post traumatic stress, all also CBT-worthy presentations. The acuity itself can be addressed using components of CBT such as relaxation, emotional regulation, anger management and de-escalation techniques. CBT is more difficult to provide to inpatients, partly because of acuity, and partly because of the usually compulsory nature of their presence on the wards. CBT principles are always useful in empowering staff to be able to try something, however, and inpatients are keen to engage in this sort of collaborative, problem-solving, pragmatic approach, whether actively in distress or otherwise.

> 'Just sticking CBT into a ward does nothing to reduce other problems, like lack of accommodation for homeless patients, morale problems within ward staff groups, employment discrimination, the list goes on. We should not waste money on CBT when we do not have the basics right.'

I can understand the sentiment here. But I believe that CBT is empowering, in that it can put the individual in charge of employing improved coping strategies initially in their psychological life, then within their broader social context. I would not advocate introducing CBT to the detriment of meeting basic local needs, but as CBT can promote self-efficacy and self-advocacy it will always be desirable. More service users coping better with distress as a result of taking part in CBT will improve the therapeutic milieu of the ward, as will more staff confident that they can introduce a psychological intervention that effectively alleviates distress.

'The evidence base for CBT is stronger with outpatients, and with people presenting with mild to moderate problems; they should get the lion's share of regional funding for CBT – inpatients are less of a priority.'

There is a tension between public health's primary care trust concerns (see Lord Layard's report 2005 on stepped care CBT approaches for primary care services) and specialist mental health care trust concerns (see the NSF). This tension can be healthy or unhealthy. Both ends of the spectrum of distress must of course be addressed. We can stand back and wait, while people suffer in acute and severe distress, while CBT researchers gather evidence for working with inpatients, or we can get stuck in. I vote for the latter.

What is being done to set national standards

The Inpatient Psychological Practitioner Network (IPPN) of the Psychosis and Complex Mental Health Faculty, DCP, has sent me as a standing member on Accreditation for Acute Inpatient Mental Health Services' (AIMS) steering group, now a standards review group, for the past few years. AIMS is a service devised by the Royal College of Psychiatrists in collaboration with the BPS/DCP and the Royal Colleges of Nursing and Occupational Therapists, alongside service user and carer representatives, that reviews member wards and rates them against its own set of standards, partly in preparation for statutory reviews by the HCC. The AIMS steering group initially agreed ambitious psychology standards, but found upon piloting that only eight out of the 15 pilot wards could meet them – seven wards would therefore have had to be deferred on the basis of very limited or no access to psychological therapies or clinical psychologists. We have since, disappointingly, lowered the standards to make it easier for wards to become accredited by AIMS, but a few key standards remain in place. AIMS remains committed to regularly raising these standards, advising participating wards in advance in order to prepare to meet them. The following information is drawn from AIMS' first edition of standards (2006).

If a ward fails to meet any of AIMS' Type 1 standards, its accreditation is automatically deferred. The Type 1 standards related to psychology state that wards must assess forms of psychological risk and must ensure that psychological assessment is a partial basis for care plans. Ward staff must undertake invitations to one-to-one sessions for all inpatients each waking shift and ensure that the delivery of this one-to-one contact is augmented by training from experienced practitioners. Ward staff must demonstrate that they are developing skills to implement the basic psychological interventions recommended by NICE, namely basic CBT interventions. AIMS have further set a Type 1 standard to ensure that each ward is served by a specialist psychology practitioner one session (half a day) per ward, per week, minimally.

AIMS' Type 2 standards, desired but not mandatory, and Type 3 standards, representative of a centre of excellence, are harder to meet but almost equally important. A ward-based service would meet Type 2 requirements if it were to provide a choice of medication which takes into account an individual's emotional and social needs. Other Type 2 standards require a ward to provide supportive counselling one hour per week, and supportive one-to-one time every day, as well as a range of psychosocial interventions and, minimally, one group activity per day. Type 2 accredited wards would typically have input from psychology within the multidisciplinary team, with access to a specialist psychology practitioner for more than one session per week. The work of this practitioner would include training multidisciplinary staff in basic psychological interventions recommended by NICE, including CBT. A ward accredited as excellent by AIMS would tend to train its staff in complex interventions recommended by NICE (such as CBT for psychosis or bipolar disorder) and would provide three or more evidence-based psychological interventions.

While working within the AIMS steering group, I had the good fortune to meet Marion Janner, a campaigner who has used mental health services in the past and who runs a charity called Bright. Bright has produced *Star Wards* (2006, available on the website www.starwards.org.uk), a document which includes a piece I wrote to promote the commissioning of psychological services for inpatients. *Star Wards*, like AIMS in a way, is primarily an effort to set basic standards for wards to follow in order to optimize the experience of inpatients during their episode of care. It is rather more written in the spirit of volunteerism and creative making do than AIMS or certainly the HCC statutory standards, and as such remains very positive and engaging to staff and service user groups alike. *Star Wards*, as mentioned before, sets out as its final objective, in terms of psychology, to ensure that every inpatient who needs psychological therapy will get it. It also sets standards that are easier to meet, including employing assistant psychologists and training staff in basic CBT. Both AIMS and *Star Wards* are receiving the government's attention, and there is hope that their efforts will influence the HCC to adopt more specifically prescriptive standards to ensure the effective delivery of evidence-based psychological therapies, principal among them CBT, to inpatients.

To this end, Peter Kinderman and I responded recently to the HCC's consultation on acute inpatient care on behalf of the DCP. The HCC is broad in its statutory responsibilities, and does not yet, to our satisfaction, require wards to meet quantifiable psychological therapy specifications. In our response, available on the BPS website (www.bps.org.uk/consult), we asked the HCC to adopt the AIMS Type 1 standard of at least one session per ward, per week input by a qualified specialist in psychological interventions, likely to be a clinical psychologist, to offer direct patient care and training and supervision to ward staff. Although this would be a tall order for the psychologist brought in, it would at least be a start, and something to build upon. We further note that, at present, every inpatient has access to medication while access to an equally and in some instances better evidence-based approach, CBT, remains very limited. We look forward to the HCC's response with some hope of progress.

Aspirations for the future

The DCP is keen to produce a document that strongly advocates the employment of clinical psychology and evidence-based psychological therapies based at least part-time on acute inpatient mental health wards. We are, in part, driven to counter anecdotal claims that some heads of psychology, in addition to commissioners of services, have overlooked the care needs of inpatients when designing services. This type of arguably benign neglect, of course, runs counter to the NSF, but is the result of many years of bias against working psychologically with the actively suicidal and those with unbalanced moods or perspectives on reality. CBT has offered us a major opportunity to work effectively with those individuals most persistently distressed and at the highest risk of relapse – alongside traditional psychiatric input – on inpatient wards. We would like to see CMHT psychologists working into their catchment area wards during 10 per cent of their working week, or, if this is not possible, for a cross-ward service to be set up. CMHT psychologist inreach tends not to lend itself well to staff training and supervision, but has the advantage of providing greater continuity of care between inpatient and outpatient settings. Cross-ward services tend to become more embedded in hospital systems and can respond more effectively to training and supervision needs, but clinical follow-up post discharge is usually capped in order to preserve the resource for inpatients. Chapters 6, 7 and 8 of this volume suggest how we can overcome some of these problems of embedded psychology.

AIMS will continue to raise its psychology standards, no doubt regularly prompted to do so by an activist DCP partner. *Star Wards* is being benchmarked on several wards across the nation. Both efforts are resulting in posts being developed for clinical psychologists and other specialist psychological therapists, and in CBT training programmes being established. With the presence of clinical psychologists increasing on the wards, assistant psychologist posts, often set up on a voluntary basis, are being developed, bringing energetic and eager future cognitive-behaviourists into the care of inpatients. As these CBT culture bearers become more prolific, there is hope that the currently somewhat small number of multidisciplinary staff interested in practising CBT will grow, and that one day all staff will employ basic CBT with their inpatient clients as part of routine care while under-going regular supervision and training updates.

Until such a day comes, and indeed, I expect, beyond then, it will remain important for those of us anticipating equal access for inpatients to CBT and other evidence-based approaches to continue to gather evidence through research and practice to strengthen the argument for firm national standards. We must do what we can to see that our local inpatient popula-tions increasingly receive basic CBT interventions from, potentially, all ward staff, and complex CBT interventions from specialists like clinical psychologists. We must involve ourselves in the shared goal of providing training and supervision to ward-based staff, as well as opportunities to practise individually and in groups. And we must lobby powerful figures, from trust executives, commissioners and heads of psychology to govern-ment leads in the Department of Health and HCC, to fund and resource the provision of CBT on wards. If we do this, we will achieve universal access to CBT for inpatient populations. We will be able to look back, with no fond nostalgia, to the old days–these days–when hardly any inpatients received evidence-based psychological interventions or met with well-trained psychological therapists. We will then hopefully never turn back.

Chapter 3

New ways of working and the provision of CBT in the inpatient setting

Peter Kinderman

Overview

Several policy developments in the UK mental health system have potentially significant implications for the delivery of CBT and other psychological therapies in both community and inpatient settings. The Government's programme for Improving Access to Psychological Therapies (IAPT) in mental health services and the related initiative of Lord Richard Layard – who has argued for increased provision of CBT both to help address mental ill health and to help people return to work – add to the drive towards more psychological ways of working. The New Ways of Working Programme in mental health services proposes radical changes in the roles of the workforce. As well as promoting distributed responsibility, the programme clearly envisages a far greater emphasis on psychological competencies throughout the workforce, psychosocial models of understanding and on the provision of psychological therapies.

The introduction in the UK of the Mental Capacity Act 2005 and the government's proposals to reform the Mental Health Act 1983 both appear to consolidate this trend, with psychologists and other professions being offered the responsibilities and (presumably) commensurate clinical leadership which were previously associated only with the medical profession. It is possible that, once the authority to develop and implement care plans is enforceable under statute law, the role of senior psychological and related professionals will develop further.

Finally, there has been a recent rapid development in the ability of clinical theoreticians to make available authoritative psychosocial accounts of personal distress that challenge and expand on medical or diagnostic approaches. These offer plausible and useful alternatives to previously dominant ways of conceptualizing 'mental illness'. Clearly, for initiatives such as these to be successful in promoting CBT and other psychological therapies, it is essential that all professions incorporate psychological and cognitive models in their work. Indeed, very many professions have CBT skills, although the opportunities to use them are limited at present.

The chapter will expand on these plans and policies. It will discuss the implications of proposals to increase substantially the number of professionals who are competent in CBT in mental health services generally, and in the inpatient setting in particular. The chapter will discuss training and continuous professional development (CPD), as well as the challenges of clinical supervision. Clinical supervision must be provided, and this is likely to come in the first instance from existing CBT practitioners and clinical psychologists. The issues around this will be discussed, with reference to the New Ways of Working discussions, proposed new roles such as associate psychologists and the possible new responsibilities under mental health legislation.

Improving access to psychological therapies

Several related policies from the UK's Department of Health have emphasized the benefits of psychological approaches to mental health (DH 1996, 2001b, 2004a, 2004b, 2006a). Service users increasingly demand psychological services (Sainsbury Centre for Mental Health 2006a) and this call has been reflected in the mass media (Pidd 2006). This reflects academic evidence of the effectiveness of manualized psychological therapies such as CBT in randomized controlled trials and of the likely cost effectiveness of investment in this area (Centre for Economic Performance 2006; Department of Work and Pensions 2006; Layard 2004, 2006).

A major programme of work within the UK Department of Health – the Improving Access to Psychological Therapies (IAPT) Programme (2006c) – is managing the development of such psychological therapy services. The initial phase focuses explicitly on mild to moderate depression and anxiety (and therefore implicitly on outpatient services). Preliminary workforce planning for these developments (Turpin et al. 2006) estimates the likely demand for psychological therapies based only on the epidemiological prevalence of mild to moderate anxiety and depression as requiring more than 10,000 additional therapists (Boardman and Parsonage 2005; Turpin, Hope et al. 2006) to treat 800,000 patients per year (Centre for Economic Performance 2006). The modelling employed typically assumes that perhaps half of the psychological therapists involved might be applied psychologists (that is counselling or clinical psychologists), with the other half being health care staff such as nurses, occupational therapists or graduate workers with additional training and experience (Lavender and Paxton 2004; Boardman and Parsonage 2005; Turpin et al. 2006).

It is likely a 'Stepped Care Model' of service provision (Simon et al. 2001; Dietrich et al. 2004; Bower and Gilbody 2005) will be adopted, where workers competent to deliver interventions at the lower levels would have different (more limited) competencies than staff able to intervene at higher levels. Turpin and colleagues (2006: 10) acknowledge that these assumptions 'are based upon the effectiveness of randomized control trials conducted under stringent conditions whereby therapists are trained to a standard of competency, adopt manualized protocols and receive expert supervision'. This work is closely allied to the policies in respect to the regulation of medical and non-medical professions (Department of Health 2006a).

Therapists, of course, must not only be trained to an appropriate standard of competency but must also receive expert supervision. Supervision requires institutional support. Brooker and Brabban (2004) found that graduates from training schemes in psychosocial intervention for psychosis relatively rarely employ their newly acquired skills within the workplace, often as a result of lack of supervision. There are obvious links to John Hanna's discussion of quality standards in Chapter 2.

Implications for IP settings

The IAPT programme and the 'Layard hypothesis' are both specifically aimed at mild to moderate depression in primary care and community settings. They are not proposals to develop psychosocial or CBT services in inpatient settings. Nevertheless, the implications may be significant here too. First, it is reasonable to see any major investment in CBT (or in psychosocial approaches generally) to have positive implications across the board. The IAPT/Layard programme is indeed major – 10,000 extra therapists were promised in the Labour Party election manifesto (Labour Party 2005), and it is a matter of simple arithmetic to see that salary costs alone stretch into hundreds of millions of pounds. Sometimes politics are important.

On a more human level, it is highly likely that emphasis on psychosocial approaches in outpatient and community services will lead to increased attention on these issues across mental health services. Clients and colleagues will both be exposed to and experience greater focus on and investment in psychological perspectives, and demand is likely to generalize across service settings. Moreover, the IAPT initiatives are not the only similar policy drivers currently extant.

New ways of working

The New Ways of Working Programme of the Department of Health, National Institute for Mental Health in England (NIMHE) and the Care Services Improvement Partnership (CSIP) is designed to help professions working in mental health to become more modern and flexible. The Royal College of Psychiatrists and NIMHE began a process of workforce development in respect to the role of psychiatrists. This work identified widespread dissatisfaction among psychiatrists who felt that a more genuinely true multidisciplinary approach with the involvement of service users and carers would deliver more responsive and appropriate services, acceptable to professionals, service users and their carers alike. The report from this work (NIMHE 2004b) strongly encouraged shared responsibility and leadership across teams, as opposed to older styles of medical leadership or even dominance. These developments have implications for other professionals in multidisciplinary teams and beyond.

The changes in what was perceived to be the medical responsibility of consultant psychiatrists for the care of all service users may be radical. Although this work stream has changed nothing in law, the General Medical Council (GMC) clarified its guidance with respect to the consultant psychiatrist's medical responsibility. It is now clear that the consultant psychiatrists are medically responsible for those patients with whom they are directly involved and for the advice given to others; they are not, however, accountable for the decisions and actions of other clinicians. This, of course, offers more professional accountability to other professionals, including those delivering psychological interventions. It is significant that these statements have been 'signed off' by all the major professional groups conjointly, and the New Ways of Working Programme has now been extended to incorporate similar discussions about the roles of many professional groups working in mental health.

In these documents, clinical psychologists are described as experts in psychological interventions. It is explicitly recognized that many professions in mental health services are highly competent in the use of psychological interventions, but psychologists are recognized as unique in having a single focus on psychological processes and the systematic study of mind and behaviour throughout a lengthy and high-level training path. Psychology, as a profession in mental health, has a longstanding tradition of skills transfer to non-psychologists, and is keen to offer consultation, training and supervision in psychological intervention to other members in multidisciplinary teams. Increasingly clinical psychologists provide group supervision to teams. Supervision may focus on how best to work with individual clients or may assist the multidisciplinary teams as a body to enable more effective working.

Clinical leadership

One of the significant aspects of the New Ways of Working Programme is the potential for clinical and professional leadership offered to psychosocial therapists. Intrinsic to several Department of Health reports is practical guidance about how to drive forward the evidence-based practice agenda, for example: *NHS Psychotherapy Services in England: Review of Strategic Policy* (1996); *Treatment Choice in Psychological Therapies and Counselling* (2001b); *The National Plan for the NHS* (2000); *Improvement, Expansion and Reform* (2002d); *Organising and Delivering Psychological Therapies*

(2004a). From these documents, good practice in the management, training, access, choice and supervision of psychological therapists includes:

- improved access to therapies to avoid long waiting time
- attention to the psychotherapeutic needs of different groups; for example, older people, people from minority groups
- involvement of users in choosing the most appropriate therapy for their condition and situation.

Systematic training in psychological therapies for mental health professionals supported by specialist supervision once they return to the workplace and clear leadership, both professionally and managerially, is best achieved through the development of an organization-wide body, i.e. a Psychological Therapies Management Committee. This advice has been developed and extended by the British Psychological Society to recommend that psychologists, by virtue of their training, competencies and experience, can lead and manage teams and take 'clinical responsibility' while supervising more junior staff. It concludes that there should be specific board-level representation for the delivery of psychological services, and services must be aligned with the vision of future service delivery and the key external drivers for organizing psychological services. This includes the need to consider how psychological therapies and approaches are organized and delivered in a multiprofessional, multidisciplinary context (British Psychological Society, Division of Clinical Psychology 2007).

Clearly, these changes appear to be part of a significant shift towards psychosocial approaches and interventions in mental health care, and towards a more democratic, multidisciplinary approach to mental health care delivery. Although the implications for CBT in inpatient settings are perhaps secondary or indirect, they could be highly significant. At present, pharmacological therapies dominate mental health care, especially in inpatient settings, and medical models of service delivery similarly take precedence. If health care shifts to a more democratic, pluralistic model, and if psychosocial therapies attain a higher profile, CBT is likely to become more valued across the board.

Mental Heath Act reform and the Mental Capacity Act

The introduction of the Mental Capacity Act 2005 and the proposed changes to the 1983 Mental Health Act are also potentially significant for the development of psychological perspectives in acute mental health. The Mental Capacity Act 2005 provides a new legal framework for decision making when people are unable to make decisions for themselves. Although, in this context, perhaps relatively few people commonly offered CBT in inpatient settings will have decisions made on their behalf by health professionals, the Mental Capacity Act 2005 is significant because the legal basis for the substantial legal responsibilities within its provisions is essentially psychosocial – being based on the individual's ability to understand, retain and use or weigh relevant information as part of the process of making decisions. This is, of course, substantially different to a medical or psychiatric basis for legal action. In consequence, the Mental Capacity Act 2005 provides for more functional and pragmatic decision making and clinical planning, and provides opportunities for a wide range of professionals to contribute to clinical and social care plans.

The government's proposals to reform the Mental Health Act 1983 are similarly substantial and significant. The proposals themselves are controversial and have taken a considerable time to evolve (Cooke *et al.* 2001). Amongst other proposals (for good or ill), the reforms include suggestions to replace the existing role of Responsible Medical Officer under the Mental Health Act 1983 with a Responsible Clinician. The Responsible Medical Officer at present is invariably a consultant psychiatrist. Under the proposed changes, the Responsible Clinician could be any properly competent, senior and experienced clinician – a nurse, a social worker, occupational therapist or psychologist.

These proposed changes are explicitly designed to permit proper use of the skills and competencies of the workforce. In the context of the Improving Access to Psychological Therapies Programme and the New Ways of Working Programme, these latter changes herald little short of a revolution. Many non-medical mental health care professionals regard the provisions of the Mental Health Act 1983 as substantiating biomedical dominance. That is, even when the individual's presenting problems appear mainly social in nature, and even if an individual is not subject to the provisions of the Mental Health Act 1983, the place of the Responsible Medical Officer (RMO), and therefore the status of the person (of course the consultant psychiatrist) holding this position appears established by statute. A new Mental Health Act, undermining these assumptions, may well lead to major changes in the power relations in acute or inpatient settings (Kinderman 2007). These changes can therefore be seen as consolidating, in law, the developments outlined above.

A psychological model of mental disorder

It is not surprising, in this context, that psychological models of mental disorder as well as mental health care have grown in popularity. Psychological authors such as Richard Bentall (2003) have criticized psychiatric frameworks, diagnostic approaches and pharmacological treatments. Alternative frameworks such as the mediating psychological processes model of mental disorder (Kinderman 2005a) have been proposed as comprehensive models of mental disorder with wide applicability to other areas of health

and social care (Kinderman *et al.* in press). The most common interpretations of the biopsychosocial model tend to assume either that social and
psychological factors mediate the effects of biological processes, or that
biological, social and psychological factors are co-equal partners in the
aetiology of mental disorder (Pilgrim 2002). In contrast, the mediating
psychological processes model proposes that distal causative agents –
biological abnormalities or physical insults, social factors such as poverty
and social deprivation, and circumstantial factors or life events such as
childhood sexual, emotional or physical abuse – lead to mental disorder
because those factors adversely affect psychological processes.

Kinderman and Tai (2006) discussed the clinical implications of this
model for the individual therapist – suggesting that psychological formulations rather than diagnoses should predominate clinical planning. Such
individualized formulations would list problems, rather than diagnose
putative conditions or illnesses, should detail the social, biological and
circumstantial factors hypothesized to lead to the disruption of psychological processes or mechanisms behind these problems and on the functional consequences of them (Kinderman and Tai 2006). Such an approach
is likely to be more person centred and normalizing than a diagnostic
approach (British Psychological Society, Division of Clinical Psychology
2000; Tarrier and Calam 2002), is compatible with the 'recovery' model of
mental health care and consequently with expressed service user preferences
(NIMHE 2004a, 2004b, 2004c, 2004d, 2005a, 2005b). Although the mediating psychological processes model emphasizes psychological factors other
than cognitive processes, Kinderman *et al.* (in press) further suggested that
access should be improved to psychological therapies based on individual
case formulations and that nurses, occupational therapists and social
workers should develop increasing competencies in psychosocial interventions. Within this, the authors recommend, psychologists should be prepared to offer consultation and clinical leadership. While psychiatry should
remain a key profession, the emphasis for psychiatrists should be a return to
the key principles of the application of medical expertise as it assists a
multidisciplinary team in the understanding and treatment of mental disorder. A theoretical approach such as the mediating psychological processes
model could have revolutionary implications for mental health care, and
particularly for how psychological therapies such as CBT are conceptualized and delivered.

Summary

Together, these policy initiatives herald major changes in mental health care
– ones which will see increased attention on CBT and other psychological
approaches. They can be summarized as follows: the UK government is
proposing major investment in psychological therapies, particularly CBT,

in the context of a shift from a medically dominated framework to a focus on multidisciplinary teams and clinical leadership by competent individuals from a range of professions, supported by new mental health laws and assertive professional and academic commentary.

Psychological and psychosocial approaches to mental health – to conceptualization, planning, service organization, training, supervision, care planning and intervention – are likely to be supported and to find a receptive milieu. It is highly likely, therefore, that CBT will increasingly be part of the picture across mental health care, including in inpatient settings.

Chapter 4

The service user perspective

Marie (introduced by Isabel Clarke)

Introduction

I invited Marie, whose mental health difficulties arose from what can best be described as 'complex trauma', to contribute her experience to this book as I had watched her relationship with the institution from the sidelines, as her therapist over a long (outpatient) therapy. I concluded that she was in a particularly good position to chart the changing relationship between therapy and the hospital, as well as having an amazing and courageous tale to tell. The interview takes place two years after the end of the therapy. As well as the individual therapy, Marie attended an adapted form of the DBT skills training programme that was being piloted in Southampton at the time (Sambrook *et al.* 2006).

Interview with Marie

ISABEL: This chapter is about hospital and therapy – something that you are an expert in, so I want to ask about your experiences and in particular what did help and what didn't.

MARIE: Well I've had mental health problems for 25 years and it only really came to the forefront after my youngest daughter was born and I went down with post natal depression and then my father died two weeks later and that's when I started going in and out, in and out of the local psychiatric hospital. I was on what they call the revolving door for about 11 or 12 years. In all that time my psychiatrist kept telling me I would never get well; I would never recover from what had happened to me and the only treatment that he could ever suggest was ECT (electro convulsive therapy) and general medication and that medication didn't work; that's one thing that definitely didn't work but he was convinced that psychotherapy, psychology or anything to do with that line would never work with me. In the end I wrote to him and said we've gone as far as we can. I've had to change psychiatrists; my new psychiatrist was more open to psychotherapy.

ISABEL: It might be useful to get the chronology of what happened before that clear at this stage. My recollection is that your childhood was mostly spent in a children's home; you were sexually abused in the home from age 15, then escaped into a marriage where you were routinely abused, terrorized, and periodically tortured, escaping at the point at which you were almost killed. You then made a good marriage with the father of your children, but one that did not survive the mental health problems, and it was those multiple traumas that needed to be faced when you chose to go into therapy.

MARIE: Yes, at the time I was first referred for therapy, I still wasn't well enough to face the traumas of what had gone on in my life and I think that was twice they tried a psychotherapist with me but it just didn't work. And then I can't remember what year you and I started and the group, I think it was about 1999 . . .

ISABEL: Let's just go back a little bit to what it was like being in hospital during those early years; was there anyone to talk to when you were in hospital?

MARIE: Not in the early years, not in the early years; in the early years you were given your medication at set times and left to vegetate on the ward. There was no occupational therapy and there was no input from the staff. There was just a place of safety and that's why I was always put in there because in those days I wasn't safe from overdoses and self-harming; that didn't improve until 1996. Then they started bringing in staff that were more friendly; more open to being with the patients and not sitting in the office having cups of tea all day. From 1996 to now I would say that things have improved in working with patients and carers; there's a lot more involvement from the staff to the patient, there's a lot more occupational therapy going on now; but in the early years (we're talking about 1990 to 1996) no; it was just vegetation on the ward.

ISABEL: And when the occupational therapy came in, was there any sort of talking therapy, such as cognitive behaviour therapy?

MARIE: No, not in 1996; that didn't actually come in until I started working with you. The earlier psychotherapy I tried was based on my dreams, the nightmares I was getting, and the flashbacks. My therapist at that time said that he couldn't work with me because I had just moved home and he thought that I wasn't ready to cope with both the trauma of the move and living on my own again, and looking after my children on my own. But I must admit I hold the psychiatrist and the hospital responsible for not getting me the help I needed sooner and for me losing custody of my children; and them having to go to their father. I looked after my children when I was well but that wasn't very often. Every eight weeks I was in hospital for six weeks ECT and then I was out and then four weeks later I'd be back in for another course of ECT. That went on from 1990 right up until 1998.

ISABEL: So how many courses of ECT a year were you getting?

MARIE: I was getting at least six. At one point when I was living in a group home for mentally ill people when I first divorced the father of my children, my psychiatrist had me going three times a week for a year on what he called preventative ECT. So every Monday, Wednesday, Friday I was picked up from my house by taxi, taken to the hospital, had ECT, spent the day on the ward and then went back to the house I was living in; and that went on for a whole year.

ISABEL: What sort of effect did that have on your life?

MARIE: A very bad effect because my daughters were very young and my youngest daughter was only six and because I couldn't remember how to do things as a mother she wouldn't come with me. I only ever saw my eldest daughter; she would stay with her grandmother rather than come to her mum; so it had a very bad effect. And it was very restrictive, three days of the week for a year; I couldn't do anything and my memory has been shot away; there's an awful lot of my memory of my children when they were babies and young children that I can't remember because of the ECT treatment that I've had and that's why I say that ECT is not the answer for everybody. It works for some, but my psychiatrist believes that was the only answer. He is very pro ECT. He made me have it when I was admitted to hospital this year, but I soon stopped it.

ISABEL: It sounds as though those were wasted years.

MARIE: Yes, I wasted a good nine to ten years of my girls' lives in and out, in and out of the psychiatric hospital and having ECT and not being a mother. Not being able to be a mother; only looking after the children when I was well, but even then not being able to do normal things with them like swimming and taking them to the beach and anything like that. I was just there and they stayed with me; we used to play games like Scrabble, but I could never leave the house and take them out. I was never confident in those years, so yes there was a lot of wasted years.

ISABEL: So, tell me about the decision to enter therapy; you were offered therapy a couple of times before we met and my memory was that you were quite cautious at the beginning with me as well. What do you remember of that?

MARIE: I remember that I had an assessment with you and I think my eldest daughter was with me actually when I came to the assessment. Then you made the decision that you thought that you could work with me and I said that I would give it a try but my psychiatrist didn't believe that I was ever going to get through any kind of therapy. For the first six months of working with you I was only seeing you once a month. You offered it more frequently but I couldn't cope with the idea of that. It took me a good six months to build up the relationship close enough to you to put my trust in you and say okay let's get it down to two weekly and then, eventually, it was weekly.

ISABEL: Tell me what was that like being in therapy?

MARIE: Being in therapy at times, certainly at the beginning, was confusing. I remember you asked me about my time in the children's home and that was difficult.

ISABEL: As I remember it, we did go through what I would call the exposure work – all the traumatic memories – towards the end, but we had done a lot of other work first. It could be that you don't remember so much of the earlier part; you were quite spaced out or dissociated when we first met.

MARIE: That could be.

ISABEL: Before you were ready to do that work of revisiting the things which formed the material for your flashbacks, we had to actually get you living more normally and deal with the self-harm, so that you could hold it together and not self-harm when reminded of those memories which triggered the self-harm. Do you remember doing that work?

MARIE: Yes I do remember doing that. I remember doing the DBT (dialectical behaviour therapy) classes at the same time. I was seeing you twice a week then – in the group and individually. I was coming to group on a Tuesday I think it was and then seeing you on a Thursday. I can remember learning that there were skills: other ways of coping than self-harming. One of the biggest memories I have of DBT is learning to put things like thought, memories and feelings on a conveyor belt and let them go up to the top, fall over the top and then go away. From that day on learning that, my self-harming didn't stop but it did get reduced dramatically and my seriousness of self-harm was not as intensive as I used to do in the early days.

ISABEL: My memory is that the first things that we worked on were about altering some quite basic things that you were doing; for instance, you were washing your mouth in bleach and you had problems with using bathrooms and that sort of thing. We were just looking at ways to approach doing very ordinary things, or not doing things like the bleach.

MARIE: I think the washing out of my mouth with bleach started when I was 15 because of what had happened in the children's home and it was probably a year after I started working with you that I got the confidence up to tell you that I was no longer doing that; only occasionally was I doing it – not every day of my life. Which was a big improvement because I was 40 when I started working with you and this abuse had started in the children's home when I was 15, so for a good 25 years I had been washing my mouth with bleach. That stopped; we talked an awful lot in the very early sessions about me not being able to use the bathroom. It didn't take long for you and I to figure out how to get me able to use the bathroom.

ISABEL: I think that was the first thing we did because it seemed so important. We started with very concrete things; working on doing things differently before we talked about anything much deeper. It was behavioural to start with, and then we went on from there to the work on learning the skills to be able to cope with feelings . . .

MARIE: Yes, I don't actually remember some of the skills I learned; I know I learned the mindfulness of either letting things go on the conveyor belt or, how to go through making a cup of tea in my mind and going through the motions in order to distract myself when things were difficult. They became my two major sources of coping skills.

ISABEL: Do you remember the self-soothe table, your lilac table? At the beginning it was very hard for you to look after yourself or give yourself nice things.

MARIE: Oh yes, I made a lilac table and everything on it was given to me by a very close friend of the family and I still do love the colour lilac but I have come so far ahead now that I no longer have a lilac table, but I do have a lilac bathroom and my lilac stuff is up in the bathroom, which is very helpful for me to go into the bathroom any time of the day or night. I used to be frightened to go in at any time because of the flashbacks of the abuse.

ISABEL: So you were very much using skills of looking after yourself and then, when you felt strong enough, we did the exposure work to the trauma memories which was what you remembered first. Let's go back to the hospital because the hospital was always in the background wasn't it?

MARIE: The hospital was like a second home to me – for 16 years.

ISABEL: While we were working together, though you were living in the community, you did have frequent stays in the hospital. Do you remember how that fitted in with the therapy?

MARIE: It didn't fit in too well with the therapy when I was still under the original psychiatrist that liked ECT to be the answer, because you yourself felt that we couldn't do any work during the course of ECT because it affects your memory. Not just long term, but short term as well, so I was in a Catch-22 phase. I wasn't safe to be at home so I needed the safety of the hospital but I couldn't convince my psychiatrist that I didn't need ECT, and though I had changed psychiatrist in the community, I had to have the original psychiatrist when I was admitted to hospital. It took me a good couple of years working with you before he no longer prescribed ECT for me whilst I was working with you. Then my stays in hospital were still quite frequent but I was able to come down off the ward and still have my appointments with you. And that made a huge difference because that's when the continuity of therapy carried on through the hospital and when I was able to be out living in the community.

ISABEL: That is right: I didn't carry on seeing you through the ECT simply because your memory for what happened between one week and the next wouldn't have been sufficient that you could really have made use of the work, and this was temporary obviously, while you were having the ECT.

MARIE: It was only every six weeks; whenever I went into hospital while I was working with you, it would be a six-week course of ECT so it would be a six-week break. But I changed psychiatrists and I think I stopped having ECT, probably the third year into working with you, and that's when we really managed to get a grip on what we were dealing with and going through right to the end of therapy.

ISABEL: I got the impression that your relationship with the hospital changed more generally over time and became more of a partnership. Was there a change between being admitted involuntarily and choosing to go in?

MARIE: I was only ever sectioned once and that was when I was really, really ill and I was still married to my second husband. I wasn't sorry to go in even then – I was living in my one-bedroomed flat and my girls were seven and nine. It was the first year after my girls' father and I had split up and I was having such a bad time. I had a social worker at the time who was also an approved social worker. She called my general practitioner (GP) who couldn't convince me to go into hospital so my psychiatrist came along and between them all I was put into hospital. But that section only lasted three days; then I stayed there voluntarily. Otherwise I went in voluntarily. In the end I had such a reputation on the ward that all the staff and my psychiatrist, at the time, knew that if I needed to be in they always found me a bed and if I said I was ready to go home they always let me go home. There was never any question of 'You're not well enough to be at home and if you insist on going we're going to section you'. They learned to trust me to say when I did and did not need help. So that was an improvement in the hospital trusting the patient instead of sectioning them because they said they're going home.

ISABEL: During the last year or so of the therapy there were also nurses on the ward who had received DBT training weren't there? How did that work and affect things?

MARIE: That affected things very well and I would like to mention one particular nurse by name because she was my primary nurse; her name was Sue and whenever I was on the ward she always had me as her patient for the hours she was working; she always gave me an hour at a time to talk to her. She was also trained in acupuncture and she did acupuncture on me; she helped me calm down so I could go to sleep and she'd had the DBT training. She played a big part in the times I went into hospital in the last years of working with you, helping me carry on the exposure work that we had been doing. So my stays in hospital, even though they were still quite frequent even towards the end, her work with me as well was working in conjunction with what you did meant that they were really helpful.

ISABEL: She was able to remind you of the DBT skills when you were in hospital, didn't she? Because my memory is that when we felt that you had, by and large, stopped the self-harm and that it was safe to revisit those traumatic memories, we made the decision to do the exposure work. Can you recall that now?

MARIE: I remember we started before the flashback abuse memories and went back to when I was little. You asked me to go back to memories from the age of five in the children's home and I found that quite difficult to actually do because I had tried to block out my early years, my early memories of the children's home. But now when I look back on it I think it's good that I went back as far as five years old and my earliest memory of the children's home, because it's pieced together some of my childhood. My feelings as a young child and being in the children's home brought on a lot of stress because the lady who looked after us was very abusive, very violent and wouldn't think twice about smacking us about the slightest thing. They can't do that these days, but in those days that did go on. My sister who was in the children's home with me had a lot of verbal abuse from this lady and it affected her life as well as mine.

ISABEL: When we had gone through those memories, you were feeling brave enough to face the major trauma memories. I recall that you were then able to use the hospital positively to assist the therapy. You made a conscious decision to go into hospital when we were revisiting the worst of the memories. Up until then you had been regularly destabilized on the anniversaries of the worst traumatic things that happened to you and you had always had to go into hospital and stay, so we knew that it was going to be quite disturbing for you to really look at that stuff. How did that work, using the hospital in that way?

MARIE: It was good because like you say while we were doing the work on facing the anniversaries of certain dates of the year, I was able to use the hospital to my advantage; still work with you because ECT was stopped and work with Sue on the ward. That was a big step forward in how the hospital would allow me to take control.

ISABEL: Because you were essentially negotiating that with the hospital weren't you? So, we went through all the major traumas and I left that job in about May 2004. We just had some months to work on the ending, because we had been working together for four years, although at the beginning it had been not that frequent meetings; it was really quite a long time.

MARIE: I would say that out of those four years we probably spent half of those years working intensively; for the first 18 months it was just really building up my trust that I could face the traumas and the flashbacks. There were many, many times during those two and a half years when I nearly gave up and said I just can't do this anymore. And with your encouragement and your determination not to give up on me, I didn't give up either and that's where I am today as a result.

ISABEL: Yes, and it took a lot of courage on your part to carry on. Also there were times when the team were a bit discouraged; I can remember your GP was very good in standing by your decision to stay with therapy, but there were times when questions were asked when it had been going on a long time and was not appearing to be getting anywhere. Suggestions were made that something else should be tried. I remember those meetings.

MARIE: Yes they did once suggest that I stop working with you and have EMDR instead. I actually had a friend who'd had that done at a private hospital, and she told me that it was very intense and very, very traumatic and I said, 'No, I don't want that done. If Isabel is still prepared to carry on with me I'll carry on with her. If she doesn't give up I'm not giving up!'

ISABEL: Yes, I think the EMDR idea was a bit of a counsel of despair, I think they just didn't know what to do; I don't think there was any suggestion that would have made it any easier really.

MARIE: My psychiatrist kept saying to me, 'Don't you think you ought to give up therapy, you aren't getting anywhere, you're still coming in, still self-harming', and I kept saying to him, 'Don't you see the pattern that's going on over the last two and a half years. My stays in hospital are less frequent and they are less dependent and they don't last for so long.' I had many, many arguments with my psychiatrist about continuing with you, many arguments. But in the end I won the arguments, because I am a very determined woman when I want to be. I thought I am worth more than this, I am worth a proper life.

ISABEL: Absolutely. That determination and that vision were crucial, because you needed huge courage to face all the things that had happened to you in the past and to come through as you are today, with a happy marriage and going back to work.

MARIE: Yes, now I only see my community psychiatric nurse (CPN) every six to eight weeks; I only see my psychiatrist once every four to six months and as I say, in the last two years I've had two inpatient stays and three treatments of short periods from the home treatment team that is now involved. The home treatment team is a big improvement in the NHS because the home treatment team can keep people, like myself, safe at home and not need the environment of the hospital. So that was a good move for the NHS. This means I have got a chance

now of having a different life that doesn't revolve around the psychiatric hospital, and now two years down the line I've had two jobs,
I'm happily married, I very rarely go the hospital and I very rarely self-
harm or need input from my CPN or psychiatrist. That proves that,
although it took so long, my traumas had gone on from the age of 15,
and they were very severe with what my first husband did; that I had to
give it that time to get through. Now I have got a proper life.

Comment

Marie's account illustrates the following issues that are pertinent to this
book.

Therapy as exit from hospital dependency

Marie described herself as a 'revolving door patient' for many years. Her
story illustrates the role that therapy can play in breaking that cycle, even in
a case that could have appeared intractable. Marie's flashbacks that drove
her self-harm and suicidality were of delusional intensity, and previous
attempts to engage her in therapy had not worked.

Neurological insult and therapeutic pessimism

Research into the neurological impact of early severe emotional deprivation
(Schore 1994, 2001) can lead to therapeutic pessimism. In Marie's case, such
deprivation preceded the early sexual abuse in the children's home, and
continued sexual abuse and life-threatening torture in her first marriage. It is
therefore significant that, with sufficient attention paid to engagement (the
long period of spaced sessions that preceded the more intensive therapy),
and a commitment to a longer than average length of therapy, it is possible
to overcome these hurdles.

Hospital used collaboratively to support therapy

Marie was able to request planned admission to support the most challenging part of the therapy. By this time, the team had come to respect her
ability to make constructive use of admission, so were prepared to accede to
this request. With this support, it was possible to do the most challenging
part of the exposure work safely, which validates this use of admission.

Chapter 5

The use of formulation in inpatient settings

Fiona Kennedy

Introduction and summary

This chapter examines the inpatient setting as a system, where the dominant conceptualization of behaviour is as manifestation of illness, but confused messages are sent to clients. Psychological formulations offer alternative understandings of clients' problems. The nature and status of the activity of formulating is discussed and CBT formulations are used as illustrations. The need to formulate client–staff–environment interactions is emphasized, as well as transitions between inpatient and outpatient life. Psychological formulation, it is argued, should provide a more compassionate narrative than the medical model, leading to benefits for the client and for those in helping roles. Shared formulation is seen as an intervention in itself, which can be effective at many levels, from the individual client, through staff thinking, to organizational structure and power relations.

What is formulation?

Meyer and Turkat (1979: 261–262) defined case formulation as 'an hypothesis which (1) relates all the clients' complaints to one another, (2) explains why the individual developed these difficulties, and (3) provides predictions concerning the clients' behaviour given any stimulus conditions'.

The literature on the nature of formulation itself is rather scanty, considering the importance afforded it as a central activity in CBT and indeed in many other modalities. Within the behavioural tradition, functional analysis represented one of the first attempts to identify the nature of 'variables' which might affect the clinical presentation of a problem. These included the social-cultural-physical environment, social relationships, incentives and aversive consequences, biological and behavioural changes in the person's history, behavioural 'excesses and deficits', and self-control. Cullen (1983), within the behavioural tradition, made a plea, in response to papers by Slade (1982) and Owens and Ashcroft (1982), that 'functional relationships must be demonstrated, not merely claimed', and that 'clinicians should be wary of superficial analysis'. The 'functionality' of the relationship between external and internal events implied some causal relationship between the variables identified in the formulation and the problems the clinician is trying to treat. Demonstrating such causality is indeed an immense, if not impossible, challenge.

Researchers in the field of clinical psychology also face this problem. How to demonstrate scientifically that an observed correlation (for example, between bulimia and a history of childhood sexual abuse) may also involve causality? Statistical solutions, such as structural equation modelling, regression analysis and distinguishing between mediator and moderator variables (Baron and Kenny 1986), help the researcher in this field, but are beyond the scope and interest of many clinicians.

A major contribution that Beck (1976) made to the psychological endeavour was to free us from the shackles of the reductionism associated with behaviourism and allow introspection but with a scientific base. CBT prescribes introspection upon thoughts and feelings alongside the behaviours and physiological reactions allowed in the behavioural tradition. Thus, the 'variables' which are the building blocks of the CBT formulation include both outside and inside events and experiences.

Bieling and Kuyken (2003) question whether cognitive case formulation follows the process of scientific inquiry. They suggest that formulations should be valid, reliable and that cases worked based on formulations should have better outcomes than those without. They point out that the literature on validity is non-existent and on that on reliability is conflicting. There is no compelling evidence that cognitive case formulation improves outcome.

Butler (2006) argues that two different CBT therapists could develop two different case formulations, both of which could be valid, because the mind of the therapist introduces selective bias based on their own life experience, knowledge and therapeutic learning. She claims the most important aspect of shared formulation is that it opens up options for change for the client, increasing hope, providing information and preparing the person for therapy. There are different ways of applying theory to practice and at present we do not know which kind of formulation is best, either clinically or for research purposes.

The inpatient context

The nature of people's experience of inpatient psychiatric services is little explored, but the government emphasis on service user involvement (*National Service Framework for Mental Health*, Department of Health 1999a) has given us some insights. Marie's account (Chapter 4) contains the following desperate description of a pessimistic illness model:

'I was on what they call the revolving door for about 11 or 12 years. In all that time my psychiatrist kept telling me I would never get well; I would never recover from what had happened to me and the only treatment that he could ever suggest was ECT and general medication and that medication didn't work; that's one thing that definitely didn't work but he was convinced that psychotherapy, psychology or anything to do with that line would never work with me.'

Such an account is by no means uncommon. John, 45, described his experience:

The environment is very cold. It's very alienating. You just get put into the system. The way they treat you is they know your symptoms and they know how to treat you and you are just part of the system. The system deals with you and you have little input into your care. They put you off because they know what you are going to say to them but they have no power to change your medication, to change your regime without the psychiatrist.

(BBC News 2004)

Dolly Sen, another inpatient, said some nurses on the ward were extremely supportive but others were of little help. 'We only saw [some] staff at medication time or if someone was acting up in a really violent way . . . Often the staff would be at one end of the ward and we'd all be at the other. I wanted to get out of the ward, so I lied. I wasn't feeling better at all but I told them that I was', she said. 'People would often lie just to get out.'

Mind's Ward Watch campaign (2004) collected self-reports from inpatients over two years and found only 20 per cent reported being treated with respect and dignity by staff. Seventeen per cent reported never being treated with respect and dignity during their stay. A joint national visiting programme by the Mental Health Act Commission and the Sainsbury Centre found intense pressure on beds, understaffing and a lack of basic humane treatment. On a quarter of wards the nurses were not in contact with patients during the visit. Women and ethnic minority members were subject to harassment and nurses needed more training in psychological interventions (Department of Health 1999a).

The reasons for the poor conditions on many mental health wards are complex and include funding decisions which prioritize more obviously life-saving health care activities and the stigma and devaluing attitudes surrounding mental health work. More recently the move to home assessment and treatment services may mean inpatient wards are dealing only with those with very severe distress and disturbance. In addition to under-funding, the problems may be to do with lack of clarity about why a person is admitted and what needs to be done while they are there.

Consider the clues that lie in the environment and experiences encountered by a person during the process of admission. The person will usually already be in crisis, perhaps having attempted to die, perhaps having isolated themselves at home without eating for days, perhaps having been arrested for threatening or harming someone else. During assessment there will often be pressure to agree to admission. In order to avoid sectioning the person, the assessment team may offer a 'choice' of voluntary admission or sectioning. The Mental Health Act 1983 allows more liberties to be taken with a person's human rights than any other legislation, including the Prevention of Terrorism act. In no other circumstances can a person who is not suspected of committing a crime be detained against their will for an indefinite period of time. This author would argue that such a violation of rights (sectioning) should never take place unless the person's life or that of others is in danger.

From the person's point of view, upon admission they become a 'patient'. Their 'choices' are not genuine, there is really no alternative on offer. The 'hospital' has many aspects of a prison about it, unlike a physical health ward. Possessions are likely to be removed and, on locked wards the cutlery and crockery may be plastic. Patients on 'observation' may find themselves being watched even when bathing or going to the toilet. Thus admission can be seen as a ritualized induction marking transition from the usual family/ work/social 'outside', former freedoms of normal life to a restricted and controlling system. These events are just as reminiscent of joining the army, or going to prison, as to entering a medical ward.

From this disempowered and helpless state patients may be expected to attend ward rounds with up to ten people in the room, when they may be discussed as if they are not present, with a slot in which to speak. Anxiety levels are likely to be very high and the person's ability to use this opportunity greatly reduced. Simultaneously, patients may be expected to care for themselves wherever possible and engage in therapeutic activities. Or else they may be left alone for long periods of time, with little to do. They may be asked to explain their behaviour and their explanations may be given disproportionate credence. At the same time they may be given messages about illness which imply they are helpless to help themselves. Drugs may be changed in response to complaints about them 'not working', often without discussion of what is meant by such a statement. So simultaneously, the messages received by the patient include that they are helpless, out of control, unable to manage without being (forcibly if necessary) detained and drugged, while being asked to explain their own behaviour, take responsibility for their actions and 'get better'.

Models of disorder

Open systems theory (Katz and Kahn 1966) suggests that it is important to think about the roles and expectations sent to and received by individuals in the context of an organization and the wider society in which it is embedded. The model of psychological disorder as mental illness may have consequences for the expectations of and roles played by both the providers of services and the receivers, or clients. Although nurses may have a variety of beliefs about what their role should be, the administration of drugs is still the central treatment intervention. The absence of psychologists and presence of psychiatrists on most inpatient wards (see Peter Kinderman's Chapter 3) may partly be a result of this.

The biopsychosocial model (Engel 1980) sees psychological disorder resulting from biological (nervous system) and psychosocial elements. The biopsychosocial model has been widely recommended as a way of integrating psychological and medical approaches (e.g. Department of Health 2004a, 2004b, 2004c), but has not yet had the desired effects on psychiatric practice (Read 2005). The biopsychosocial model has been seen as inadequate to challenge biomedical approaches (Pilgrim 2002).

The recovery model (Jacobson and Greenley 2001; Anthony 1993; Sullivan 1994) stresses individual autonomy and responsibility and improved quality of life as outcome. The impact of this has yet to be felt in the UK, judging by the findings quoted above. Criticisms of the model are ongoing within psychiatry and the wider mental health system, in terms of its applicability to those with the most severe problems who have lost touch with their selves and with the external world (e.g. Frese *et al.* 2001). Recovery from what has yet to be elucidated.

Kinderman (2005b) suggested that the biopsychosocial model fails to address the nature of psychological factors themselves. He suggested that, instead of assuming that biological, social and psychological factors are co-equal partners in the aetiology of mental disorder, disruption or dysfunction in psychological processes is a final common pathway in the development of mental disorder. Kinderman's 'mediating psychological processes model' proposes that biological and environmental factors, together with a person's personal experiences, lead to mental disorder *through their conjoint effects on these psychological processes*. He suggests that this approach would allow integration of many perspectives, medical, psychological, social and many therapeutic orientations, by requiring the formulation to specify which psychological processes and normal functions are disturbed by these factors (Kinderman and Tai 2006).

Formulating in the inpatient context

Within the inpatient context, the reinforcement contingencies differ from those naturally occurring outside. For example, expressing an inability to cope will often, understandably, result in a prolongation of inpatient stay. This prolongation means the client does not get the opportunity to acquire or practise coping skills in the environment in which they will finally be expected to survive. The observation of a duty of care which is quite reasonably a requisite of all mental health services means that it may be necessary to enforce a Mental Health Act section detaining the person against their will, in order to prevent suicide or harm to others. This may act as a positive reinforcer for suicidal or threatening gestures for those who are better adapted to life inside than out, or for those whose major sources of caring are the inpatient staff. It may act as a negative reinforcer for those who cannot manage the stresses of life outside, who are coping with, for example, divorce, homelessness or hearing voices using escape and avoidance strategies. Being sectioned may act as a punisher in the technical sense (that is, serving to reduce the likelihood that the behaviour will occur again), which is preferable, since inpatient services are not officially in the business of encouraging long-term stays.

A successful inpatient intervention needs to teach new behaviours, thoughts, feelings and physiological responses in the inpatient context and then enable transfer of these new skills to the natural environment in which the client normally exists. In order to do this, formulation is necessary for both environments enabling predictions as to what might change when the environments, with their differing contingencies, change.

It is of course essential that formulations be based on thorough CBT assessments. In the inpatient context this author has found the Millon Clinical Multiaxial Inventory III (MCMI III, Millon 1997) useful as a screen for personality problems as well as Axis I symptoms. The Brief Symptom Inventory (BSI, Derogatis 1992) gives a range of scores including anxiety, depression, obsessional-compulsive tendencies and others with relatively few questions, and is normed for inpatient as well as outpatient populations. The Clinical Outcomes in Routine Evaluation (CORE, Barkham et al. 2006) provides a benchmark to compare outcomes with those of other treatment centres. The inpatient setting also facilitates access to relatives and friends of the client (with consent) and to direct behavioural observation and recording as well as behavioural experiments.

Case example: Sarah

Sarah, a 25 year old who had not been admitted before, was working as a sailing instructor. She began self-harming, cutting herself on her arms and legs with a razor. This got worse and she cut her face and stomach. She drove her car towards an oncoming lorry, swerving at the last minute. She got drunk and her parents found her surrounded by vomit in the bath tub. She stated on assessment that all she wanted was to die and would not give assurances she could keep herself safe. She said she was a coward because she had failed to kill herself. She was sectioned and admitted to the locked ward. She often tried to escape, throwing herself against the doors when staff or visitors came and went, self-harming with a broken toothbrush, trying to hang herself with a stereo lead.

Sarah had received diagnoses in the past of anorexia, schizoaffective disorder, and depression. The self-harm seemed to have begun after she had been rejected by a heterosexual woman with whom she had fallen in love. Sarah expressed disgust towards herself for having homosexual feelings.

Ward staff paid attention to the 'planned' nature of Sarah's attempts to escape (e.g. she watched for times when people were coming and going so that she could try to escape), and concluded that this was evidence against 'mental illness'. The psychiatrists focused on the 'voices' in Sarah's head which told her she was worthless and deserved to die. Sometimes Sarah agreed they were voices, at others she described them as powerful thoughts. The psychologist focused on Sarah's inability to recall many details of her past before the age of 16. During relaxation classes at occupational therapy (OT), Sarah reported two flashbulb images, one of her younger sibling being taken, dead, from their cot; one of some beds in the back of a lorry in which she had travelled with her uncle, a long-distance lorry driver, when a child. She did not like to think of or discuss these images.

At first, Sarah was given several doses of a drug designed to knock her out and have an antipsychotic effect at the same time. She was restrained and placed in seclusion many times. She injured herself and the nurses because of the intensity with which she struggled. She agreed to work with the psychologist, who she knew from a previous admission, after which her attempts to escape and self-harm suddenly stopped. Sarah's developmental history is formulated in Figures 5.1 and 5.2.

The two formulations shown in Figures 5.1 and 5.2 represent hypotheses about the cognitive and behavioural processes that are operating to produce both the observable and self-reported reactions and inter-reactions between Sarah and the world around her, while she was growing up and while in the inpatient system. The information presented is highly selected and the hypothesized relationships between internal and external events are based on expert and informed guesswork: 'expert' in that there is evidence in the clinical and experimental literature showing the prevalence of negative early experience in the development of eating disorders and of dissociative disorders, for example; 'guesswork' in that there is selection and exclusion of reported life events and in the construction of the story, or narrative, about their influence on Sarah's present problems.

The formulation of Sarah's development hypothesizes that the death of her younger sibling along with her parents' reactions to the death, were early experiences of loss and abandonment, possibly with self-blame, which still

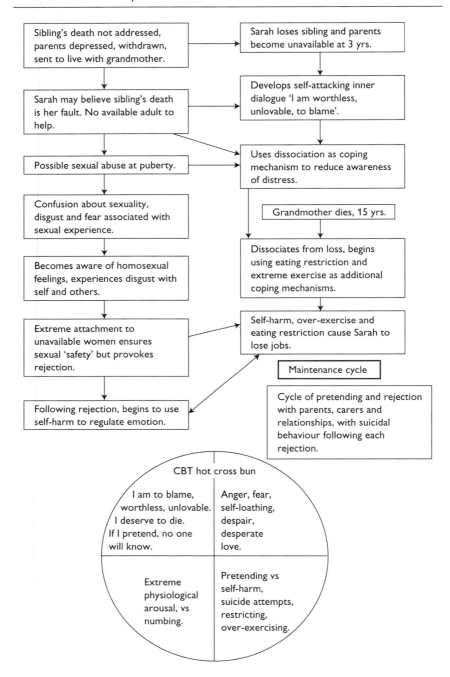

Figure 5.1 Formulation: Sarah – developmental history

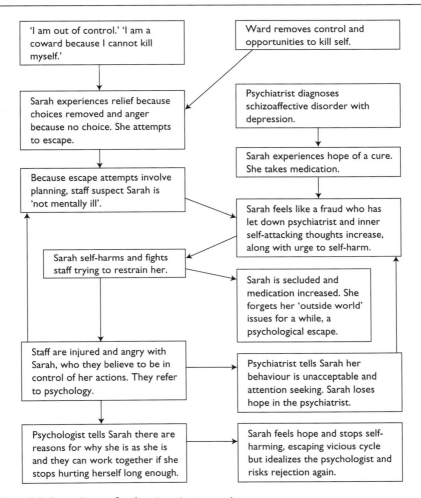

Figure 5.2 Formulation: Sarah – inpatient experience

affect Sarah's experience of herself and others today. The isolation and dissociative coping meant she was vulnerable to sexual abuse while growing up and most unlikely to disclose its occurrence (having carers whose distress was worse than her own, and cutting off from the reality of her own experiences). However, it is not known whether such abuse occurred.

The formulation of inpatient experience hypothesizes that inpatient workers, each with good intention, struggle to make sense of Sarah's behaviour, as does Sarah herself. Their professional training and personal assumptions produce different understandings and attributions, resulting in contradictory messages and perverse incentives being given to Sarah.

How to make a CBT formulation

There are as many ways to make a CBT case formulation as to make a chair; to this extent the activity remains as much a craft as a science. Bruch and Bond (1998) describe this craft by presenting several approaches with illustrations of their application in a variety of settings. In the case of CBT, the understanding of what is happening is predicated on the presumed influence of past (e.g. in the case of schema-focused formulation) formative and current maintaining factors. The cycle of thoughts, feelings, physiology and behaviour must be part of the formulation. For many presentations, there are evidence-based 'template formulations' (e.g. Salkovskis 1985; Wells 1997) for obsessive-compulsive disorder; Beck (1976) for depression and anxiety. The clinician can adapt these to make best-guess hypotheses about factors maintaining an individual's problems.

Various authors have laid down guidelines for making CBT formulations. Kinderman (2005a) and Kinderman and Tai (2006) present a 'mediating psychological processes model' stating that because psychological processes mediate the effects of environment and biology, formulations rather than diagnoses should predominate clinical planning. Formulations should detail the hypothesized disruptions to psychological processes or mechanisms. Medical, social and psychological interventions are most likely to be clinically effective if they are designed on the basis of their likely beneficial impact on underlying psychological mechanisms.

One famous approach is laid out by Judith Beck (1995). Simply stating that the essentials of formulation are predisposing (vulnerability), precipitating and maintaining factors will summarize the key features of a formulation. Sarah's issues would be summarized thus:

- *Predisposing*: loss of sibling at an early age; parental depression leading to loss of care from mother and father; family coping by suppressing and punishing emotional distress; possible sexual abuse by trusted family friend at puberty; internalized family/social attitudes to homosexuality.
- *Precipitating*: rejection by female objects of affection and attraction; perceived criticism from authority figures; weight gain resulting from antipsychotic medication.
- *Maintaining*: coping by eating restriction, over-exercise and self-harm. Assumption that no one is available to help. Avoiding disclosure/ discussion of problems. Dissociating (cognitive avoidance) from negative emotions. Attaching emotionally and sexually to unavailable heterosexual females.

Persons (1989) and Persons and Bertognolli (1999) developed a framework for conceptualizing cases from a CBT point of view. The Cognitive

Behavioural (CB) Case Formulation model emphasizes identifying all overt problems and specifying the underlying schemas or core beliefs that, when activated by life events, are postulated to cause the overt problems. A similar approach is used by Young (1990) in CBT for personality disorders. Sarah's case example could be formulated in terms of early learning about abandonment, emotional inhibition and mistrust/abuse (schemas). Sarah may have developed core beliefs that others cannot be trusted and she herself is worthless and defective. She may assume that if another person gets close to her this defectiveness will be recognized and repel the other. She may assume that there is no one available to share her emotional pain, and that even if there was that person could not be trusted not to take advantage.

Linehan (1993a) drawing from the behavioural tradition, emphasizes the importance of the transactions between individual and environment and stresses the ever-changing nature of things. This approach is most helpful in the endeavour to formulate the inpatient environment, particularly in terms of contingencies of reinforcement in operation. The cognitions of the staff also drive the interactions (for example, the belief that personality disorder does not constitute 'mental illness' and is untreatable, or the belief that talking about hallucinations will result in increasing intensity of hallucinatory experience for the client). Meta cognitions (beliefs about the nature of psychological processes) are also important. Believing that clients must understand about behavioural intervention for them to work effectively may lead to staff giving up on intervening in this way if the client is out of touch with reality or has a profound learning disability.

The third level of formulation necessary for a complete description of factors leading to the creation or maintenance of problematic experience and behaviour for inpatients is the level of the organization itself. The NHS is most often the organization responsible for inpatient care. Over the past 20 years a dramatic shift away from long-term 'asylum' care to short-term, brief intervention, community care and cost awareness had meant the general acceptance that admission should be brief, focused on 'treatment' and a last resort in most cases (*National Service Framework for Mental Health*, Department of Health 1999a). There is often lack of clarity about reasons for admission and discharge, but there are certain features which predominate in the majority of inpatient wards. These may be summarized as follows.

The psychiatrist's opinion and treatment plan take precedence. Other professionals may disagree and say so, but the final decision will rest with the psychiatrist, especially the consultant psychiatrist. This may stem from the widespread confusion about the term 'Responsible Medical Officer', which in fact has meaning only in the context of legal sections, but is often interpreted to mean that the psychiatrist has responsibility for all aspects of treatment (not just medication and ECT) for all clients. Even establishments such as coroners' courts fall victim to this misapprehension, calling the psychiatrist to account over unexpected deaths and suicides, as if they were the sole professional involved, so that psychiatrists can with justification insist that, since they will be hauled over the coals in case of disaster, we had all better do as they say.

The interactions between the professionals in the multidisciplinary team and the ward environment are complex. Good practice guidance dictates each member listens to the rest and respects their views and opinions. But the levels of emotional intensity combined with daily familiarity on the wards can contribute to strongly held, passionate opinions which can become personal. The more difficult the problem, the more intense these feelings can be. Overt criticism in front of clients does not often occur, but there are often power struggles occurring behind the scenes which can result in the client's treatment becoming substandard. At times clients may join one camp against another, for example, if the client prefers one diagnosis because they perceive it only involves taking pills rather than another diagnosis they think might involve taking risks.

The target and benchmarking culture that pervades the NHS at present may place perverse incentives on the care of the client. For example, reducing length of admission may be achieved by better interventions or by premature discharge. Patients' rights to complain may lead to employers 'sacrificing' an employee at the centre of a serious complaint, to protect the good of the organization. This may produce a reluctance to take risks and a practice of 'covering one's back'. Thus, to formulate the whole picture requires a willingness to name and discuss these issues and their potential effect on the outcome for individual clients.

Case example: Archie

A 24-year-old man was admitted from the general hospital following treatment for severe injuries after an intense episode of self-harm carried out within a prison cell, where he had been held on remand for allegedly setting fire to his flat. He had cut his body from head to ankles with a razor, including partially severing his penis. The client had a pre-existing diagnosis of paranoid schizophrenia, based on his hearing voices, with onset around 14 years old. He had no previous history of self-harm except for smashing his fists into walls when upset.

Archie stated that he did not wish to live, for now his life was ruined because of the harm he had done himself and he might never have a normal sex life again. He also repeatedly criticized himself and said he had always been a bad person and there was nothing he could do about it. He had a history of abusing street drugs and alcohol and petty crime.

He described the self-harm incident as follows. He was in his cell and heard inmates in his neighbouring cell tell him he was a paedophile and responsible for the abuse of a young relative of his. They told him to punish himself severely and he did. It is unclear where he got the blade but must have had it concealed about him. The prison guards said there was no one in the neighbouring cells, but Archie believed they were lying. The day before the self-harm he had been visited by the young relative, who did not smile at him as usual. He found this very distressing.

The lead-up to the arson incident involved several events. He said he was housed in a tough area, and became the victim of taunts from the local children, who called him a paedophile whenever he went out. This made the voices he heard worse. The day he set fire to his flat he received a letter from the local council, refusing to rehouse him. He became desperate and enraged. He thought he would destroy the flat and then the council would have to rehouse him. He warned the neighbours about what he would do in case he put them in danger. He had said to the neighbours the previous day that he would set fire to the place if his request for a move was denied.

Archie was the eldest of four children. His father was mostly absent earning a living and his main memories were of his mother. He said he had always made her life a misery. He recited a long list of misdemeanours which he carried out as a child. The first, when he was four, involved making a hole in the glass front door by throwing a stone at it. Most of the incidents were of this nature and Archie described catastrophic reactions by his mother. He felt these were deserved and appropriate, but it seemed they were unrealistically severe and age inappropriate. Archie described a lifetime of criticism and accusations by his mother which he accepted without question as factually accurate.

We hypothesized that he came to believe he could never do anything right, would never amount to anything, would cause trouble wherever he went and when people got to know him they would recognize his defects and abandon him. This may have been the reason for his possessive controlling jealousy towards his ex-girlfriend, who ended the relationship because of Archie's verbally aggressive behaviour towards her a week before the incident.

The psychiatrist involved in the case tended to believe that most of his patients were malingering until he could be convinced otherwise. In this case, because there was a trial pending, there was indeed an obvious reason for Archie to lie. Archie was very clear that he preferred the hospital environment to the prison. In addition, the community nurse who visited Archie reported him 'well' two weeks before the incident. Archie, however, claims he was very 'unwell' before the incident, that is, the voices he heard were becoming more frequent and more abusive and he was restless and agitated. He began hiding in his house in order to avoid the taunting children in the street.

A debate ensued on the ward concerning whether or not Archie was lying about being unwell in order to avoid prison, including harming himself severely for this purpose. There was another debate about whether he was lying about being 'unwell' before he committed the arson offence. The staff were divided on these issues.

The urologist confirmed that Archie would be able to have a normal sex life in future, and after a period of disbelieving this, Archie did accept it and seemed to be more optimistic. At no point did he express suicidal thoughts or urges and claimed the self-harm incident was not done with thoughts of dying as the outcome. Apart from very low mood he appeared symptom free during his stay on the ward, saying he felt safe there.

Archie said he was unwell before the arson incident but did not claim the voices told him to set fire to the flat. He said he 'just did it', 'without thinking'. It seemed that if he had wished to lie the most effective thing would have been to say the voices told him to do it, since this would be part of his 'illness'. He reported hearing no voices at all following his admission. A debate ensued about whether he was lying about this also. The psychiatrist's view was that he was 'well' at the time of the offence and there was evidence of premeditation according to the neighbour's report. The psychologist's view was that he may have been ruminating in an obsessional way on the outcome of his request for a move, but that if he had been truly planning he would have worked out he would be arrested as a result. He may have been planning to be imprisoned but he had always shown a horror of prison previously. The psychologist's formulation involved arson as an impulsive act, triggered by multiple stressors including the loss of his relationship, the refusal of the council to rehouse him, the taunting of the children and consequent worsening of the voices.

Archie did not seem to have any delusional belief system about his voices (apart from misattributing them to inmates in neighbouring cells), saying he had had them as long as he could remember. He did not feel obliged to do what they told him, but always agreed with the horrible things they said about him. He was open to discussion about where voices might come from and the nature of the phenomenon and was interested to know how common hearing voices is (Pearson *et al.* 2001). See Figures 5.3, 5.4, 5.5. and 5.6.

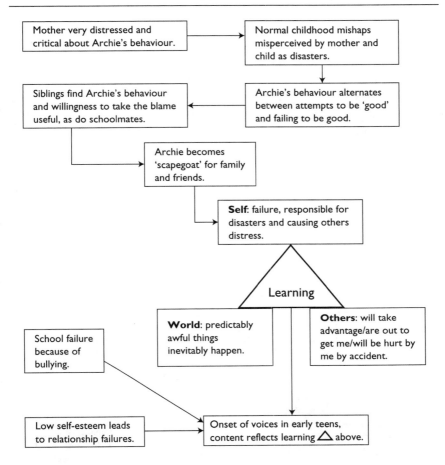

Figure 5.3 Formulation: Archie – development

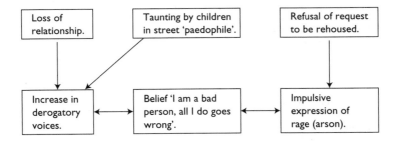

Figure 5.4 Formulation: Archie – precipitating factors for arson

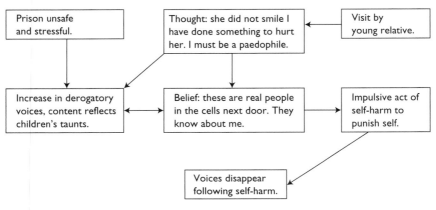

Figure 5.5 Formulation: Archie – precipitating factors for self-harm

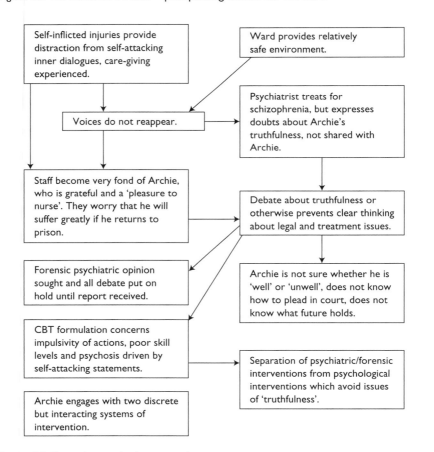

Figure 5.6 Formulation: Archie – ward environment

Effectiveness of formulations

Paul Gilbert (2005), in his work on compassion, stresses how important the shift to a compassionate view of the self and others is within the therapeutic process. He describes compassion thus: 'Compassion . . . involves being open to the suffering of self and others, in a non-defensive and non-judgmental way. Compassion also involves a desire to relieve suffering, cognitions related to understanding the causes of suffering, and behaviours – acting with compassion. Hence, it is from a *combination* of motives, emotions, thoughts and behaviours that compassion emerges' (Gilbert 2005: 1, original italics).

CBT formulations in inpatient settings need to encourage such shifts towards a compassionate stance, not just in the clients themselves but in those around them within the hospital and outside it. There is evidence, for example, from the learning disability field, that staff attributions and beliefs about the causes of a person's behaviour, in particular about whether the person is in control of their own behaviour, affect the outcome of treatment and the behaviour itself (Hastings and Remington 1994).

Because the inpatient unit can be viewed as a closed system, in theory contingencies of reinforcement should be easier to observe, analyse and manage; likewise cognitive rules and assumptions, explicit or implicit. To this extent the *whole environment is the client*. Formulation of client behaviour, staff behaviour and managers' behaviour is necessary to get results. It is the contention of this chapter that a compassionate position is an essential ingredient in and outcome of any formulation, i.e. that the effect of the formulation should be to increase compassion towards the client. A medical (paternalistic) explanation that does not lead to effective treatment can easily transform into (equally paternalistic) condemnation of the client. A compassionate formulation allows forgiveness of self and others, understanding and empathy, all of which are needed for attachment, trust, collaboration and the human relationships which form the basis of mental health.

This means that an alternative narrative to that of madness or badness is provided. If shared collaboratively with client and multidisciplinary team, a compassionate narrative can emerge which is validating for the client and staff and allows the team and the individual to be active in changing the situation. For example, should staff and/or client not perceive any improvement, frustration may set in. Often the contingencies of reinforcement in operation lead to deterioration in the client's behaviour, and attributions are made which follow directly from the medical model. For example, in the case of Sarah, the comment 'she/he is not mentally ill' represents a cognitive categorization with consequences. One (mistaken) consequence is that 'if she is not mentally ill she must be in control of their behaviour'. Therefore, she is being deliberately manipulative and needs to be told off. Linehan (1993a) discusses this confusion between the effect of a behaviour such as self-harm (making staff feel manipulated) and the conscious intent of a behaviour (e.g. making oneself feel better). Such attributions affect staff behaviour towards the client and the transaction between client and system can become mutually invalidating. In the case of hearing voices and having delusional beliefs, an attribution that this is an illness may have corollaries for staff behaviour which mean that the effects of the environment are ignored, as in the case of Archie.

There has been little interest in researching clients' reactions to collaborating or sharing in formulations. Chadwick *et al.* (2003) studied patients' reactions to a shared formulation. They interviewed 11 patients with psychosis who had been treated with cognitive therapy which included a shared formulation. They reported positive (reassured, encouraged and hopeful) and negative (saddened, upset and worried) emotional reactions, based on patients' increased understandings and seeing a way forward, but also on their new perceptions of problems as long term and complex. A client writing in *Clinical Psychology Forum*, told of his own experience: the 'meta messages' he received through sharing his formulation with his therapist were: 'I am sorry you have had all this trouble; you had some negative experience a long time ago; you shouldn't have; that was the cause and these are the effects; this is how to fix it.'

When formulation is collaborative, shared, and owned by all participants, it amounts to the creation of a shared conceptualization of reality which previously did not exist. This 'shared narrative' is the equivalent of the generation of replacement thoughts in cognitive work with individuals, and *requires the same efforts to make it the preferred or 'default' conceptualization.* In reality, several world views are in operation at once and this author has found it useful to formulate this also, as illustrated in the case examples. The shared narrative should be validating, not just to the client but to all concerned. Validation – finding the truth in what each of us feels and thinks – allows us to bear witness to the other person's thoughts, feelings and behaviour, to the fact that their suffering, their point of view, their passionately held opinions, mean something to us (Leahy 2005).

The impact of formulating like this with different levels of the system has rarely been studied. The author's clinical work largely takes the form of sharing assessments and formulations with client, staff and significant others, along with discussion of possible interventions and their likely effects, partly because there is little time to do more in the brief admission period. The average number of sessions in our inpatient work is two. An audit of client and staff perceptions of this service showed high levels of satisfaction and perceived benefit from this intervention. Themes of clients' comments included having an increased understanding of themselves and their problems, some ideas about how to work towards change, being treated as a valued person. Staff ratings also showed high satisfaction levels and comments showed changes in thoughts and feelings towards the client following a shared session: for example, 'I always like the client better after sitting in on a session.' 'I feel more competent to deal with the person's behaviour after discussing the formulation' (Kennedy *et al.* 2003). The audit did not directly address separately the effects of formulating the ward's political and social environment itself, but staff wrote comments such as 'talking openly about conflicts helped me be more balanced in my views'.

Other research supports this, showing that the major effect of therapy usually occurs in the first few sessions (during which collaborative formulation is usually the principal activity). One change which might mediate this impact is the enabling of the individual and system to take a compassionate stance towards the self/client. As Gilbert's work shows, the reduction of shame through compassionate stance leads to great improvements in the self-attacking dialogues and behaviours which often maintain dysfunctional lives (Gilbert and Irons 2005).

Case examples: the effects of formulation

Sarah

In the case of Sarah, the formulation identified rejection by loved ones as the trigger for many self-destructive coping behaviours such as self-harm, eating restriction, over-exercise and violence to others. The hypothesized development of beliefs about herself, the world and others included that no one is there to help, that Sarah herself was defective and unlovable, that she tended to assume the blame for anything that went wrong. Her meta beliefs included that she could not manage her emotions and that her cognitions about herself were all factually correct. Psychological processes hypothesized to be involved in maintaining the problems included dissociation from intense emotion, resulting in inability to recall important facts about her life and failure to experience emotion fully, as well as failure to anticipate and plan for threatening situations. Her disgust at the concept of being gay and her cognitive and behavioural avoidance of the issue resulted in her falling in love with unavailable heterosexual women who rejected her, strengthening her belief in her own defectiveness. On the ward, her attempts at self-harm and escape were driven by her despair at being able to bear her emotions, negatively reinforced by their natural consequences (escape, avoidance of emotion) and intermittently positively reinforced by some staff reactions (care giving and restraint allowing her to feel safe). The negative attitudes shown by some staff strengthened her beliefs in her problems as minimal and her behaviour as melodramatic.

On building and sharing these formulations, several changes were noted. First, Sarah herself stopped self-harming and trying to escape and began to engage with the psychologist and the nurses (albeit in an idealizing way). Second, a debate about diagnosis began, with borderline personality disorder as a possibility, with consequences for the medication and therapeutic regime. Third, a plan not to physically restrain Sarah in future was developed with her involvement. Fourth, psychological therapy (except for borderline personality disorder, BPD) was not recommended in view of her dissociative coping and belief that she could not manage her emotions. The staff were able to give validating messages about being uncertain about one's sexuality and several gay staff discussed their own struggles with Sarah. This had the effect of reducing her shame around the issue. Fifth, the reported voices were discussed and it was decided to approach these by acknowledging Sarah's uncertainty about whether they were thoughts or not, but normalizing the phenomenon and working alongside rather than trying to change it. Lastly, it was predicted that Sarah would probably develop a sexualized attachment to a heterosexual older member of staff and a plan was made about how to handle this when it happened.

Archie

In the case of Archie, the CBT formulation suggested Archie learned early that he was responsible for bad things happening, which caused stress to others (his mother in the first instance) and meant he was a bad person. His efforts to 'be good' invariably failed because they were based on being perfect. He learned that he was not to be trusted and would always fail and do bad things. Later he learned at school that others were out to get him. He believed he did not deserve to be loved, which fuelled a conviction that his partner would leave him for almost anyone else (who would, by definition, be better than him). This produced severe anxiety and jealous, controlling behaviour, which usually resulted in his partner leaving, a self-fulfilling prophecy.

The content of the voices, which had always been derogatory, changed to focus on the theme of Archie being a paedophile when the children taunted him. Being in the habit of believing his voices were correct about him and not questioning their veracity meant he most naturally thought what he heard was true. His delusion that there were prisoners in neighbouring cells rather than voices when he self-harmed was also understandable, since there really had been children saying these things around his flat. This, following or triggered by the unusual coolness of his young relative towards him during the prison visit, produced emotions that were too difficult to bear and a strong urge to harm himself which he acted upon impulsively. The non-appearance of the voices in the ward environment supported his own statements that he felt safer there than anywhere he had recently been. His thoughts, however, continued along the same ruminative lines about his uselessness, worthlessness and culpability, now focusing on the hurt and worry he had caused his family, his mother in particular. The ward environment, when messages about his not being trustworthy were being transmitted to him indirectly, served to strengthen his belief system about himself, as prison would have earlier.

Through the formulation process the staff, including the psychiatrists, became aware of our focus on whether or not the client was malingering and its effect on our relationships with each other and with him, and also the effect on our ability to think clearly about needs for intervention. By creating two separate streams of thinking – one about the legal aspects including whether or not he had been 'ill' at the times of the fire setting and self-harm incidents, and one about the development and maintenance of his problems – we were able to refocus our efforts on providing effective help.

The formulation liberated our thinking and allowed us to start work normalizing the experience of hearing voices and discussing various interpretations of the phenomenon. The normalizing of behaviours and experiences around voices is just one example of the potential for transformation that psychological formulation offers (Morrison et al. 2004). We were also able to carry out behavioural experiments about the truth or otherwise of the content. Mindfulness work on accepting the voices without fighting them or acting on them was also done by staff. Archie was an exceptional artist and work began on how he could use this skill commercially, at first voluntarily and later for financial reward. This work could be done alongside the legal processes and meant we could demonstrate therapeutic progress when the time came for the courts to decide how to proceed.

We predicted that if Archie returned to prison his behaviour would most certainly deteriorate and he would be at high risk of harming himself severely again. We also predicted that if he was discharged from hospital back into his former housing area he would not manage the taunting and might pose a risk to himself and other people. We recommended a combination of supported housing with therapeutic input around his self-attacking inner dialogue and management of voices, possibly with legal sanctions should he reoffend.

In both cases, a shift was observed from disagreement and potential acrimony among those in caring roles towards a more compassionate stance: that is 'being open to the suffering of self and others, in a non-defensive and non-judgmental way. . . . also a desire to relieve suffering, cognitions related to understanding the causes of suffering, and behaviours – acting with com-passion' (Gilbert 2005: 1).

Making formulation more effective

Although there is no research available on this topic, the author has found that extending the principles and practices of CBT with individuals to the wider system is effective. Therefore, in order to develop a shared narrative, it is important that all key figures in the client's ward environment are included. The practice of *having the key worker included in the assessment and formulation sessions* (usually the primary nurse) means they feel con-sulted and collaborative in developing the shared psychological under-standing. Sadly, there are few inpatient settings where there are sufficient CBT practitioners to attend all ward rounds, and indeed the nature of these, as discussed earlier, often precludes open and mutually validating discussion.

Guidance on New Ways of Working for Psychiatrists (NIMHE 2005a; see also Kinderman, Chapter 3) makes recommendations that, if implemented, may *change the balance of power* within inpatient and other settings. At present, the acceptance of the psychiatrist's word as final creates difficulties for the whole team (including the psychiatrist) as well as for the client, as illustrated in the case examples.

The boundaries of confidentiality are often blocks to effective formu-lation, in that if too narrow they preclude sharing of information. The practice we have implemented involves asking for *client consent to wider confidentiality*, to the team of professionals who are involved in the client's care, on the ward and in the community. This has not yet been refused, but in the case of refusal would be treated the same way as any other refusal, namely the client's reasons would be explored and the consequences for the effectiveness of the intervention explained.

The constantly changing nature of circumstances requires a constant review and updating of formulation. Because the inpatient setting is a unique and restricted environment, attention must be paid to formulating the likely external environment to which the client will be discharged and predicting and addressing the obstacles to generalization of progress on the ward to the normal environment. In our service the lack of psychology resource prevented this being done effectively. In an ideal service the *assessment, formulation and recommendations should be repeated around discharge planning.*

It must be stressed again that formulation is the middle step in the process between assessment and intervention, whilst also acting as an intervention in itself. With greater resource, it should be possible to formulate the client's interactions with staff and other clients throughout their stay in order to keep the interventions on a compassionate track. Reflective practice work (see Cowdrill and Dannahy, Chapter 10) may be the most efficient way of doing this.

Summary and conclusions

This chapter has set out to demonstrate that the inpatient ward can be regarded as a unique environment. Often tough and harsh for inpatients who are already severely distressed before admission, it can also offer asylum in the true sense. Staff as well as clients have restricted contact with the outside, and thoughts, feelings and behaviour can be intensified and exacerbated. This hothouse can also be seen as an ideal environment for the functional analysis and formulation of behaviour, with its endless opportunities for assessment and observation, but with awareness that these only tell us about the person in the ward context. The formulation of the effects of the ward environment is vital, given the artificial nature of the situation and the enormous potential for harm and for good that the behaviour, thoughts and feelings of the caregivers may have.

We need to describe the development and maintenance of the problems on the 'outside' and the potential maintenance of the problems on the 'inside' of inpatient life. We need to pay attention to differences in reinforcement contingencies between the two environments and take measures to ensure benefits are gained from an inpatient stay and that they generalize to the person's normal life. We need to use CBT formulations to influence the attitudes and understanding of the client, the staff and the significant others in the person's normal life towards a more compassionate stance.

Assessment, intervention and even evaluation are things we have in common with other practitioners, but as psychologists and as therapists formulation is something unique we have to offer. Our presence in the inpatient setting is sparse and we need to make it felt to best effect. Formulation as intervention with the aim of producing compassionate understanding and action seems a good place to start.

Although CBT is noted for its evidence base, there is a paucity of research on formulation. Clinical psychologists and others have recently begun a fascinating debate on the nature of formulation and its purposes. The development of explicit concepts of the processes involved in formulation and a shared value base to underpin the activity is needed. Work is urgently required to investigate the contribution of formulation work to the therapeutic endeavour. The changes in understanding and emotions experienced by those involved may be a good place to start.

As the formulators, of course, it is very easy to neglect our own attitudes, judgements, prejudices, assumptions, emotions and limited knowledge bases. Using supervision, reflective practice and other opportunities to formulate our own behaviour in the inpatient setting seems, above all, essential for effective ethical practice and for demonstrating faith in our own professional activity.

Part II

Individual CBT in the inpatient setting

Chapter 6

Pioneering a cross-diagnostic approach founded in cognitive science

Isabel Clarke

Introduction and context

Therapy is human interaction. Admittedly it is a stylized, boundaried and one-sided interaction with the aim of facilitating change in one of the parties. Conventions around the delivery of therapy have grown up in the different schools. These can become as precious to therapists as the essentials of their approach. The circumstances of the acute inpatient setting make the maintenance of many CBT conventions impossible, as these rely on predictability – of availability of the client, for instance. As a result, inpatient therapy has traditionally been confined either to institutions that keep people for longer and predictable lengths of time, such as specialist personality disorder units, or has been offered to a limited number of clients, with a set number of sessions spanning discharge, or, more frequently, is postponed altogether until after discharge. The evidence base naturally reflects current practice, so there is no evidence base for offering therapy, across diagnosis, during the period of admission, as far as possible to all inpatients deemed to be able to benefit from it by the clinical team. Consequently, we have attempted both to develop and deliver such a service and to evaluate its effectiveness (see Durrant *et al.* 2007; also Chapter 15).

Seeing someone for CBT within the hospital differs in a number of respects from the first appointment in a community setting. The referral will usually have been perfunctory and rapidly picked up: delay and the individual will have been discharged before they could be seen. Prior information in the form of medical files might or might not be available, so that often a briefing from the key nurse and the notes made by the admitting psychiatrist are the only information preceding the person. Taking an exhaustive history from the individual is not advisable at this time. They are already in crisis, so exploring sensitive areas in the past could lead to further destabilization, as well as wasting precious time. Conditions are further not conducive to the cool collaborative discussion of agenda and goals of therapy that precede the standard CBT delivery. However, the circumstances do have their own predictability and regularities which inform the therapeutic approach to be outlined in this chapter, and the two following it.

A word about the context: Woodhaven Adult Mental Health Unit is the NHS acute psychiatric hospital serving the New Forest, and the western area of Southampton known as Totton and Waterside. It currently has 24 acute beds and two six-bedded psychiatric intensive care units (PICUs), one of which takes referrals from the whole of Hampshire. It is a new-build hospital that opened in 2003 with the optimism, vision and determination to put right the mistakes of the past which comes with a new venture. Much of this optimism and vision has borne fruit. The building, which was designed in consultation with service users, carers and staff, has won a design award. The refocusing initiative and training in solution focused conversation that was part of the inception of the hospital has oriented the institution towards the therapeutic and away from some of the more restrictive elements of traditional nursing practice. These initiatives were ably facilitated by the nurse consultant, Nick Bowles (Bowles *et al.* 2001). Part of this orientation towards the therapeutic was embodied in a singular skill mix, with more occupational therapists than usual and provision for a consultant clinical psychologist and a CBT therapist. The latter post was opened to clinical psychologists as well as nurse therapists and was filled by my colleague, Dr Hannah Wilson.

In many ways, therefore, we are privileged, in particular in having two full-time, CBT-oriented clinical psychologists working in one relatively small hospital. However, the pressures and dynamics of working in the acute sector have not passed us by. Positive risk management and therapeutic approaches are undermined by the inevitable critical incidents and pressure from management following these. Staff move, so that many of the founding contingent are no longer with us. Not all were convinced of the brave new approach in any case, particularly on the PICUs, where the pressures are felt most keenly. 'Modernization' – meaning more pressure on beds and the closure of a ward – is upon us, leading to more staff movement and vacancies. Part of modernization is the establishment of the new teams designed to keep people in the community for as long as possible (e.g. crisis resolution and home treatment).

The effect of these developments is to reduce admission times and concentrate the most severe pathology within the hospital. Along with the relentless pressure of admissions and discharges, and the financial constraints that make finding suitable placements for those with complex needs almost impossible and so consign them to long periods in the unsuitable (for the long term) care of the acute hospital, the daily life of the institution is fraught with stress and unpredictability which will be familiar to anyone with recent experience of inpatient work in the UK. It is a direct result of our greater therapy resource, which could well be under threat as modernization gathers pace, that we can spare the time to see a significant number of individual referrals at the same time as providing the indirect consultation work that can absorb most of the energies of our colleagues in other institutions. Under indirect work I include reflective practice, care planning and behavioural management consultation, staff training and supervision – all of which we are currently able to provide.

A cross-diagnostic approach to working with crisis

The basis for the approach is the CBT for severe mental illness model developed while working in an inner city tertiary outpatient department during the 1990s, and written up for publication (Clarke 1999). Throughout the 1990s, CBT was developing rapidly to meet the challenge of treating client groups with far more severe pathology than ever envisaged by the founders of the model. Different practitioners responded to this challenge by adopting an eclectic mixture of developments within and beyond CBT. The Interacting Cognitive Subsystems (ICS) model of Teasdale and Barnard (1993) presented itself as the ideal theoretical foundation to provide coherence between mindfulness-based treatments, attachment and transference theories, direct work with emotion, and all the other elements that had found their way into the latest CBT practice.

On first encountering ICS, I assumed it would soon sweep the board. I was wrong. I had not allowed for the tendency for each authority to produce their own information processing model, or for slowness in grasping the scope and potential of ICS – but then I am a convert! However, most branches of CBT now accept the need for a multilevel processing explanation – it is just that such explanations proliferate. I would argue that wherever mindfulness is at the heart of a cognitive approach, as in all the third wave approaches (see Chapter 1), ICS provides possibly the cleanest theoretical rationale for its utility. Barnard (2004) has provided a thorough and cogently argued review of this field.

The prominent place accorded to mindfulness, or an equivalent (see Wells' 'attentional training', Wells 1997), is a feature of the recent developments in adapting CBT for severe mental health problems. ICS provides a clear explanation for the role of mindfulness as it places two, not one, higher order meaning making subsystems at the heart of its cognitive organization. These two central subsystems are called the 'implicational' and 'propositional' subsystems. Thus, the subsystems processing input from sensory and body state channels directly inform the implicational subsystem, whereas the propositional subsystem gets its input from the verbal centres. This provides a solid theoretical underpinning for the difference in kind between emotional processing, 'hot cognition', and the verbal, analytical 'cool' cognition noted by CB therapists from Ellis onwards.

It further maps neatly on to the DBT distinction between 'emotion mind' (the implicational) and 'reasonable mind' (the propositional; Linehan

1993a, 1993b). The DBT category of 'wise mind' can be identified with the situation where the two main subsystems are working smoothly together. This mode of operating is labelled by Teasdale and Barnard as 'the central engine of cognition' (1993: 76) and is the norm. However, one or other of the central subsystems (propositional or implicational) can become dominant, which narrows the information base on which the individual is operating at such times. For instance, where the implicational dominates, new propositional material, such as cool appraisal of a situation, will be difficult to access – hence reactions such as irrational panic. Similarly, where emotional material is felt to be too dangerous or threatening to the self, it can be blocked, leading to incomplete processing and so to the complications of grief and trauma reactions.

Conventional (first wave in Hayes' terms) CBT relies on harnessing the propositional appraisal – in other words getting the person to become aware of and be critical of how they are thinking about the situation. Where emotion is overwhelming, or the schema is too entrenched, this approach falters. ICS has a clear explanation for such entrenched schemas which are produced by a restricting interlock in the communication between the two central meaning-making systems (Teasdale and Barnard 1993: 105). The therapist encounters this situation when the client declares that they can see the logic perfectly, but their fear/obsession or whatever remains just as compelling. Teaching the technique of mindfulness enables the client to gain distance from both the overwhelming affect and the propositional appraisal, and so find a way into the continuous transaction between the two and take charge.

ICS-based formulation

When someone who finds themselves admitted to hospital in crisis is referred to a therapist, the priority is to create a simple and intuitively valid way of making sense of their situation. They need to know how it is that they find themselves in this predicament, in such a way that indicates clearly how they can participate actively in the solution. This rationale needs to be clear enough to penetrate a state of panic and confusion. It needs to be compelling enough to persuade someone to take charge of the process of working on change for themselves, when they might have been accustomed to passively allowing their 'illness' to be treated by the psychiatrist and team. It needs to be able to sidestep powerful self-critical schemas when normalizing the negative feedback loops that have produced and deepened the crisis. Such people can sometimes react to a CBT formulation by feeling criticized for making themselves 'ill' by thinking the wrong thoughts. Such a reaction is a powerful motivator to reject the psychological perspective in favour of a narrowly medical one.

The ICS model is helpful here. According to this theory, the implicational level is always alert for meaning in relation to the self. It is closely connected to the arousal system, so reacts to perception of threat to the self with a self-perpetuating and reinforcing cycle of autonomic arousal and increased vigilance to threat. For human beings, as with higher animals such as apes, information on place in the social order and therefore relationship is perceived as threat, or proof of value (see Gilbert 1992 for this evolutionary approach to human social order, arousal and psychopathology). I find this formulation of human motivation more convincing than the frequently encountered 'goal pursuit' hypothesis (e.g. Austin and Vancouver 1996). Rationally derived goals are the province of the propositional subsystem, whereas the situation of the self – whether about to eat or be eaten – is in the domain of the implicational, and therefore most relevant for disorders with an emotional origin.

To return to the effects of a perception of threat, ICS is particularly helpful in providing an explanation for the way in which memory of distant trauma is converted into a current sense of threat. According to the model, each subsystem has its own memory store, coded in its particular coding modality. Thus, the implicational memory is coded in a multimodal way, representing all the senses. This means that information on previous threat situations is preserved along with the sights, sounds and smells of the original experience in all its vividness. It also means that, being quite separate from the verbal propositional memory store, the information that all this happened a long time ago and is not a current threat is absent. Such implicational memories are triggered and experienced as immediate in matching high states of arousal. The propositional ability to distinguish time and place gets lost along with the flexible connection between the two main subsystems at such times. In extreme cases, this results in the type of delusional flashback that Marie experienced (Chapter 4). Her hospital admissions were necessitated when her conviction that one of her abusers was present became overwhelming, and she would feel compelled to attack herself in the same way that she had been attacked. She was so convinced that her abuser was present that she would call the police, and on one occasion cut off contact with her sister for many years when she was convinced her sister had brought her abuser to her flat.

The person finding themselves in hospital is mainly aware of an overwhelming sense of affect, which can be perceived as external threat, or as internal threat in the form of unacceptability of the self. This sense of threat is registered as visceral discomfort rather than specific thoughts. Where thoughts such as 'I am unworthy' are accessible, they are given power through the arousal reaction they provoke. Naturally, the person will seek to escape this intolerable affect in some way or another. They might attempt to block the affect through alcohol or street drugs. They might withdraw (cease to compete in Gilbert's ethological terms) and become

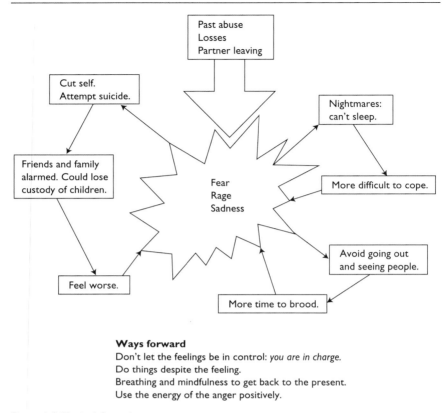

Figure 6.1 Typical formulation

vegetatively depressed. They might maintain high anxiety through worry, or respond to anxiety with compulsions, or eating disorder.

Perhaps more controversially, psychosis can be seen as the facility that people on the higher end of the schizotypy continuum have to escape into an alternate reality when faced with a crisis (see Claridge 1997). Mike Jackson (among others) has named psychosis a 'problem solving' response (Jackson 2001: 187). All these varied responses, which map on to the different psychiatric diagnoses, have the following feature in common: the person will have found ways of coping with a bad situation that appear to offer short-term relief or escape, but which maintain and intensify the problem in the longer term. Self-harm is a classic example of this sort of response.

The ICS-based formulation that we employ at Woodhaven names the central sense of threat and constructs a simple diagram (see Figure 6.1). At the centre of the diagram, the sense of threat is represented graphically by a spiky blob. This is an attempt to represent what it feels like for the individual – like an emotional wound at their very core, that they seek to escape, but make worse in the process. The earlier threat circumstances that have been retriggered in the current crisis are named at the top of the diagram, without elaboration – abuse, critical messages from parents, bereavements and other life events, etc. The maintaining cycles are drawn at the bottom.

In some ways this is only different from the conventional, Beck-type CBT formulation diagram in that the core is drawn jagged and spiky rather than in a neat box, and overall meaning (i.e. threat) is emphasized more than specific thoughts. On the other hand, it has proved to be a style that communicates very directly, at a visceral level, in line with the ICS prediction that the only way to influence at the implicational level is to use implicational styles of communication. It obviates the necessity for a lot of explanation of the model, aimed at the propositional. True to the emphasis in ICS, most of the rationale comes from an explanation of the body's arousal system and the effect this has on concentrating thought on to threat, limiting ongoing appraisal and so cutting out the rational, propositional part of the cognitive system. This type of formulation has been found to have three advantages:

1   There is the central naming of the felt sense as the problem.
2   It leads to simple ways out of the vicious circles that have been named; arousal reduction work, facing rather than avoiding affect and practical behavioural steps towards change.
3   It provides a rationale that is simple and powerful enough to have a chance of persuading people who are looking for 'them' to provide the right medication to make them feel better, that they themselves have a role to play in the process – a point of view that is welcome to many but not to all.

The next chapter goes into the approach in more detail, illustrated with clinical examples.

ICS and psychosis

The ICS model also offers a way of making sense of psychosis that is complementary to the conventional CBT for psychosis approach. CBT for psychosis has made a powerful argument for normalization through the continuity of thinking processes (see Garety *et al.* 2001 for a recent review of the field). Taken to extremes, this can appear to ignore the different quality of experience in psychosis, though works such as Gumley and Schwannauer's (2006) book on preventing relapse do acknowledge the importance of the nature of the experience (e.g. p. 23). ICS provides a possible basis for understanding this different quality. Barnard (2003) has extended the model to account for psychosis, identifying desynchrony between the two central meaning-making systems as an explanation for anomalous experience. This makes sense, as the individual relies on the propositional subsystem for precise meanings, and where this part of the cognitive apparatus is temporarily unavailable, the implicational can hold sway with its powerful sense of meaning and significance but lack of distinctions.

This is further in line with other authorities who link disruption in information processing to the psychotic experience. Frith (1992) suggests an explanation at the neuropsychological level in the form of a self-monitoring deficit that leads both to a breakdown in willed intention, and anomalous conscious experiences such as heightened perception, thought broadcast and synchronicities. Gray, Hemsley and others (e.g. Gray *et al.* 1991) also link the characteristic difficulties observed in psychosis/schizophrenia to possible underlying neurological difficulties. Problems such as perceptual disturbances and disruption of activity can be ascribed to 'disturbance in the moment-by-moment integration of stored regularities with current sensory input' (Hemsley 1993: 635). Fowler (2000) has identified confusion between inner and outer origin of stimuli as a way of understanding the confusion between voices and inner speech among other phenomena. All of these explanations contain an element of the disruption of the part of the mind that gives stimuli their current context, which would fit well with the idea of desynchrony between the propositional and implicational subsystems.

I have argued elsewhere (Clarke 2001) that this dissolution of context and boundaries, combined with a heightened sense of meaning, can produce a sense of oneness and participation in the whole which can be exhilarating in the short term (as in a spiritual or drug-induced experience), but frightening and persecutory in the longer term. This can be seen as the source of psychotic experiences such as the instability of the sense of self and openness of the mind to intrusion from outside (through the television, for instance). Such a perspective both provides a normalizing explanation for someone's unnerving experiences, and a rationale for mindfulness as a treatment. Another third wave approach to psychosis, featuring mindfulness, is being pioneered by Chadwick (see Chadwick 2006 for details of the approach; Chadwick *et al.* 2005 for the latest research on this).

Psychosis and emotion

The link between psychotic experience and the dominance of the implicational subsystem suggests the applicability of aspects of the dialectical behaviour therapy (DBT) model and skills approach to psychosis, because of the easy mapping between the DBT distinction between 'emotion mind' and 'reasonable mind' on to the two central subsystems, with the connection between them, facilitated by mindfulness, corresponding to 'wise mind'. Of course, the focus of DBT is on the regulation of emotion, and at first sight, there appears to be a considerable gulf between overwhelming emotion and the more dissociated states characteristic of much psychosis. However, there has been recent advance in the sophistication of our understanding of the relationship between emotion and psychosis. Research such as Morrison's on the overlap between anxiety disorders and intrusive thoughts and psychotic symptoms (Morrison 1998, 2001) points to a close relationship. My own clinical experience of the monitoring forms completed by participants in the voices and symptoms groups I have run over many years demonstrate that vulnerability to these phenomena is correlated with states of high and low arousal. These are precisely the times when the propositional subsystem is most sidelined, and therefore the implicational is to a greater or lesser extent in charge – as is the case at times of over-whelming emotion.

Research has also demonstrated that even in the case of negative symptoms, apparent lack of emotion being a prime example of these, strong emotion is present but not betrayed. Myin-Germeys et al. (2000) found that, comparing intensity of emotion experienced between a group of people with a diagnosis of schizophrenia and controls, the experimental group experienced more intense negative, but not positive, emotion. The authors concluded that flattened behavioural expression of emotions does not accurately reflect inner emotional experience. This fits with the hypo-thesis regarding negative symptoms that they are a protective withdrawal in the face of hypersensitivity to stimuli, as opposed to an absence of reactiv-ity. This is in line with the high schizotypy, and therefore greater openness to a variety of stimuli, way of understanding psychosis (Claridge 1997). Watkins (1996) argues this perspective both persuasively and accessibly.

These factors suggest a new perspective on the relationship between psychosis and emotion where the empathically expected emotional reaction is absent, not because emotion is absent, but because it is blocked or dis-placed. In the absence of accurate propositional appraisal of an emotional situation, the person in a psychotic state of mind will either act on the emotion without being aware of it or without appraising it (leading to arbitrary acts of violence, for instance), or will construct a delusional expla-nation for the emotion. It becomes reasonable to draw a parallel between such states of mind and the DBT concept of 'emotion mind'. Mindfulness can therefore be employed to reach the more balanced 'wise mind'.

Treatment

Viewing psychosis in this way provides a number of useful openings for therapy, in the form of the new normalization of the psychotic quality of experience, collaboratively exploring the two types of experience (shared and idiosyncratic); using mindfulness and other skills to navigate between them, and in understanding and working with emotion and the self in psychosis. It also facilitates motivational work where the attractions of the psychotic reality for the individual lead to risk and continued hospitalization.

Normalization and negotiation of acceptable language are core skills for CBT for psychosis, and are particularly helpful in the inpatient context where the team might be struggling to make a therapeutic alliance with somebody. The concept of illness is frequently not intuitively obvious to someone who is aware of unusual experiences but no physical debilitation or damage. In earlier writings on ICS and psychosis (Clarke 2001, 2002a), I have linked the tendency to subsystem desynchrony with the well-researched concept of schizotypy. Claridge and his associates (see Claridge 1997 for a comprehensive overview of the research here) of course track the relationship between schizotypy, a greater openness to unusual experience, to proneness to psychotic breakdown, but also link it to high creativity and spiritual experience (Brod 1997; Jackson 1997).

I frequently use these ideas to normalize the vulnerability to this type of openness, at the same time as being realistic about the difficulties it brings. This provides a non-threatening way into discussing the idea that people who are 'sensitive' in this way often have the choice to inhabit either the shared reality or their own reality, but that being able to distinguish the two is useful for survival (and hence for getting out of hospital/off their section – frequently the most powerful motivators for this group). I often track this idea with the person using a simple diagram with two columns. People soon get the idea and can point to the right column for a particular turn in the conversation (their new idea to save the world = 'their reality'; being firm with the person who keeps asking for cigarettes = 'shared reality').

This formulation makes it easier to discuss with people that their particular conceptualizations of reality might not be shared by others, and to invite them to check things out, in the usual tradition of CBT reality testing. The idea that 'the feeling is real, but the story might be wide of the mark' lies at the heart of this approach, and links closely with the earlier discussion of psychosis and emotion. This leads naturally into emotion and arousal based skills work, as discussed earlier. It also provides a way into talking about the confusions around the self that abound in psychosis.

Negotiating a language that is acceptable to the individual, rather than imposing an external language, is also crucial. The individual who is adamant that they do not have schizophrenia can often identify times of 'confusion' or even 'weird thinking', to give clinical examples. Mindfulness is taught as the skill that can ground them in the present, view internal experiences such as voices or convinced ideas dispassionately, and enable them to discern whether they are in the shared or the individual sphere of experience. Drawing out the characteristics of the non-shared reality, such as a sense of super-specialness of the self, or of the supernatural, is further useful in normalizing bizarre experiences and putting them into perspective. I have published a case illustrating this elsewhere (Clarke 2002b).

Another advantage of this approach is that it opens the way to working motivationally with people who are either ambivalent about joining the dominant reality (which characteristically offers someone with a diagnosis like schizophrenia an undesirable position in the social order), or frankly prefer their own reality. While working with distress is the main rationale for CBT for psychosis, a positive adherence to a psychotic reality can entail issues that lead to continued hospitalization (i.e. self-neglect, violence, greater accessibility of distressing symptoms, etc.). In such cases, it is useful to be able to start with an even-handed discussion of the advantages and disadvantages of the two states that can appreciate the positive aspects of the idiosyncratic reality, in line with motivational interviewing principles (Miller and Rollnick 1991).

Continuing the therapy and providing continuity

While individual sessions with the psychological therapist might continue during the person's stay in hospital, the formulation and approaches described in the preceding sections breaks down the next stage into elements that can be delivered or supported by group work available within the occupational therapy or psychological therapies programme of the hospital, or by other members of the team. Arousal reduction has been stressed, and this is ably delivered by the relaxation and anxiety management groups offered by occupational therapy and other staff. Where problems regulating emotions, self-harm, impulsivity, etc. are an issue, the DBT-based emotional coping skills programme is crucial (see Chapter 14). The approach described makes this programme applicable across diagnosis, and not just for self-harmers. Because of the link between 'emotion mind' and the state of non-shared reality described above, it is also relevant for some people with psychosis. The practically based self-esteem group described in Chapter 13 and the psychotic symptom programme in the same chapter are further possible routes for referral, depending on the person's particular difficulties.

The formulation routinely reveals practical issues that need tackling in the person's life. These can either be communicated to the team through the care programme approach (CPA) process, or by handing on the rationale of the psychological approach via a joint meeting with the community key worker. Often relationship issues are revealed to be at the heart of the problem, so that family meetings, joint sessions with partners, etc. are arranged, with or without the direct participation of the psychological therapist. The practice of having other members of staff present at assessments, whether named nurses from the ward, or staff who are interested in developing therapeutic skills such as trainee mental health practitioners, means that these professionals can continue to support the person with individual sessions during their stay on the ward. Such staff have the advantage over the therapist of being able to catch someone at a good moment, or talk to them while undertaking another activity, which is helpful where there are engagement issues. A certain proportion of referrals will be already in contact with the community psychological therapies service. In this case, close liaison with the therapist concerned ensures a complementary approach. In other cases, a previously unrecognized need for psychological therapy is uncovered by the hospital referral, and this route can then be pursued by referral to the psychological therapies service following discharge.

Chapter 7

Working with overwhelming emotion

Depression, anxiety and anger

Isabel Clarke and Hannah Wilson

This chapter is designed to illustrate the brief Interacting Cognitive Sub-systems (ICS) based intervention described in the previous chapter with a couple of clinical examples. In both cases, the therapeutic contact was very short; four sessions in the case of the first example, Emma, and only two in the case of Alan, the second example. In both cases, the brief individual work was complemented and reinforced by attendance at the DBT-based, six-session emotional coping skills group that we run in the hospital. Chapter 14 gives more detail about this group.

Case example: Emma

Emma was referred for psychological therapy because she was clearly struggling with overwhelming and conflicting emotions, to which she some-times reacted with self-harm (cutting) as well as battling strong suicidal urges. In addition, there was a history of sexual abuse. In terms of diagnosis, Emma had acquired the label of bipolar disorder, and the purpose of the admission was stated as management of a manic episode. In Emma's case, as in that of many of the people I see, I would suggest 'complex trauma' as a more helpful descriptor of the recurrent distress that interfered with her life from time to time. Whatever the diagnostic label, it was the emotional turmoil that Emma was struggling with which was stopping her from getting on with her life, and had led to admission to hospital.

It is important to keep in mind that Emma's ordinary life came to this sort of a halt only 'from time to time'. Emma is a musician and gifted artistically. Periodic breakdown is only one part of her life, and one she strives to stay on top of by participating in an active, recovery-oriented, self-managed relapse prevention programme. The work we did together was designed to help her to take control when things were particularly difficult, and to increase her insight into her individual vulnerability. Hopefully, this will help her to be more understanding with herself and less self-critical in future episodes, and so make it easier for her to take control of her process for herself in the future.

Engagement

Meeting up in my office was not easy for Emma. She was anxious about leaving the ward and going with me, even though she was accompanied by a mental health practitioner she trusted, who was present during the first two appointments. This enabled the practitioner to continue to support the approach with Emma on the ward between our meetings. Emma also found it hard to sit on a chair for any length of time, and would ask permission to shift to the floor when the session touched on a sensitive topic. She related this difficulty directly to the traumatic memory of being forced by her physically violent father to sit on a chair for many hours as a child. These memories had come to the front of her mind because of her current emotional vulnerability.

Though the first session was brief because of Emma's degree of anxiety, we were able to arrive at a formulation, following the pattern outlined in Figure 6.1 (p. 70). 'Fear, rage, horror' occupy the spiky centre of the diagram, which produce the voices, nightmares and desire to self-punish that drive behaviours that perpetuate the core feelings. Early trauma is named but not explored as the source of these unmanageable feelings, which are preserved as a sense of threat in the implicational memory, ready to be unleashed when some current upset triggers the memories. Interpersonal difficulties with a member of the music group Emma was part of was the destabilizing event in this case. The self-perpetuating patterns that arise as attempts to ward off the intolerable affect are targeted as the points for intervention. Self-harm is an example of such a pattern. If these patterns are followed, they serve to keep the problem emotions alive. If they can be successfully resisted, Emma can get a sense of taking charge and can experience previously intolerable feelings as bearable.

In that first session, there was no time to introduce mindfulness, so we settled for the simple relaxation breathing that encourages the individual to concentrate on the outbreath, and to relax on the outbreath along with the natural relaxation of the chest muscles.

Positive anger work

The most useful piece of work we were able to accomplish during the first meeting was naming and reframing the understandable anger Emma harboured. This anger was directed against the abuser, and against her mother for not believing her. She had tended to disallow anger and to turn it upon herself. I encouraged her to see it as justified, but without relevant target in the present. I suggested how it could be put to use. The anger, which mobilizes the body for action, could be owned as personal strength and its energy put into physical or creative activity in a positive way. Emma had not met this view of anger before and found it helpful.

However, unleashing the anger that had been disallowed for so long was not without its problems, and Emma went through a generally angry period before she reached the more mature control. For instance, her anger surfaced against another participant in the emotional coping skills group (this group was an integral part of her therapeutic programme), meaning that she left the group early. At our second session, she reported having been able to express her anger through shouting when out with a friend at a quiet beach, and felt much calmer as a result.

Another way in which the ICS slant on the DBT formulation of 'emotion mind' helped Emma was in making sense of the way that past trauma governed her present actions and fears. At our third meeting, we tackled Emma's fear of having access to her cigarette lighter, plastic bags or knives. She was prey to obsessively intrusive thoughts that she would set fire to herself, suffocate herself with the bag, or attack others with the knives. The latter impulse was particularly distressing to her.

We linked these fears and impulses to her activated threat system. In the past, she had been in physical danger, and specifically she had been raped after being threatened with a knife. Logically, with her propositional subsystem, or 'reasonable mind', she knew that all that happened a long time ago. However, as I pointed out to her, it is only 'reasonable mind', or the propositional, that has a sense of time. When 'emotion mind', or the implicational, is in charge that sense is lost and the threat is experienced as present.

Past/present confusion in 'emotion mind'

Similarly, it was hard for Emma to understand why, as she had been attacked in the past, she should experience urges to attack herself and others now. Again, I was able to explain that the subject/object distinction that enables us to tell who does what to whom is a feature of propositional logic, and is absent in the implicational/'emotion mind'. This point is recognized as a feature of unconscious cognition in the psychodynamic psychotherapist, Matte Blanco's, system of 'Bi-logic' (see Bomford 1999 for an accessible exposition of this system of logic). Understanding this subject/object confusion, and normalizing intrusive thoughts, enabled Emma to see how mindfulness could help her to reach 'wise mind' and so escape from these compulsions. Seeing these things as understandable in the light of implicational logic also helped her to challenge the idea that she was 'bad' for having these impulses. Negative self-beliefs like this help to activate and maintain the threat system, and so compound the problem.

With trepidation, she opted to test herself by spending the night with access to her lighter. Having passed this test, she experienced increased confidence that she could keep herself safe in general, and the way was paved towards discharge. As she came from another locality, it was not possible to do more than pass on through a letter the psychological work that had been done on the ward to those who will support her back home. However, I am confident in Emma's ability to use and develop the approach for herself.

On the subject of formal evaluation, unfortunately this was missed, as Emma's departure was quite rapid as she had been placed out of area, and the questionnaires completed at the start of therapy were not repeated at the end. (By the time I sent her this write up, it was too long after the therapy to send the questionnaires, and experience has suggested that return rates for questionnaires sent on are low.) This is a problem we frequently encounter, which will be discussed in Chapter 15.

Case example: Alan

Alan is a middle-aged man who came into the hospital following a serious and quite determined suicide attempt. This was his first contact with mental health services. I think it is an example of how providing a short piece of work at this point of acute need can be a highly effective and efficient way of achieving life changes at a time most relevant for the client. Alan and I only met individually on two occasions alongside his attendance at the emotional coping skills group.

Recent history and background

I met Alan for the first time a few days after he was admitted to the hospital having taken a significant overdose. He had written a suicide note to his wife and had high intention at the time to take his life. He was currently unemployed due to a back injury and was trying to hide considerable debt from his wife. He had previously been self-employed running his own business but also had to give this up due to the back pain. After a long and painful illness, Alan's father had also recently died with whom he had had a difficult relationship. Alan had been married for 14 years and had two children aged nine and twelve. An additional stressor was that during this time he had been trying to complete an Open University (OU) degree.

These pressures increased Alan's vulnerability to unresolved emotional issues from earlier in his life. Alan recalled that in his early childhood his father had treated him differently and less favourably than his younger sister. He recalled finding his father having sexual intercourse with a neighbour when he was about seven years old. Since this time he recalled how his father had been more or less constantly angry with him, opening criticizing him in front of others. Alan's memories of these early experiences were highly accessible to him. He had a felt sense that it was best to keep things to yourself and that to be a 'real man' meant hiding your emotions; not talking openly about your innermost thoughts and feelings. He recalled that in recent years during his father's illness, his father had been in a lot of pain and frequently asked for forgiveness. Alan felt he had been unable to tell his father what he really wanted to say and as a result repressed a lot of his anger about the way he had been treated as a child. He continued to carry the belief that he was not good enough and a failure.

Alan had been coping with these stressful life issues and strong emotions by avoidance and hiding his innermost thoughts and feelings from those he loved. This was understandable given his history and strong messages that to be a man you should hide your feelings, deal with difficulties alone or face rejection for finding the truth. However, this way of reacting meant that Alan was left overwhelmed with his emotions and isolated without support. The fear of becoming 'discovered' was intense and rather than be discovered he opted to take an overdose.

Naming 'emotion mind', normalization and acceptance

Alan and I first shared together what a huge amount of emotional pain he had been carrying over many years. We acknowledged together that this heavy burden had led him to feel that there was no other way out other than to end his own life. Living life as he had done had become intolerable. We explored how this had thrown him into 'emotion mind' and that this way of thinking had made avoidance, self-criticism and suicide seem like the only options available to him. 'Emotion mind' thinking had confused the past and present, making him feel the humiliated little boy once again and convinced that the only way of responding was to 'hide' and cover up his mistakes.

Together we then looked at new, alternative ways of facing difficulties rather than avoiding them. Alan and I worked on ways of being able to face difficult, strong emotions rather than run away from them. This was achieved through the teaching of simple breathing exercises and short mindfulness exercises. By learning how to be mindful of emotion, notice its impact on the body, acknowledge its presence, accept it and watch it like a curious observer, Alan learnt that emotions were more like waves coming and going rather than a foreboding presence that needs pushing away or suppressing. I also encouraged Alan to be gentle on and accepting of himself. He had been through major life changes and losses (i.e. his father's death, loss of his business, etc.). I normalized that feeling vulnerable and fragile at these times was part of the human condition. Therefore, what he needed was acceptance, time and space to build up his strength once more rather than more self-chastisement.

Alan also attended the emotional coping skills group in the hospital to help practise and consolidate these new skills. We talked about the importance of facing practical difficulties in life by breaking them down into small steps and manageable chunks: balancing addressing the difficulties with hobbies and ways to unwind. In addition we discussed how he could let others in to help and support him when feeling stressed and overwhelmed. The more he struggled alone, the more Alan struggled.

In between our two sessions, Alan was able to talk things through with his wife and, with support from the Citizens Advice Bureau, found a way of tackling the debt problem. He also considered a self-referral to Relate to continue to explore ways of improving his communication style with his wife. By using the breathing techniques and mindfulness exercises, Alan also had been able to face talking about his true feelings about his father with his mother and sister. He allowed himself to express his anger about his childhood experiences in a letter to his father and take it to the grave. Dealing with these issues freed Alan to be more accepting of praise and allowed him to acknowledge his own successes (e.g. the OU degree, helping with his son's rugby team) as well as to hear how much others valued him (e.g. accepted that his niece thought he was 'the best uncle'). By accepting himself and his emotions he also recognized that this was making him a more open and loving father and husband.

Alan and I acknowledged how much he had achieved in this very short space of time. He stated that the way of understanding his problems that we arrived at together had helped him see why he had become so stuck. In this understanding also came the answers on how to get unstuck, which he was motivated and ready to employ.

Evaluation

Alan completed a series of questionnaires before we met for the first time and after the second session. The results are shown in Table 7.1. These results and Alan's anecdotal reports suggest that this very brief intervention

Table 7.1 Changes in Alan's questionnaire ratings

	Mental Health Confidence Scale: total score	Living with emotions	Core total score
Before	60	13	1.53
After	70	19	1.15

was highly successful. It targeted his specific psychological and emotional needs at a time of crisis. It highlights that the CBT therapist working in the inpatient unit can facilitate the individual to both weather the immediate crisis and attain a better adaptation in their emotional life.

Chapter 8

Making sense of psychosis in crisis

Bernadette Freemantle and Isabel Clarke

Introduction

Recent advances in CBT for psychosis have often arisen through making connections across diagnoses. For instance, Morrison (2001) has investigated the overlap between intrusive thoughts and ego dystonic voices; both Morrison (2001) and Hemsley (1993) have highlighted the role of arousal in psychotic symptomotology, and Gilbert *et al.* (2001) have identified connections between critical voices, negative automatic thoughts in depression, and social hierarchy. These are probably a sample of what is becoming a gathering trend. The examples of working with psychosis in the inpatient context given here further illustrate the way in which creative therapeutic approaches to psychosis can develop through cross-borrowing from CBT approaches originally developed for other diagnoses. Both examples represent therapy with people detained on the psychiatric intensive care unit (PICU), demonstrating that fruitful work can take place in this setting.

The first example, Daniel, illustrates the potential for the dialectical behaviour therapy (Linehan 1993a) skills training approach to be applied to people with a diagnosis of psychosis. Given the strong association between cannabis and other drug use and psychotic breakdown, it is particularly relevant that this young man, detained on the intensive care unit, was able to recognize for himself that drug use was a major factor increasing his 'vulnerability to emotion mind' (Linehan 1993b: 154). This is a message which is frequently advanced, but just as frequently resisted by this client group. Consequently, a conceptualization that makes clear sense to this service user group has obvious utility. In the second example, the crossover was even more unlikely on the face of it between CBT anger management and religious grandiosity. Both case histories use the 'two ways of experiencing' conceptualization of psychosis introduced in Chapter 6, which maps neatly on to the DBT distinction between 'emotion mind' and 'reasonable mind'. Daniel's case, which follows, is presented by the therapist, Bernadette Freemantle, a DBT-trained staff nurse on the PICU.

Case example: Daniel

Daniel is a young man in his early thirties with a history of psychotic illness. These episodes were characterized by both paranoid ideation and auditory hallucinations. A deterioration in his mental health was triggered by non-compliance of prescribed medication and illicit substance use. He reported that using amphetamine helped him to 'feel better'. He described the effects of amphetamine use as producing clear thinking, confidence and a feeling of being focused.

Although an articulate individual, Daniel would inhibit strong emotions and disturbed thinking through fear of saying 'the wrong thing', which he felt would lead to longer admissions or higher doses of medication. This fear had a negative effect on his mental state as it created a constant state of arousal which fuelled his paranoia and put him in a state of mind where he was more vulnerable to psychotic experiences.

The value of validation

Daniel reported that he finds it difficult to talk about his psychotic 'experiences' because he has found that people often tell him that his 'experiences' are not real. This invalidation of his reality triggered strong emotions of anger, frustration and feelings of confusion about the world around him. He described that this invalidating experience only added to his lack of trust and feelings of suspicion. With this in mind it was helpful when building a therapeutic relationship to at first validate his experience by actively listening, allowing Daniel to tell his story; then reflecting back my understanding of what he had communicated. This process built rapport, allowing me to explore with Daniel the idea of two reality states, the one we share together and the one that only he experiences. This framing of reality states both validated Daniel's experiences and gave an alternative perspective.

States of mind

Using Linehan's mind states model (Linehan 1993b), I introduced the concept of 'emotion mind' and 'reasonable mind'. We explored 'emotion mind' as a state of high arousal that would influence thoughts, physical sensations and behaviour. Daniel was able to recognize that when in 'emotion mind' he was more likely to act impulsively and use illicit substances in order to inhibit these strong emotions. We also linked the high arousal experienced in 'emotion mind' to an increase in racing and intrusive thoughts, auditory hallucinations and feelings of paranoia. The process of problem solving and logical thinking that would occur in 'reasonable mind' would be affected by the aroused state and paranoid thinking, limiting his ability to problem solve in a way that was in his best interests.

Vulnerability to 'emotion mind' and psychosis

We discussed vulnerability factors to 'emotion mind'. This was beneficial in working towards promoting change as it highlighted that both illicit substance use and inhibiting emotions resulted in Daniel being in 'emotion mind'. This aroused state increased his vulnerability to paranoia and auditory hallucinations. He also identified that being detained in hospital itself increased his vulnerability to 'emotion mind' as he described feeling intensely angry and frustrated. Validating this difficult experience formed a therapeutic alliance working towards using the energy of the emotion to work towards his recovery.

Activating 'wise mind'

When introducing 'wise mind' to Daniel, I explained it as a state of mind where 'rational mind' and 'emotion mind' are integrated, achieving a balance or synthesis. By introducing the skill of mindfulness we were able to observe and describe emotions, thoughts, body sensations and urges. Mindfulness exercises appeared to reduce Daniel's arousal state. He reported that it allowed him to have more control and have a choice over how he responded to these emotions. We continued to use these exercises to be mindful of emotions and practise letting these emotions go, working towards reducing suffering and developing a greater understanding of how heightened arousal states increase vulnerability to psychotic experiences.

Applying dialectical behaviour therapy skills training to psychosis

Alongside the skill of mindfulness, we formulated his experiences using an emotion circle (i.e. the Padesky 'hot cross bun' diagram, Greenberger and Padesky 1995: 4; see also Figure 5.1, p. 46 of this book), breaking down emotions, body sensations, thoughts and urges and linking this to psychotic experiences. He described how when he is around people at times he feels sensitive and has paranoid thoughts and feelings. At such times, he states he feels alienated, self-conscious, nervous and anxious, thinking: 'Do they think I am a bad person? Do they think I'm on drugs? What are people thinking about me?' Daniel would describe auditory hallucinations of people making comments about him as he walked by, which further fed into these paranoid thoughts. This triggered an action urge to withdraw and lock himself away, to avoid people. Additionally, he would have urges to use amphetamines to gain the confidence he felt he lacked to face the world. Daniel and I worked on formulating a plan based on DBT skills training to cope with these thoughts and feelings.

1   Reduce arousal with breathing techniques.
2   Use mindfulness to observe and describe thoughts, emotions and conse-quential judgements you make about yourself.
3   To work towards letting these judgements go.
4   Use distraction to focus attention on music or physical activity.
5   Take care of yourself by eating, wearing nice things and not taking illicit substances.

Conclusion

Through acceptance of what is, we can work towards change. Validating Daniel's experience was a way of accepting where he was at the moment; allowing him to accept himself, which in itself is change. He concluded that the amphetamine use was increasing his vulnerability to relapse. By increasing emotional regulation skills and reducing emotional reactivity there was a marked improvement in Daniel's mental state, both in a reduction in symptoms and in his ability to express himself by observing and describing emotions and urges and noticing judgements. This increased Daniel's confidence, sense of control and further developed skills of active problem solving. There was a marked reduction in auditory hallucinations and paranoia. The combination of medical and psychosocial interventions resulted in a shorter admission and sped up the recovery process. Most importantly, we worked towards developing tools for wellness, which could be used for relapse prevention work in the community after discharge.

Case example: Martin

Martin had been admitted to the intensive care unit with an aggressive form of mania some weeks before I first met him. He was a burly man in his early forties, with a shaved head. His diagnosis varied between bipolar and psycho-affective disorder, with religious delusions in the acute phase. As well as messianic ideas, he displayed a short fuse, particularly when faced with the taste in loud dance music favoured by a younger fellow patient. He had demolished a couple of reinforced doors on the unit and aroused considerable apprehension early in his admission. However, he had a level-headed and sensible side to him. He quickly calmed down and regretted having frightened people and requested help with his anger – which was where I came in.

Anger management

As luck would have it, Martin was very angry when I met him for our first session, but not to the uncontrollable extent of earlier in his admission. He had just been refused leave that he had been counting on, and reacted by feeling that the whole world was against him. At the same time, he was keen to have our session and to master his anger enough for that. As we started to talk, a large lorry began to reverse just outside the window, beeping loudly. This reignited his fury and he got up, swearing at the driver and declaring that the man was doing this specifically in order to enrage him. I introduced Martin to my standard relaxation breathing and he was fairly soon able to see that such a notion was absurd, and we laughed together about it.

This proved to be an extremely fruitful introduction, first to anger management and then to psychosis work, as I was able to link this graphic illustration of there being two styles of thinking, one emotion driven and idiosyncratic (implicational dominated in ICS terms) and the other logical and shared (or propositional). Reference to the lorry always raised a smile, and so helped to cement the therapeutic alliance.

In a couple of sessions we got most of the way through my 12-session anger management programme (Bradbury and Clarke 2006), so I tried my luck with applying the same model to the psychotic ideation. As Martin was relatively in remission when I met him, this intervention was aimed at laying the foundation for effective relapse prevention, by developing a shared and agreed way of understanding the ideas that dominated when his psychosis was active. For this reason, I encouraged him to talk about these ideas.

Reconceptualizing the religious delusions

Martin recognized that his religious ideas got out of hand when he was high, and that he alienated people by insisting on his mission to predict the imminent end of the world, etc. However, a vision of angels he had experienced in his youth was precious and important to him, and he considered that the profound conviction behind his messianic ideas must mean that he was 'right', even though he had now calmed down. He recognized the role played by medication in enabling him to keep such ideas more to himself.

It is generally recognized that religious and spiritual concerns are frequently present among the preoccupations of people whose presentation invites a diagnosis of psychosis (see Kingdon *et al*. 2001: 224 for a discussion of the prevalence of religious delusions in studies conducted in different cultures). This observed prevalence has long proved puzzling, and Chapter 6 contains a fuller exposition of how the ICS model can be used as a way of understanding this religious and spiritual content in psychotic thought, and indeed the confusion between the two areas. That exposition is based on Barnard's ICS-based formulation of psychosis (Barnard 2003) and more detailed exposition of the relationship between the two areas in Clarke (2001 and 2002b). Chapter 6 argued that, though this exposition is necessarily speculative, and indeed it is hard to know how to verify it more precisely, it does have clinical utility, and Martin's case illustrates this in practice.

The idea that there could be completely different ways of experiencing and making sense of the world that the reversing lorry had introduced was invaluable in getting across the subtler notion that his visions and convictions could be viewed in two completely different ways. They could simultaneously be real and important (to him) and at the same time not shared by others, nor a good guide for communication with others.

I enquired about any links Martin might have with a faith community and he said he had none currently. He referred to some contact with Jehovah's Witnesses in the distant past. I validated the existence of faith groups for whom Martin's world view would be accepted, but not necessarily his unique role within it. I suggested that such information needed to be treated differently from more conventionally derived knowledge, and introduced to him the idea of 'shared reality' and 'your reality'. I further introduced the caution with which the 'your reality' information needed to be treated. It could simultaneously be a great gift (as the vision of angels evidently was for Martin) and something that others might see differently, so that circumspection about spreading the word was advisable. Above all, the sense of unshakable conviction that apparently gave him a mission to tell the world about it needed to be viewed with great caution. Martin was able to recognize the irrational conviction he had briefly held about the reversing lorry, so could accept that he might need to sit lightly to his sense of personal mission in the religious sphere.

The 'both–and' nature of this conceptualization makes it possible to steer a course between two possible pitfalls in dealing with this sort of content. The traditional medical view is that these experiences are just an 'illness phenomenon'. This judgement is very invalidating and undermining of self-esteem. However, its opposite, an uncritical belief in their absolute validity and therefore the messianic role, is even more prejudicial to a good adjustment, and will tend to lead to continued detention in hospital. Because of the compelling nature of psychotic conviction, where the former (medical) explanation is unacceptable, the individual will be inclined to opt for the latter, and indeed will convert milder forms of collusion with the delusion (for the sake of avoiding an argument, for instance) into endorsement. Arguably it is therefore more strategic not to totally demolish the second explanation, which is where the utility of an approach that allows for 'both–and' comes in.

Preserving self-esteem

The importance of the preservation of self-esteem for recovery from psychosis is becoming increasingly recognized. Harder's (2006) recent research has revealed an interesting negative correlation between 'insight' – in the sense of acceptance of a medical explanation, – and self-esteem. (The introduction to Harder's 2006 paper includes a useful review of the literature on self-esteem and psychosis.) The 'two ways of experiencing' formulation, illustrated above, provides a compromise that both recognizes the validity of the individual's experience and the mismatch between this experience and the perceptions of the rest of the world. This approach acknowledges the validity of the experience for that person, since it is difficult to argue with any sound justification that someone has not had an experience that they claim to have had. It is also possible to add where relevant, as it was in the case of Martin's angels, that such experiences have been reported and indeed valued by others, often throughout history. This then paves the way for the work of the CBT therapist in reducing distress and increasing adaptation to ordinary life through supporting the person to sideline such cognitions for the purposes of everyday living.

The work with Martin was brief, four sessions in all, and in the letter I wrote to his consultant and care co-ordinator, I recommended further relapse prevention work. He was embarking on an anger management group in the community on discharge and my hope is that the work we were able to do on his religious ideation will help him to maintain more capacity for reflection, and another way of looking at things, should he relapse in the future.

Working with psychosis in the inpatient setting

These two examples could give a misleading picture of our overall work with psychosis in the inpatient setting. Both were cases of successful engagement and productive work. Unfortunately, things do not always proceed so smoothly. Many of the people admitted to the unit with psychosis are in an acute phase and not open to a talking therapy approach. It can happen that by the time things have settled down, and they are prepared to reflect, the time for discharge has been reached so little is achieved.

The problems of a 'sealing over' style of coping, where the individual who has recovered from a psychotic episode refuses to think back on it, preferring to assume that this is now in the past and will not recur is well recognized (see Gumley and Schwannauer 2006: 87–88 for an interesting discussion of this phenomenon). In the nature of the problem, there are real motivational difficulties in getting someone to accept an alternative view, which has been well documented in the CBT for psychosis literature. Even where an initial engagement is achieved, the person can bring the contact to an end when they realize that you are not prepared to accept their world view in its entirety.

An example to illustrate this point is a man with longstanding delusions who was detained on the PICU following behaving violently towards people he believed were persecuting him. He was enthusiastic about the idea of 'both–and' logic, and could initially see that his own conviction that he was a special person, destined to save the world, could hold good for everyone else as well. We were beginning to be able to look at the mismatch between his and other people's perceptions of the violent events that had preceded his admission. He was very resistant to the idea that he had been anything but justified in his actions, but was just starting to take this possibility seriously.

My mistake was to do what I do with almost all the people I see. I went through with him the report of my work that I was intending to send to the team, as I almost always copy letters to the person I am writing about. This report explained that he had accepted the idea of another way of experiencing, with a both–and logic. It named that the team would label this way of experiencing as psychosis and recommended medication as the way to deal with it. Though this idea had been brought up verbally, set down in black and white it was too much for this individual, and he decided not to continue the sessions.

I have included this example of a therapeutic rupture to balance the picture and to illustrate the very real difficulties of working with this client group. A CBT approach will not be acceptable to everyone, and it can also be a matter of timing. It might well be possible to reopen the dialogue with the man cited above at some future time. The ward considered that the fact that his court case had been dismissed made him less amenable at the juncture at which he broke off therapy. Other outside factors could influence things in the other direction in the future.

Group work is another way in which people who are very undecided about viewing their symptoms differently can be influenced. Hearing others talk about experiences that they recognize can be more acceptable than being lectured at by those in authority. Chapter 13 gives the example of the psychosis group that we run in this unit.

Chapter 9

Working with personality disorders in an acute psychiatric ward

John McGowan

Though personality disorder has often been a controversial label (Blackburn 2006), in recent years there has been some consensus as to ways forward in treatment (NIMHE 2003a). Despite increased provision of such national guidance, the role of acute psychiatric wards remains somewhat unclear. The following discussion considers how appropriate acute psychiatric wards might be in treating individuals who have been given this label and how ward stays may be improved. In particular I wish to focus on how the provision of particular psychological therapies may affect the care provided by acute psychiatric wards. As I have worked on acute psychiatric wards for six years and seen many people who have become associated with this label, what follows is necessarily informed by my own experience. However, I will also consider the findings of the research literature on psychological approaches to personality disorder in this environment which, though extremely limited, offer clear pointers as to the way forward.

Personality disorders

In considering the label of personality disorder, and specifically the way it is often approached in psychiatric mental health services, it is difficult to disagree with the contention of Moran (2002) that 'health professionals do not agree about how best to define personality disorders, nor indeed whether the term personality disorder has any use at all'. My own experience as a psychologist in acute psychiatric wards has borne out this view, with the term used by staff variously to exclude individuals, to emotionally cut off from them, to justify accusations of attention seeking and malingering, to excuse punitive care strategies, and (as this experience is in danger of sounding unreservedly negative) very frequently to understand them, to connect to their emotional difficulties and to help plan appropriate care.

Given the complexity of the area, it is first necessary to briefly consider just what personality disorder is believed to be and define the scope of this discussion. (A recent fuller discussion of definitions of personality disorder has been provided by Blackburn 2006.) Both the *International Classification of Mental and Behavioural Disorders* (*ICD-10*) (World Health Organization 1992) and the fourth edition of the *Diagnostic and Statistical Manual of Mental Disorders* (American Psychiatric Association 1994) have defined personality disorder as enduring or characterogical traits and behaviours which lead to problematic consequences and often extreme social dysfunction. However, the label of personality disorder is still associated with strong feelings and conflicting views among professionals. As will be seen, such reactions can actually be of central importance in considering how individuals with such a label may best be helped in acute psychiatric wards. Given the strength of staff reaction, it is also important to reflect on how this may impact on those individuals carrying the label. Considerations of the views of service users (Castillo 2003; Haigh 2002, 2006), have highlighted stigma, lack of information, and concerns about lack of knowledge and care in professional systems.

Both *ICD-10* and *DSM-IV* define a number of categories of personality disorder (nine in the case of *ICD-10* and ten in the case of *DSM-IV*). *DSM-IV* has offered a useful grouping of these labels into three 'clusters' as follows:

- *Cluster A* (*odd or eccentric types*): covering paranoid, schizoid and schizotypal categories.
- *Cluster B* (*dramatic or erratic types*): covering antisocial, borderline, histrionic and narcissistic categories.
- *Cluster C* (*anxious or fearful types*): covering obsessive-compulsive, avoidant and dependent types.

It has been pointed out by a number of authors (e.g. NIMHE 2003a; Moran 2002) that individuals with a borderline personality disorder label (and those in Cluster B generally) tend to receive the most attention and input from services. It is easy to see why this is the case. People receiving a borderline label often show high levels of impulsivity and instability in relationships and moods, often combined with high risk of self-harm and suicidality. Such individuals make up the majority of individuals who are referred to me in acute ward settings and they have generally been admitted in an attempt to contain the risk they pose to themselves. How appropriate this is as a treatment strategy is discussed at greater length below. To this I would also add that I have at times seen individuals exhibiting antisocial personality disorder features (often violent disregard for the right of others). The nature of these behaviours inevitably lead the majority of such individuals to be dealt with via forensic or criminal justice routes and their presentation in general psychiatric services is therefore less frequent. The third group I have encountered in my work comes under the banner of histrionic personality disorders (excessive emotionality and attention seeking). Despite my division of individuals in this way, the distinction between these diagnostic groups is not always clear.

This review is particularly focused on borderline presentations and more generally individuals with Cluster B features. This focus is not intended to ignore or minimize the suffering experienced by individuals with other personality disorder labels, but is rather an acknowledgement of the considerable anxiety that individuals experiencing these kinds of difficulties generate in services and the way this has shaped my own experience and knowledge.

The role of hospital

Before looking at the potential roles of psychological therapies in psychiatric ward settings, I will consider in some detail the context in which such therapies may be delivered. As will be seen, contextual factors are of the greatest importance in thinking about the applicability of psychological approaches to the treatment of personality disorders. The most important question to be posed is the following.

Is hospital useful in treating personality disorders?

The use of acute psychiatric wards in the treatment of personality disorders has often been viewed as at the very least unhelpful, and at worst harmful. In a recent review of the literature on the usefulness of hospitalization for suicidal patients with borderline personality disorder, Paris (2004) concluded that there was no evidence to suggest that hospitalization in this setting has any effect in reducing risks, has unproven benefits in terms of safety and is, in many cases, counterproductive in terms of self-harming and suicidal behaviour. Other reviews have endorsed this general conclusion. For example, Krawitz and Batcheler (2006) went so far as to say that 'a strong consensus exists that overly defensive treatment measures can actually increase the long term risk in working with adults with borderline personality disorder' (p. 320). Among such measures is admission to hospital to manage risk. These conclusions are consistent with the views of the vast majority of ward staff whom I have encountered, particularly in a number of workshop-based teaching sessions I have facilitated over the last six years. In talking to colleagues I have found that views of hospitalization for individuals with personality disorder were largely negative and contained repeated references to variations on the theme of 'making people worse'. This experience is borne out in literature on nurses' attitudes to borderline personality disorder in acute settings (e.g. O'Brien and Flote 1997) which have highlighted considerable uncertainty as to the type and value of care they might provide.

It must be noted at this stage that a search through the literature also reveals several studies providing more positive outcomes of hospitalization in the treatment of borderline personality disorder (e.g. Bateman and Fonagy 1999, 2001: Chiesa *et al.* 2002; Vaslamatzis *et al.* 2004). However, such studies have been primarily concerned with units that provide a more specialized intervention than the non-specialist and diagnostically hetero-geneous environment of an acute psychiatric ward.

Though there is some research which does endorse a more positive view of acute hospitalization (discussed in the following section), it is difficult to find any support for the view that it should ever be the treatment of choice. It is in such a context of overall negativity that the most important national guidance on personality disorder in the UK, *No Longer a Diagnosis of Exclusion* (NIMHE 2003a) makes little mention of acute psychiatric treat-ment as a realistic treatment option. The accompanying *Capabilities Frame-work* (NIMHE 2003b) treated hospital very much as a marginal option where individuals are treated in the absence of more effective services.

It is important to clarify why many mental health professionals may view admission so negatively. After all, to the general public it surely seems logical that if someone is in a distressed state and posing a risk (especially to themselves), the provision of a place of safety in the form of hospital is the sensible thing to do. There are two main concerns about this as a strategy, beyond more obvious issues of stigma and curtailment of personal liberty. The first of these is the concern that hospital (at least in non-specialist units) may not actually be able to offer anything useful beyond containment and observation to promote safety. There is also a question mark over whether hospital can even provide this, as many individuals find ways to harm while hospitalized (see the case of P below for further illustration). It often seems to be a public perception that acute wards should offer safety, but it is uncertain as to just how much people in these settings can be protected if they wish to harm themselves (Paris 2004 has provided some discussion of this point).

A second concern takes this point about ineffectiveness further by suggesting that hospital admission may actually end up being detrimental to an individual's prognosis and recovery. One aspect of this concern relates to the possibility that many individuals who are hospitalized may often be seeking to elicit admission to fulfil a need for themselves (such as care or security). The means chosen to fulfil such needs may be maladaptive and extremely dangerous (self-harm, suicidal behaviour or violence). A point made with particular force by Linehan (1993a) and Paris (2004) is that admissions (and response to such behaviours after admission) are likely to reinforce such maladaptive and dangerous strategies.

A different aspect of the concern that admission may be harmful relates to the erosion of individuals' skills in the environment of a psychiatric ward. Rachlin (1984: 306; cited by Paris 2004) termed this '[denying] patients the right to learn and live'. This idea will be familiar to many clinicians contemplating the discharge from hospital of individuals who seem to have become dependent on the level of care provided in that environment. Such concerns have also featured in user literature. For example, Williams (1998: 174) said: 'It prevented me from having to make a choice to get well or even finding out that I wasn't as helpless as I believed myself to be.'

My own central concern here centres on not just the erosion of life skills but particularly on the taking away of responsibility for oneself from individuals, as may particularly happen when someone is continuously observed to try to control risky behaviour. This is perhaps inevitable in an environment of mixed presentations which is in many ways geared to taking care of people who cannot take care of themselves (e.g. individuals experiencing acute psychotic episodes). However, it often seems to lead to the most profound erosion of skills relating to the ability to take responsibility for one's own emotional reactions and behaviour.

Frequency and reasons for admission

Such figures that are available suggest that, despite the kinds of concerns identified above, the use of acute psychiatric wards in the treatment of individuals with personality disorder is nonetheless an extremely common option. For example, in my own NHS Trust during 2004–05, 16 per cent of individuals admitted to its acute psychiatric ward beds had an *identified* personality disorder, the second most common label after depression at 19 per cent. Indeed, the literature has suggested that the actual number of individuals with personality disorder in wards may be much higher. For example, Hayward *et al.* (2006) conducted a number of assessments with an existing set of psychiatric inpatients on a London ward and found that 54 per cent of them met the *DSM-IV* criteria for personality disorder. Moran's (2002) review estimated that the prevalence of individuals meeting the criteria for personality disorders in acute psychiatric inpatient care was frequently above 50 per cent and often in excess of 70 per cent among inpatients with drug, alcohol and eating disorders.

It is clear, therefore, that despite little evidence of therapeutic benefit, and serious concerns as to the effects on service users, acute psychiatric wards are used repeatedly in the treatment of individuals with a range of personality disorders. Lack of specialist facilities and gaps in the knowledge and skills in general mental health services (both identified by NIMHE 2003a) are important in maintaining this picture. However, in thinking about why acute wards in particular might be chosen to fill such gaps, the inescapable conclusion of both research (e.g. Hull *et al.* 1996) and clinical experience is that it is a direct result of the risks posed by individuals exhibiting borderline and other Cluster B presentations. In particular, serious suicide attempts, suicidal threats, threats of self-harm, violent acts and the threat of them lead to hospitalization (and often detention under the Mental Health Act) as a way to try and move individuals to a place of greater safety. While it is important to note that not all admissions are simply a reaction to risk, the numerous circumstances where they are can result in difficult consequences. The anxiety stemming from an individual's risky behaviour may make it difficult to plan care beyond admission: admission itself being the only plan. Thus, concerns which relate to the inadvertent reinforcement of dangerous behaviours and the erosion of personal responsibility are particularly relevant. In such circumstances, minimizing short-term risk is prioritized over an individual being helped towards a position where they are encouraged to manage their own risk.

Can acute psychiatric wards ever be useful in this context?

Thus far, a largely negative portrait of hospital admissions for personality disorders has been offered. It is now time to consider if hospitalization in an acute psychiatric ward can be beneficial. After all it is clear that (as Fagin 2004 has pointed out) regardless of whether people with a personality disorder label should or should not be treated in this setting, they clearly are and in significant numbers. While a range of initiatives has been under way to improve the quality of acute psychiatric care generally (e.g. Department of Health 2002b; Sainsbury Centre for Mental Health 2006b) it is clear that these potential improvements (while useful in making wards more therapeutic) do not necessarily make wards an ideal treatment setting for personality disorders. Such literature as there is suggests rather that if wards are to be effective a number of conditions relating to the basis of admission and good case management should be met. Several such conditions have been outlined, based on clinical experience, by Bateman and Tyrer (2004). They have suggested that, if such conditions are met, then the kinds of erosion of emotional self-containment discussed above may be avoided (as observed by Gabbard *et al.* 2000). The conditions they set out were that admissions should be:

- informal, with patient-determined admission and discharge
- organized around specific therapeutic goals agreed by the care team and the service user
- arranged with clear agreement of the ward nursing team
- brief and time limited
- individual can be discharged if admission goals not met.

These conditions have been elaborated further by Fagin (2004), who stressed the importance of rules and contracts around tolerable behaviour, the need to involve carers and other agencies, and the importance of group supervision to help staff make sense of strong feelings which may be raised.

In considering these conditions a number of areas are worth emphasizing. The stress on informal admission, in Bateman and Tyrer's (2004) first recommendation, addresses the danger that use of detention under the Mental Health Act powerfully takes responsibility away from individuals who are detained. Other professionals would, I suspect, have some reservations about the second part of this recommendation (which seems somewhat at odds with their last one) as *organizations* may also often wish to be able to take some responsibility for whether or not they would offer a particular service. However, I would strongly endorse their second point relating to the involvement of service users in care plans. As well as affording individuals dignity and respect, such involvement crucially passes some responsibility back to the user for their own recovery and this may be one of the most effective ways of addressing the erosion of responsibility for oneself. Furthermore, the idea that discharge should follow if admission goals are not met further strengthens the notion that the user has some responsibility for maintaining the treatment contract and can be discharged if they do not. Such a stance combines the offer of treatment with clear limits and requires the active engagement of the individual in their own treatment plan.

In addition to those conditions mentioned above, I think it is also worth adding three more:

- the central importance of communication and consistency across the *whole* care team (ward team and community services)
- the importance of a clear formulation (with psychological conceptualizations central to this)
- the importance of ongoing staff training in addition to supervision.

In many circumstances ward services and community services can fail to communicate. Sometimes ward staff may perceive that patients have been admitted to give community staff a break. In other circumstances ward staff may fail to communicate their ideas to the broader team. Such occasions have been all too frequent in my working life and in such cases the dangers of an inconsistent and damaging response is increased considerably. The importance of the whole care team moving forward as a unit cannot be overstated. The second condition, clear formulation, is intended to help this. It should be easier for a team to act consistently if there is both a plan and a rationale for that plan available to everyone. The importance of training has been highlighted by NIMHE (2003b) in its personality disorder 'capabilities framework' and the skills deficits have been made clear. Wards, like all services, must address this.

Overall, despite reservations about hospitalization of individuals with a personality disorder diagnosis in conditions of high risk, there is some force in the view of Fagin (2004) that sometimes 'there is a role for the in-patient unit where patients are often taken in an emergency, *if a graded and well informed response can be agreed between staff and patient'* (p. 103, my italics).

Psychological treatments in acute psychiatric wards

The question of whether wards may offer something therapeutic (the very theme of this book) prompts consideration of the role that psychological therapies may have in improvement of services. After all, the most recent national guidelines (NIMHE 2003a) recognize both the appropriateness of psychological therapies in treating personality disorder and a growing evidence base for a range of therapies. The supporting review attached to the NIMHE document (Bateman and Tyrer 2002) reviewed the evidence, a range of treatment options suggesting that psychodynamic treatment, dialectical behaviour therapy (DBT, Linehan 1993a), and therapeutic community treatments (Campling and Haigh 1999) have the strongest evidence of efficacy in the treatment of personality disorders. A later meta analysis (Leichsenring and Leibing 2003) has also provided support for both psychodynamic therapies and cognitive behaviour therapy (CBT) in the treatment of personality disorder. It is not overstating matters to say that the NIMHE report appears to envisage psychological approaches as the major vehicle for achieving positive change for individuals with a personality disorder label and of considerably more importance than medication. The National Institute for Clinical Excellence (NICE) has not yet published its guideline on borderline personality disorder, but psychological approaches are mentioned in their self-harm guideline (2004d) and it would be extremely surprising if a range of psychological approaches to personality disorder treatment were not given prominence in the forthcoming guideline.

Given the emphasis of current guidance and key literature, it may be assumed that the provision of evidence-based psychological therapies in acute wards is bound to make them a more effective treatment environment for personality disorder presentations. Before discussing just how realistic this assumption is, it is first necessary to briefly describe the kind of psychological approaches which have been employed to treat personality disorder, and in particular those approaches I am most familiar with as a practitioner.

Two psychological approaches to personality disorder

The two approaches I will discuss here are dialectical behaviour therapy (DBT, Linehan 1993a) and cognitive analytic therapy (CAT, Ryle 1997). While the evidence base for each of these is still emerging (see Robbins and Chapman 2004 and Ryle 2004 for reviews) there are three important reasons (beyond my own familiarity with them) for choosing these two therapies for consideration here. First, and most importantly, they have both to some extent evolved as treatments specifically designed for borderline personality disorder presentations and have been recognized as such by NIMHE (2003a and others). In the case of CAT it has been applied to many other diagnostic categories but Ryle's (2004) own development work has particularly concentrated on this area. Second, both approaches provide formulations that can be made accessible to multidisciplinary teams in making decisions about case management. The third reason for selection is that both therapies involve an emphasis on dealing with cognitions which makes them of particular relevance in a book focused on cognitive behaviour therapy.

Dialectical behaviour therapy

DBT is a variation of cognitive behaviour therapy, developed by Linehan (1993a) and her colleagues specifically as a means of treating borderline personality disorder. Like CBT, it focuses on working directly with problematic cognitions and difficulties with information processing systems such as attentional mechanisms. However, a number of quite distinct elements have been integrated into the therapy. In particular it places an emphasis on learning theory (looking carefully not only at behaviours but particularly at their antecedents and consequences). There are also specific concepts such as validation and dialectics (discussed below), and an emphasis on the therapeutic relationship and behaviours which interfere with therapy. All of these are points of difference with more traditional CBT models.

In the DBT conceptualization, borderline personality disorder is primarily viewed as being based in pervasive and profound skills deficits. The primary area where these deficits occur is in the capacity to regulate emotions. This is seen as resulting from interaction between a vulnerable temperament and an invalidating environment. An 'invalidating' environment (see Linehan 1993a, Chapter 2) is presented as a place where a child fails to learn the key skills of emotional management as a result of a failure of its carers (for example, through thoughtlessness or lack of consistency). Skills deficits are also postulated in other areas such as interpersonal relationships (e.g. instability of relationships), behavioural patterns (e.g. where maladaptive behaviours such as self-harm have become dominant) and cognitive processing (e.g. where cognitive processes such as problem solving break down in states of emotional arousal). DBT also stresses the concept of dialectics, a threefold idea involving a holistic view of the individual's difficulties, the management of extreme tensions in the individual's world view, and adaptability to evolving treatment goals.

In terms of techniques used in DBT, the primary emphasis is on skills acquisition and the translating of those skills into new environments. These skills are learned via both individual therapy and group training where possible. Other techniques employed include mindfulness (an adaptation of a central technique in Zen Buddhist meditation), validation (an empathic understanding of the patient's responses), dialectical strategies (a range of techniques based on acknowledging and holding the polarities in the patient's feelings), and fine-grained behavioural analysis of actions and responses. It is noteworthy that the DBT model envisages an explicit case management role (across other professionals as well as friends and families) as part of the treatment package. This is seen of central value in maintaining consistency of approach and preventing the undermining of progress through inconsistent reinforcement of maladaptive behaviours. A useful up-to-date account of the elements of a DBT programme has been provided by Moorey *et al.* (2006).

Cognitive analytic therapy

Like DBT, CAT (Ryle 1997) also has some commonalities with a CBT approach. In particular it uses a model of problematic sequences of thought and action which lead to unhelpful or distressing results. Where CAT moves away from more traditional CBT thinking is in its adaptation of psychoanalytic object relations theories (see in particular Ogden 1983). This aspect of the theory, termed 'reciprocal roles', utilizes templates of relationships derived from early childhood experience. Such templates are seen as involving an internal conception of being both a receiver of an experience (e.g. being nurtured) and the provider of the experience (e.g. being nurturing). In borderline personality disorder an individual can be understood in terms of having a very limited range of such reciprocal role templates based on very negative roles (e.g. abuser/abused). The third important aspect of CAT theory, which evolved specifically in the context of working with borderline personality disorder, is that of multiple self-states. This concept recognizes a separation or even dissociation of mood states in conscious awareness and an often abrupt and uncontrolled shifting between them (e.g. a shift from idealization to rejection).

The techniques of CAT are initially focused on developing a detailed formulation (actually termed 'reformulation') of an individual's difficulties in the first few sessions. The reformulation seeks to outline problematic patterns of thought and actions based on thought/action sequences and linked to problematic reciprocal roles and multiple self-states. This reformulation, which takes place over several sessions, is then offered back to the patient in the form of a letter from the therapist, retelling the person's history and outlining key problematic patterns (termed target problem procedures). A diagram of the reformulation is also often employed (see the case of C below). Reformulation is intended to capture the elements of the therapeutic relationship such as transference where reciprocal roles may be re-enacted by both therapist and patient in the session. Once the reformulation has been agreed with the patient, the subsequent therapy (usually a fixed contract of sessions of no more than 24 weeks) is based on enhancing awareness of and seeking to change the target problem procedures. A wide range of methods may be employed including cognitive behavioural, psychoanalytic and gestalt techniques. In recent discussion of CAT, Ryle (2004) has acknowledged the importance of utilizing CAT reformulations in more institutional settings so as to provide a basis on which to plan care and to guide other staff.

It is difficult to give more than a basic sense of many of these ideas in the brief space that is available. In particular, it is difficult to do justice to the complexity of concepts such as dialectics and reciprocal roles. Readers are encouraged to consult primary sources such as Linehan (1993a) or Ryle (1997), as such abbreviations of these ideas inevitably leave out a great deal of important detail.

These two therapies have several points of difference. It seems to me that DBT more clearly emphasizes skills acquisition while CAT lays stress on the roles of early relationship templates in the development of an individual's difficulties, and in the here and now. The use of dialectical thinking provides a distinct flavour to the DBT approach, as does the development of shared written and diagrammatic formulations in CAT. However, there are a number of areas of common ground between the therapies: perhaps unsurprising given that DBT (and to a certain extent CAT) have evolved to treat similar presentations. In particular, both therapies have a framework for considering the therapeutic relationship; both acknowledge the tensions of extreme shifting mood states; both acknowledge the importance of looking at chains of causality and consequence in behaviour; and both provide a means to develop a treatment plan with a broader care team. However, perhaps the greatest commonality between the two approaches is that both view problematic behaviours as direct attempts to manage feelings which are difficult to tolerate. The main therapeutic goal of both is to seek relatively concrete ways to look at behaviours and thoughts which have been impulsive, repetitive, painful and unconscious, and help individuals become more explicitly aware of such behaviours and seek to change them within conscious awareness. Engaging with such treatments involves both motivation and a willingness to take responsibility for the behaviours and the process of changing them. As will be discussed below, the way in which a ward does or does not foster these factors is central to their applicability in this setting.

The application of DBT and CAT in the acute ward

Returning to the assumption that psychological treatments enhance the care provided by acute psychiatric wards, the limited literature available confirms that other authors have reached similar conclusions. Broadly these are along the lines of 'psychological therapies are effective, evidence-based treatments, therefore they should be provided in acute psychiatric wards where they will also be effective'. This assumption appears in varying forms to support the arguments for greater psychological provision in this setting produced by Holmes (2002), Rathbone and Campling (2005) and Hanna (2006a).

There is in fact very little evidence base for psychological therapies in acute psychiatric wards. Some of the reasons for this and the difficulties of acquiring it have been discussed elsewhere (McGowan 2007). This lack of hospital-based evidence is important because of the significant differences between the circumstances in which the majority of evidence of therapeutic effectiveness was gathered and the actual conditions on wards. Some of these are considered below:

1   *Brevity of ward stays*. In the UK it is likely that the length of ward stays is briefer than ever before as a result of the creation of crisis resolution and home treatment teams (Department of Health 2001a). These teams have a remit to provide an alternative to hospital admissions and, as part of this, have the explicit function of shortening acute inpatient stays. It is not unusual in the present climate to hear of NHS Trusts setting targets of 30 days (discussed in my own Trust) for an optimal stay. Both DBT and CAT envisage a number of sessions over several weeks even in the first phase (a three- to six-week pre-commitment phase in DBT or a four-session assessment phase in CAT). Thus it may be very difficult to achieve the goals of even the earliest phases of treatment during a brief ward admission. In his book on inpatient therapy groups Yalom (1983) addressed this point with a warning that 'overly ambitious goals are not only ineffective but often anti-therapeutic' (p. 52). In the current climate of brief admissions, the relevance of this point even to individual therapies must be emphasized. Ultimately one may be confined to (as Yalom has suggested) simple engagement and the introduction of some of the ideas of psychological therapies.

2   *Uncertainty of time frame*. A related aspect, which complicates the delivery of psychological therapies in wards, is uncertainty over the length of the individual's stay. While it may be possible for a therapist to influence this to some extent (via multidisciplinary team discussion), it has often been my experience that this is difficult and that individual length of stay can also be dictated by a number of other hard-to-control factors (such as availability of housing or family circumstances). This leaves the therapist in a state of uncertainty over the scope of what may be pursued in the time available.

3   *Levels of medication*. It has frequently been my experience that, when hospitalized, individuals are often not only on higher levels of medication than they might be in the community, but also that they are given supplementary medication in the form of 'prescription required

as needed' (PRN). Often this PRN is given when people become upset or are struggling to function normally (e.g. to go to sleep). While sometimes helpful, medication given on this basis can be at odds with a psychological intervention designed to help bolster an individual's capacity to bear feelings or develop the skills to deal with a particular issue. There is a danger that the issue is dealt with by the medication rather than by the individuals developing the capability to start to deal with it themselves. Though this issue may be partly dealt with by team discussion, it may not always be possible to achieve the desired result.

4   *The appropriateness of hospital.* Points (2) and (3) above are also both aspects of what may be the most important factor for delivering therapies in inpatient settings: the appropriateness or otherwise of the acute psychiatric environment for people with personality disorders. Issues such as medication may reflect broader team dynamics where individuals may have different purposes in the admission. A similar dynamic may apply to informal talking therapies provided by different members of a ward team (see the case of C below). Perhaps of most concern, however, is the scenario discussed earlier where the containment of risk is the primary motive underlying admission. In this situation the emphasis appears to be on taking all responsibility away from an individual. This runs counter to the most fundamental goals of both DBT and CAT, where engagement and commitment to taking responsibility for one's own behaviour are paramount. In a context where such team dynamics operate it is unsurprising that Linehan (1993a: 510) has advised that 'hospitalization should be avoided wherever possible' if an effective treatment is to be delivered.

The clear upshot of these four points is that acute psychiatric wards often may not (and one might argue should not) offer therapies such as DBT and CAT in the sense in which they were originally envisaged. My own experience has been that therapies must be radically adapted, or that it is ideas from the therapies which can be used in a very different way to achieve specific goals.

Swenson *et al.* (2001) have discussed a number of useful ways in which DBT can be adapted and extended to an inpatient setting. These include: focusing on skills for staying out of hospital; supporting staff to provide reinforcement around certain target behaviours; and (equally important) thinking about how to stop reinforcing problematic behaviours such as self-harm. Also emphasized is staff support and reflection and ongoing skills training. Swenson *et al.* (2001) conclude that the DBT therapist must act as a 'quarterback' (p. 321 – the lead strategic position in American football), for the patient's treatment team. In a similar vein Ryle (2004) has suggested the importance of using the written formulations of CAT to provide a basis of shared understandings between different professionals in a hospital care team and to minimize collusion with a person's dysfunctional procedures.

The clear argument underlying all of Swenson's suggestions is the need for the therapist to work with the system surrounding the individual, to create conditions where the therapy is supported rather than undermined. Referring back to the conditions which should be met for an admission to an acute psychiatric ward, it is clear that these conditions are vital to a programme such as the one Swenson *et al.* have outlined. Clearly what may be achieved through direct therapy with a complex presentation in a short space of time is limited. Trying to enhance the impact of that work through collaboration with the broader care team may be useful. However, the key point here is that working with the whole system in the circumstance of a brief admission is not simply desirable or helpful but essential if there is to be a realistic chance of progress.

A particularly useful service model has been outlined by Nicholson and Carradice (2002). This model outlines three levels of working in the acute psychiatric setting:

- directly with the individual or group
- indirectly (working with the team to think about the person concerned)
- more strategically with the care system.

Direct work

In the circumstances of a brief admission it is clear that the aims of direct contact will be extremely limited. It may often be that conducting an assessment only is the most appropriate way forward. The complexity of presentations of individuals with a personality disorder label bring the limits of what can be achieved therapeutically into sharp focus, and any goals beyond assessment must be realistic and clearly defined. The formulation of goals (or even whether to become involved at all), require careful consideration. As Clarke (Chapter 6) has pointed out, referrals may have been 'perfunctory and rapidly picked up'. However, I must disagree with her suggestion that in this short time frame a limited briefing from nursing or medical staff must often suffice. In all cases, but particularly in cases labelled 'personality disorder', I would suggest that it is vital to find out as much as possible of the person's history, of the circumstances of their admission, of other potential involvements with psychological therapies, and of the views of the community care team (if there is one). Without such information it is impossible to gain a clear sense of how one's own contact may inappropriately reinforce problem strategies or enact established and problematic roles without realizing that this is what is going on. It has often been my experience that, particularly in admissions driven by risk, other members of the team do not always give consideration to such factors.

However, a psychological practitioner must consider such matters fundamental to their formulation and goals.

Indirect work

Though the circumstances which seem essential to a productive admission have been outlined above, it is quite normal in my own experience for none of these to apply. Being the 'quarterback' in an admission of this type requires a great deal of formal and informal liaison with staff. Both DBT and CAT can provide an accessible way for other staff to engage with the formulation emerging from a psychological assessment. Of central importance is the psychiatric ward round: a (usually) multidisciplinary meeting where the main care planning decisions are usually taken. Often ward rounds provide a place for essential contact and discussion with carers and the care team outside of hospital. Ideally, this forum should also provide a place to consider the basis for the admission and the treatment contract. If, for example, a decision which may involve significant risk is appropriate (e.g. discharge in the face of failure to engage) then it is here that this should be discussed and documented, preferably as openly and transparently as possible with the individual whom it concerns. This allows any such decisions to be owned by the whole team and for the patient to exercise responsibility for managing their own risk. If decisions relating to the care plan whilst the individual is in hospital can be taken by those present at the ward round, then the kind of team approach suggested by Swenson *et al.* (2001) has a firm foundation.

Strategic work

This model provides a framework to extend the suggestions of the kind of programme outlined by Swenson *et al.* (2001) beyond individual case management and incorporate them into the culture and strategies of the broader organization. Matters such as supervision and training must clearly be backed by organizational management. However, working at more strategic levels can also provide an opportunity to gain multiprofessional and organizational support for using hospital in a way which is less reactive to risk and more concerned with aiding therapeutic progress. If the need for the kinds of principles outlined by Bateman and Tyrer (2004) can be established at a broader organizational level, then both the milieu of acute psychiatric wards and the function of psychological therapies within them can be made considerably more satisfactory.

Case examples

It is traditional to report material from cases where a therapeutic approach is employed successfully to resolve the highlighted problem. However, it is also important to consider such cases where the outcome is less successful and to reflect on the reasons why. In the area under discussion in this chapter it needs to be emphasized that achieving therapeutic change is often extremely difficult at both the level of the individual and in working with the anxieties experienced by the care team. With the acknowledgement of such difficulties in mind, two cases with very different outcomes are reported below. Both individuals were given a label of borderline personality disorder. A number of details have been changed to preserve anonymity.

The Case of C

C was a 39-year-old woman with a 20-year documented history of regular self-harm (predominantly via cutting herself) and suicide attempts (usually overdoses of medication). As a child she had lived in Mexico. She had come to live in the UK with her parents at the age of 15. Her history indicated that she had been sexually abused extensively as a child and a teenager. Her father appeared to have been the main perpetrator, though he also had apparently used her as a prostitute in the town where they lived. At the time when a psychology referral was initiated C had been a voluntary acute ward inpatient almost continuously for over 18 months. Periodic attempts had been made to discharge her but these had been followed, always within 24 hours, by a suicidal act. At one point she had jumped off a bridge over a busy road (though into the grass verge at the side), and had broken her ankle. Her current admission followed the end of lengthy therapeutic contact with a clinical psychologist, parting from a boyfriend and a change of manager in her residential setting. She had been admitted as a direct result of the risk she posed to herself, and during her stay it had been impossible to establish her engagement in any care plan involving goals of developing greater independence from the ward.

In her demeanour on the ward (and at her initial presentation to me), C behaved like a young child in terms of a show of helplessness and a continual need for reassurance and physical contact. Ward staff would regularly hold her hand while she walked around with them. She had a number of soft toys on the ward and some staff would periodically bring her more. At times she would withdraw from staff and reject all offers of help. There was also a pronounced split in the ward team between people who seemed to treat her as 'poor little C' (who needed to be cared for) and others who described her as a 'manipulator' and suggested (often quite angrily), that she be discharged as soon as possible.

In my direct work with C we began by trying to describe her difficulties within a CAT style reformulation. This provided a clear focus and gave us

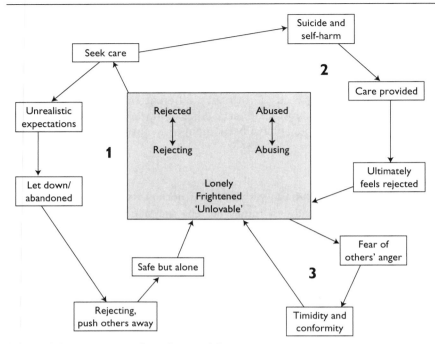

Figure 9.1 Diagrammatic reformulation of C

some cognitive material to work on while helping to avoid opening up too much painful material from her past (which may have been inappropriate given that the time frame for the work was uncertain). After four sessions we agreed a diagrammatic reformulation of her difficulties as a basis for further work (see Figure 9.1). This provided a collaborative and fairly simple understanding of target behaviours which appeared to be failed escapes from a painful emotional core state (traps). It also afforded a framework to understand more psychoanalytic processes such as transference (in this case feelings of need), and splitting (in this case experiencing individuals around her as either idealized or rejecting), which appeared relevant both within the therapy and in her relations to the ward team. C engaged well with this formulation and showed some capacity to think about the primary concepts between sessions. In particular we were able to consider her need for idealized caregivers and the sense of let down she usually experienced in such relationships (marked 1 in Figure 9.1) and the purposes of her self-harm as a way of seeking care (marked 2 in Figure 9.1). I met with C for 14 sessions (the longest contact I have ever had on a ward).

This diagrammatic reformulation also provided a useful tool to share with the team to help in considering C's care plan. Providing a concrete understanding of C's risk behaviours proved useful in thinking about reactions of either collusion or rejection in the team. It also offered a focus on the problems of continued admission and a basis to consider the potential therapeutic benefits of working towards discharge. The team agreed a plan to discharge C with an offer of further planned admissions: one week every four months irrespective of what self-harming behaviours she engaged in. She was discharged six weeks after the beginning of my own involvement. A package involving further brief psychological input and vocational training was offered. Following discharge C initially struggled, but eventually took encouragement from the fact that she had been able to manage her own risk prior to her first planned admission. She used the first three days of the planned admission, then discharged herself. She did not request admission again for five years.

The case of C was instrumental in several key developments in the ward and the NHS Trust concerned. These included the establishment of a ward staff supervision group (facilitated by me and an external supervisor); a programme of training on the ward which included strong input from specialist personality disorder services and personality disorder user groups; support from senior management for the use of planned admissions; and the adoption of clearer criteria for admission of people with a personality disorder label.

In many aspects the outcome of this case was and may serve as an example of both a shift towards a more considered and reflective position by the service user, and a shift in the multidisciplinary care team which allowed a greater level of responsibility for treatment outcome to be held by the service user. In the end, both the user and the system were able to work together to progress.

The case of P

P was a 40-year-old woman with a history of suicide attempts dating back to her teens. Her notes indicated that there was some possibility of sexual abuse (perpetrated by an uncle) between the ages of 7 and 15. She also appeared to have experienced neglect from her parents who had failed to act on her disclosure of the abuse and who had consistently favoured her two older brothers. She had lived near the hospital all of her life and had had multiple admissions over the last 20 years. With rare exceptions these were in the form of detention under the Mental Health Act and in circumstances where she repeatedly stated that she wanted to die and did not wish to be admitted. P's presentations on the ward (usually after significant life events), invariably provoked both gloomy and hostile reactions in the ward team, many of whom expressed the view that her incidence of suicide attempts became more frequent during her stays. In my review of P's extensive history one particularly noteworthy psychological report (from 12 years previously) offered support for the views of the nurses who said this. The report stated that P tended to be at less risk when she had clearly boundaried and limited contact with mental health services. In the intervening years, however, it appeared that P had had little else but such contact in the form of a slew of different interventions and team involvements as well as her repeated hospitalizations.

My own assessment of P (conducted over six sessions and two admissions) focused primarily on establishing her potential to think and understand her suicide attempts and working (in the style of DBT) on establishing the antecedents of suicidal behaviour, the nature of the behaviours themselves and their consequences. My service undertook an extensive review of her risk history along similar behavioural lines. While P was unforthcoming in the verbal investigation (merely repeating 'I just want to die'), her notes were revealing. As well as (obviously) still being alive, virtually all of P's suicide attempts had occurred in circumstances where she would be easily found and prevented. On several occasions, for example, she had placed a plastic bag over her head in a crowded room. At one stage she made a similar attempt in a session with me, waving a plate at me and saying she could break it and kill herself and that I wouldn't be able to stop her. Despite her explicit reluctance to be in hospital she also repeatedly self-harmed prior to Mental Health Act review tribunals, virtually guaranteeing that they would not be in a position to lift her detention. My formulation regarding P was that, rather than being attempts to die, her suicidality was more akin to a means of obtaining care which she found impossible to ask for more directly. While I was and remain uncertain of her potential to move from a position of repeating such suicidal acts to a position where she might be able to think about the possible purposes of the acts, it was my feeling that such thought was impossible within the context of hospital and repeated risk-driven admissions.

This case may be considered as less successful in that there appeared to be little discernible change in the presentation. It also appeared very difficult for the care team to move beyond a position where the attempt to minimize risk through repeated hospital admission was a major aspect of the care strategy. Both the care co-ordinator and the psychiatrist involved, while they were prepared to say to P that she needed to take more responsibility for her behaviour, were ultimately reluctant to risk actually giving her such responsibility. Though she subsequently managed to engage with a psychological intervention in a community service, no contract relating to hospital admissions was agreed and she was regularly readmitted to the ward. In such a position P's prognosis appeared likely to remain poor.

Conclusions

It is clear that the therapeutic effectiveness of hospital in helping people labelled with 'personality disorder' is questionable. Despite this, the hospital is frequently used as a treatment strategy. While treatments such as dialectical behaviour therapy and cognitive analytic therapy offer potential to improve this position, it is clear that working with the context as well as the individual is imperative in creating the potential for success. Ultimately, personality disorders are treated through relationships which are containing and promote insight and personal responsibility for recovery. Though hospital often appears to run contrary to this ethos, there can be circumstances where, if focused properly, it may help provide these things. Though psychological approaches are often employed in the most unpromising circumstances, perhaps their greatest asset is that they may be able to help psychiatric wards achieve such a change.

Part III

Working with the staff group to create a therapeutic culture

Chapter 10

Running reflective practice groups on an inpatient unit

Vivia Cowdrill and Laura Dannahy

> Do your work, then step back – the only path to serenity.
>
> (*Essence of Tao*)

Acute psychiatric inpatient services have received bad press from many quarters, from the media to the government (BBC News 2005; Department of Health 2002b). The Department of Psychiatry (inpatient services) in Southampton has not escaped the negative comments and criticisms from staff, service users and their families. Although there is a tendency for acute psychiatric services to be scapegoated, the dedicated professional staff within these services face a challenge if acute inpatient care is to be perceived as being a positive therapeutic environment where people with severe and enduring mental illness can receive safety, respect and appropriate treatment and care.

With the introduction of extended community services such as crisis resolution, home treatment, early intervention and assertive outreach services, people admitted to hospital represent the 'sharp end of the market'. They are admitted at times of crisis, with immense distress and in the most acute phase of their illness. It is often reported that society cannot tolerate people who are mentally ill and behave unpredictably, and therefore these individuals should be 'put away'. According to the social anthropologist and psychoanalyst Elisabeth Bott, admission to a psychiatric hospital is an agreement between themselves and wider society with an assumption:

> that madness cannot be contained and accommodated as part of ordinary personal and social life. It is beyond the pale, or it should be beyond the pale. If it is kept inside it will destroy: destroy the individual, the family, the fabric of society. At all costs it must be separated off and sent somewhere else and the main task of the mental hospital is to be that 'somewhere else'.
>
> (Bott 1976: 121)

It is not surprising that, as highlighted in Isabel Clarke's introductory chapter, hospital staff face an uphill struggle, with staff morale reported to be low. In order to cope with high levels of distress and extreme crisis, there is reversion to the traditional approach: the nurses become task driven and rely heavily on symptom management. This approach, however, does not take into account the effect that exposure to extreme crisis has on staff. Observations by Hinshelwood (2002) noted that nursing staff responded to stress in a negative manner. They tended to react in ways that were cold and uncaring, shutting out aspects of understanding and empathy from patient care. This has led to a hierarchical, mechanical and dehumanized institution that is anything but therapeutic. In view of this, it is not unexpected that in a national survey of acute inpatient mental health wards by the Sainsbury Centre for Mental Health (2005), the report illustrated that there was high staff turnover, staff shortages, failure to provide any form of therapy and an inability to offer the quality of care services that users wanted, needed and deserved.

Despite this grim picture there are many dedicated health professionals on the front line who are determined to change the negative experiences of service users. Although nurses make up the majority of the health professionals on the ward, no one profession can hope to change the culture in order to create the necessary therapeutic milieu. It is a multidisciplinary effort and the clinical psychologist or cognitive behaviour therapist has much to offer. According to the World Health Organization (1953): 'The creation of the atmosphere of a therapeutic (*milieu*) is in itself, one of the most important types of treatment which the psychiatric hospital can provide.' The therapeutic milieu is defined as the creation of a supportive and nurturing interpersonal environment that teaches, models and reinforces constructive interaction. It supports peer/staff feedback to service users on strategies for symptom reduction, increasing adaptive behaviours and reducing subjective distress. It encourages service users' participation in decision making and collective responsibility for ward events (Gutheil 1985). To change from the traditional to the therapeutic milieu approach, attention must be given to the quality of relationships, not only between staff and service users but also between different disciplines within the team. Hinshelwood (2002) argues that attempting to dismantle the traditional way of working is futile. As an alternative, he suggests that staff need to create space to reflect, so that the anxiety of working with risky patients in extreme distress and crises can be comprehended and contained. It is against this backdrop that the consultant and clinical psychologists at the Department of Psychiatry in Southampton developed reflective practice sessions for staff on each ward and a separate session for ward managers.

The aim of this chapter is to describe our experiences of setting up and running reflective practice groups in an inner city psychiatric hospital. Nursing staff, qualified and unqualified, make up the majority of the staff within the hospital. They are therefore instrumental in developing the therapeutic milieu. This chapter will briefly examine the importance of reflection on nursing practice and then look at the technical and practical aspects of reflective practice. We will then present the ingredients required to establish a reflective culture before describing our experiences of putting theory into practice. However, before we begin it would be prudent to define what is meant by the concept of reflective practice.

What is reflective practice?

In the UK, reflective practice has increasingly been advocated as a key component of practice within the current health and social care climate. Both health policy guidelines and professional education programmes promote reflection as a practical tool for the integration of theory to practice. In the Department of Health (2002b) document *Mental Health Policy Implementation Guide: Adult Acute Inpatient Care Provision*, for example, the importance of reflection within the working environment is highlighted:

> Time should be identified within the working week for an ongoing programme of structured multidisciplinary learning opportunities . . . creating a space that allows for reflection, thinking and understanding and the thoughtful application of skills, knowledge and timely interventions.
>
> (DH 2002b: 21)

In its broadest sense, reflective practice involves the critical analysis of everyday working practices to improve competence, promote professional development, develop practice-generated theory, and help professionals make sense of complex and ambiguous practice situations (Johns 1995; Wilkinson 1999; Clouder 2000; Driscoll and Teh 2001).

In order to understand reflective practice, it is important to consider what is meant by the term reflection, and how it relates to professional practice. Reflection is by no means a novel concept. The origins of reflection as an experiential learning process can be traced back to Dewey (1933), who saw reflection as 'the active, persistent and careful consideration of any belief or supposed form of knowledge' (p. 9). It may be argued that the ability to reflect on, reinterpret and reanalyse past events is central and indeed unique to human learning (Wheeler *et al.* 1997), and is perhaps the most important mechanism by which we learn (Bennett-Levy 2003). Reflection is therefore important in our professional practice as it is a process in which our professional knowledge base can be developed. This notion is supported by Carper's (1978) identification of four fundamental processes by which knowledge is acquired:

1 *Scientific knowledge*: technical, factual or scientific knowledge gained through formal education, reading and research.
2 *Personal knowledge*: knowledge acquired through life experiences.
3 *Aesthetic knowledge*: subjective knowledge gained through unique and particular situations.
4 *Ethical knowledge*: knowledge based on our moral values.

Professional practice therefore is not a simple process of applying evidence-generated theory to practice, but a much more complex process involving knowledge, intuition, experience and values. In an exploration of the nature of professional practice, Schon (1983, 1987, 1991) further suggests that although knowledge and experience are essential bases for learning, reflection is a critical component in the learning process because it bridges the gap between theory and practice, allowing the practitioner to make sense of and extract meaning from their experience. Similar to the distinctions made by Carper's (1978) patterns of knowledge, Schon identifies two approaches to knowledge: 'technical-rational' (theoretical and scientific knowledge) and 'tacit' (knowledge generated by experience). Schon argues that although practitioners require a good theoretical knowledge base to inform practice (technical-rational knowledge), practice is often not the straightforward application of theory. Our moment-by-moment decisions made during our day-to-day practice are often informed by our previous experience interacting with our knowledge base, a process he defines as 'reflection-in-action'. Reflection-in-action is the ability to reflect critically in those moments where the practitioner encounters complexity and unfamiliarity; where 'theory prescribed actions hit their limits' (Lavender 2003).

In addition to 'reflection-in-action', Schon describes another mode of reflection, namely reflection-on-action, occurring after an event and in a variety of ways. Van Manen (1991) also advocates that in addition to recollective reflection, reflection before an event (i.e. 'anticipatory reflection') can also be invaluable in that it allows practitioners to plan and approach situations in a prepared way. At the Department of Psychiatry, our reflective practice groups very much focus on both anticipatory and recollective reflective processes, with the aim of bringing about a greater level of understanding. In support of the importance of reflecting on our professional practice, Lavender argues:

If a profession is to reach maturity, there must be a recognition that practice continuously exposes the limits of science, and ways need to be developed to help professional practitioners deal with the uncertainties and complexities of the reality of practice. This is why the development of reflective practice is so important.

(Lavender 2003: 11)

A number of models have been developed, predominantly within the field of nursing, which aim to provide a framework in which reflective practice can be facilitated (e.g. Atkins and Murphy 1993; Driscoll 1994, 2000; Johns 1996; Ghaye and Lillyman 1997). Although an examination of these models is beyond the scope of this chapter, Ghaye and Lillyman (1997) summarize the commonalities between models of reflection by suggesting that all such models can be seen from one or more of the following perspectives:

- *competency based* – focus on clinical skill development and improving practice
- *personal* – focus on self-study and enhancement through a greater sense of self-worth and identity
- *experiential* – focus on an active exploration of experience
- *transformatory* – focus on challenging the status quo with the aim of reducing or removing barriers to improvement.

It may be suggested that the central tenet of all reflective models is the idea that reflecting on clinical practice is an active process which may contribute to increasing understanding and awareness, empower practitioners, extend personal practical knowledge, and subsequently enhance clinical practice. It should be recognized that there are critics of reflection who suggest that there is no conclusive evidence that nurses who engage in formal reflection provide a higher standard of patient care than those nurses who do not. Those who choose to discount the growing evidence base (Paget 2001) should note that reflection forms part of the nurses' legal and professional accountability.

Topics for reflection

In consideration of the nature and models of reflective practice outlined above, we shall now turn our attention to our experiences of how reflective practice groups can be utilized by practitioners. We chose a group format rather than individual sessions for two reasons. First, the Department of Psychiatry has a large number of permanent staff and therefore the heavy demands on our time would make our job impossible if individual sessions were offered. Second, adopting the group approach has contributed to the development of a strong professional cohesion and identity amongst the nursing team on each ward. The nature of nursing practice is complex and varied, and this has been mirrored in the content of our reflective practice sessions. We have identified a number of key areas upon which nurses reflect, which are outlined below.

Reflection on direct clinical practice: working with patients

Our reflective practice groups have provided an opportunity for practitioners to think about patients, particularly concerning how optimum delivery of care may be best achieved. In accord with the content of reflective practice sessions outlined by other authors (e.g. Shepherd and Rosebert 2007), reflective practice has allowed the chance for the nursing team to consider and define any dilemmas that the patient may pose, and to think about how these issues may be resolved. In our experience, we have found the application of psychologically based formulation skills, incorporating cognitive behavioural therapy (CBT) and dialectical behaviour therapy (DBT) principles, particularly useful in helping the team to generate a greater understanding of the patient. These approaches can help to place the patient's problems in context, explore patterns of behaviour, identify triggers and maintenance factors, and help the practitioner examine the consequences and meaning of behaviours. The provision of time and 'space' away from routine clinical practice to think about the patient's difficulties and needs enables the practitioner to synthesize and evaluate practice. Ross (1990) advocates that reflective practice should generate hypotheses; question what, why and how one does things; explore consequences of actions; and seek alternatives. Similarly, this 'spirit of enquiry' is encouraged within our sessions, with practitioners prompted to consider questions such as:

- Why do we practise in this way?
- Why do we choose these particular methods?
- What theories or experiences prompt our decision making?
- What other methods could we consider?
- If a particular intervention is not working, what might be the reasons behind this?
- How can I apply my knowledge and experience to this/other situations?

This collaborative reflection process can allow practitioners to draw upon both their theoretical knowledge base and practical experience to assist in planning, predicting and implementing informed courses of action, with the aim of enhancing individual skill development and improving practice.

Reflections on functional aspects of work

Reflective practice sessions can be used to consider the ordinary and everyday practice events. Johns (1995) suggests that practitioners have a tendency to pay attention to practice situations perceived as difficult or uncomfortable. In effect, clinical practice perceived as routine or unproblematic tends not to be reflected on. The concerted effort of practitioners to contemplate and evaluate routine practices can, however, provide a catalyst for change (Driscoll 1994, 2000). Examples of everyday practices that our groups have reflected on have included the following:

- *Handovers*: exploration of how the nursing handover can be made more effective in terms of time and information presented.
- *Clinical risk assessments*: how nurses can organize their time to ensure that clinical risk assessments are kept up to date, and discussion of how to conduct an accurate and meaningful clinical risk assessment.
- *Nursing notes*: discussion of what should be included in nursing entries within patients' day-to-day notes.
- *The 'patient's day'*: consideration of the day-to-day experiences of patients, and discussion of how routine practices may be perceived by patients. Reflective practice has also been used to propose, plan and develop nurse-led ward-based activities.
- *Care planning*: discussion of how the team can ensure that sufficient time is given to trained staff to have one-to-one time with patients on their caseload, and subsequently devise appropriate patient-centred care plans.
- *Improving communication*: between members of the multidisciplinary team (MDT).

The above list is by no means exhaustive. It is our experience that by considering existing working routines reflective practice can encourage the team to think about the discrepancy between ideal and real-life practice situations, and allow opportunities for practitioners to discuss and be open to alternative methods. The aim of this is to generate nursing practice that balances the demands of the day-to-day running of the ward and the individual needs of both the nurse and the patient.

Self-reflection

An important dimension of knowledge upon which the practitioner can reflect is the knowledge of self (Clarke *et al.* 1996). In our sessions, we recognize that as individuals we each hold moral values and judgements. Reflective practice can encourage practitioners to explore how their personal beliefs, attributes and experiences impact on clinical aspects of care. An example of self-reflection might include exploring how practitioner's core beliefs and rules for living impact on their work with a patient who has a history of violent or sexually assaultative behaviours. Self-reflection in this context has the potential to enhance the practitioner's self-understanding (Carper 1978), by identifying personal boundaries, expectations and limits.

122 CBT for acute inpatient mental health units

The role of the facilitator

As reflective practice is a multidimensional process, the use of Socratic questioning is a useful tool to understand or resolve a particular issue. Clinicians with a CBT background will already possess this tool. However, as stated above, the topics brought to reflective practice sessions are varied and the clinician will need to draw on a wide range of models and theories such as CBT, solution-focused or systemic approaches and the influences of countertransference in order to be effective. We have also found the principles of acceptance and commitment therapy (ACT) in particular to be very useful in facilitating the process of reflection and encouraging a learning culture.

Challenges of establishing a reflective group – the organizational culture

John Dewey (1933) stated: 'We do not learn by doing . . . we learn by doing and realizing what came of what we did.' The organizational culture can have a significant influence on whether reflective practice actually occurs. Clarke et al. (1996) stress that a non-reflective organizational ethos will inhibit and positively discourage the practice of reflection in individual practitioners.

The CBT clinician and clinical psychologist are familiar with different models and are therefore adept at looking at situations from disparate standpoints. As a consequence, we are good at generating positive ideas that can improve clinical practice. If the organization does not recognize or value these ideas, however, then they wither and die (Driscoll and Teh 2001).

According to Clarke et al. (1996), the dominance of women in the nursing team increases the likelihood of establishing and maintaining a reflective culture. Our experience concurs with this view. It has certainly been easier to set up reflective practice sessions when the ward manager has been female. Women have a tendency to be more willing to be open and have a readiness to share ideas than their male counterparts. Although this view needs to be tested empirically, it may be argued that these characteristics are necessary components if 'reflectivity' in the work environment is to flourish. Clarke et al. (1996) go on to point out that nursing environments tend to be dominated by what they term a 'life strategy of agency'. This reflects a 'male culture' which is characterized by 'a desire to control, a tendency to separate off the non-controllable aspects of life and to deny the life strategy of communion' (p. 179). What makes reflective practice particularly challenging is that many nurses, male and female, work in organizations that are dominated by this 'life strategy of agency', wanting quick solutions to problems without going through the process of reflection.

In setting up the staff reflective practice groups we found a number of solutions to these difficulties. There is nothing more effective than finding an ally with whom to work to encourage the rest of the team to follow. The support of the ward manager is also important to ensure the involvement of staff members. In our experience, the attendance of the ward manager in sessions increases the perceived significance and value of the sessions, and encourages other staff members to attend. Devising a contract and terms of reference describing the requirements and expectations of staff promotes commitment and formalizes the process. Although the articulation of commitment to reflective practice by the staff team is all well and good, it can nevertheless become redundant when ward demands increase. It is interesting to note, however, that although reflective practice and other activities such as supervision can be easily postponed, even when the shift is at its busiest doctors' ward rounds are never cancelled. In light of this, reflective practice needs to be promoted and viewed as an integral part of the working life of the ward. The timing of when sessions occur needs to be negotiated, again with the support and approval of management. We have found that the facilitation of reflective practice groups during the lunchtime handover session to be the most effective as this maximizes numbers, with staff from both the morning and afternoon shifts available to attend. The greater the number of staff in attendance, the more effective the group will be (Shepherd and Rosebert 2007).

There are a number of challenges that may be specific to different settings. Our aim is to consider those challenges that we have encountered. Due to shift patterns and the rota system of working, not all staff will have access to reflective practice group sessions. Keeping an attendance log helps to identify those members of staff who have had difficulty in attending and this issue can be discussed during their personal supervision.

Another challenge to be considered is that staff members need to see the benefits of participating in the process. This may be problematic for some people who want detailed instructions in how to resolve a problem rather than an approach that explores a problem and comes to an understanding rather than a clear definitive answer. Reiterating the purpose of reflection through periodic reviews of the contract may promote the intended function of reflective practice. Staff will need to feel that this process will assist in making sense of difficult and complex practice and perceive improvements in patient care.

The last issue to be addressed is that of trust amongst the team. The idea of reflective practice can be intimidating and stress inducing if the belief is that this is a process for monitoring performance. This view could be further strengthened by the attendance of the ward manager who makes decisions about a person's job or promotion prospects. The facilitator will need to foster a reflective atmosphere by positively reinforcing the following aspects:

- challenging the status quo
- suggestions about alternative ways of thinking/working
- admissions of not knowing
- when someone reveals their vulnerability or a certain level of self-disclosure, particularly by a senior member of staff
- supporting and validating the lone voice in the group
- encouraging and supporting staff when difficult choices are made.

Putting theory into practice

The following two vignettes represent examples of our reflective practice sessions. The vignettes are intended to give a flavour of the work undertaken and are not comprehensive accounts of the sessions delivered. For the purposes of confidentiality, case descriptions for individual patients are kept to a bare minimum.

PICU

The psychiatric intensive care unit (PICU) situated on the ground floor of the hospital is a nine-bedded secure facility, which provides care and treatment for the most disturbed and vulnerable inpatients within the locality. The ward has a dingy environment despite the fact that it had been recently decorated. It is fairly dark due to limited natural light. The majority of the patients are male with a primary diagnosis of psychotic illness and a secondary diagnosis of substance misuse and personality disorder. Many are potentially aggressive, antisocial, and violent, presenting with challenging and unpredictable behaviours. The reflective session described below took place when I (Cowdrill) had just arrived at the hospital as the new consultant psychologist. I was, however, a novice (despite having over ten years' experience of working with people with severe and enduring mental health problems), as I had limited experience of inpatient settings. Nevertheless I was seen as the expert who had all the answers to the difficulties on this ward.

Previous weekly reflective practice sessions had been facilitated by the specialist psychologist (Dannahy). Staff were familiar with the idea of discussing whatever was important to the team at that particular time. On this occasion, the issues concerned one inpatient. He was a 45-year-old man of Caribbean origin, whom we shall call Marc, who had been admitted under a prison order (Section 37). Marc was experiencing psychotic and delusional symptoms and displaying ritualistic behaviours. He was also attracted to fires and therefore fire setting was a risk. What was most concerning, however, were his unpredictable and threatening physical and verbal behaviours. The staff stated that Marc would make demands that could not be met and then become argumentative and obstructive. He seemed to enjoy creating scenes with other patients and then standing back and watching the result of his interventions. On a number of occasions this had resulted in other patients fighting with each other. Sometimes Marc would identify a patient or member of staff he perceived to be vulnerable and would then attempt to isolate and intimidate them. Marc had a tendency to focus his attentions on staff that were of African origin. He would shout and berate them and was often racially abusive towards them. If the staff member was from a Caribbean background they were treated favourably, and those from a white European background were treated with indifference. With visitors and the consultant psychiatrist he was extremely charming. He was often described as having a 'Jekyll and Hyde personality'.

Staff were split on racial lines in how they viewed and treated Marc. The African nurses felt intimidated by him and reported feeling unsafe at work and unsupported by both the team and management. They felt helpless to change the situation and a number of these nurses wanted to resign from their posts.

As a cognitive behaviour therapist by knowledge and training, I could have approached this problem with the idea of setting goals and finding out what the team wanted to achieve by my involvement. However, using a reflective practice approach, I decided first to explore the staff's cognitions and emotions. Giving staff the time and space to vent their concerns revealed that the white and Caribbean staff were also angry at the patient, but expressed feelings of helplessness in being able to make any changes. These members of staff also felt guilty at their own powerlessness, but also frightened that Marc would target them if they intervened. Thus, all the staff were united in their belief that they were trapped and the situation was hopeless unless Marc was discharged. Validating and showing acceptance of their emotional experiences created an atmosphere of safety, which allowed staff to be more honest and open in disclosing their vulnerabilities. By exploring their experience in depth, the individual team members were able to appreciate the difficulties of their fellow nurses. Listening to the concerns of their colleagues allowed individual members to evolve into a team, and changed their pessimistic responses to expressions of enthusiasm with the belief that a solution could be found.

This was a fairly new team made up of some experienced staff that had previously worked together on different wards, and others that were new to the hospital. Drawing on empirical and ethical aspects of reflective practice, I asked the more experienced team members whether they had encountered similar experiences, and encouraged them to think about what had worked in the past. This had the result of strengthening the team's confidence with the realization that some members possessed the knowledge and skills of working successfully with challenging behaviours. They identified that having strong leadership made a difference to solving the problem. They were then able to identify a leader amongst the senior members of staff who would be able to unite the team. It was disclosed that as colleagues they did not really know each other and the only identity they had was based on race. The shift rota enhanced segregation on racial lines as mainly nurses from one racial group were on duty at any one time. It was agreed that the shift pattern had to be altered to reflect the diversity of the team.

Time was then spent reflecting on what aspects of their practice reinforced the divisions amongst the team, which in turn had encouraged Marc's challenging behaviours. Challenging by use of questioning promoted a reflective stance, which was necessary to enable staff to step back and systematically detach from the situation. As a way of enhancing more positive behaviours and reducing dysfunctional and challenging behaviours, the team devised a behavioural plan. It was also identified that further training in working with challenging behaviour would be necessary.

This reflective practice session demonstrated that although the staff located the problem in the patient's dysfunctional behaviours, the real issue concerned the feelings of fear, impotence and the lack of support and trust amongst the staff. This was the beginning of building confidence and trust amongst all the team members.

Male acute admission ward

There are two 25-bedded acute admission wards located on the second floor of the hospital. In line with government policy guidelines regarding gender, the wards have been redesigned and refurbished within the last year to accommodate one ward designated for males, the other for females. Prior to the opening of the 'new' wards, nurses were asked to state a preference for which ward they would like to work on: male, female or PICU. In consequence, this has led to the development of new nursing teams. Patients on the acute admission wards tend to present with a range of difficulties including bipolar affective disorder, psychosis, affective disorders, and personality disorders. A number of patients also have co-morbid substance misuse difficulties. The reflective session described below took place on the male ward approximately five months after the opening of the new wards. At this time, the ward manager and nursing team had agreed that reflective practice sessions could be used to provide an opportunity to examine their day-to-day routine practices, with the aim of improving the efficiency of the team.

This particular reflective practice session had started later than usual due to the lengthy handover that had preceded the session. It is of note that there is a two-hour handover period between the morning and afternoon shifts, the first hour used for the traditional 'handover' with the aim of allowing the team to exchange pertinent information. The following hour is used to organize the afternoon shift, which may include preparing for ward round, organizing staff duties (e.g. observations and breaks), reading care plans, and providing an opportunity for individual supervision sessions. It is also within this time that weekly reflective practice sessions are offered. The staff identified that they would like to discuss the nursing handover. They described handovers as being overlong, on some occasions taking up to two hours. This was subsequently creating difficulties for the afternoon staff to have adequate time to prepare their shift. The team identified that there had been a recent change in the way in which handovers were conducted, with nursing staff encouraged to bring in each individual patient's notes, give a brief description of the patient's presenting difficulties, section status, level of observation, and risks and behaviours observed within the past 72 hours. Although the nursing staff recognized the importance of handovers being detailed, they expressed frustration at the amount of time this was taking.

Initially, nurses were encouraged to reflect on their experiences of being in handover. A number of individuals disclosed that they found themselves 'drifting off', leaving the potential to 'miss' important information (e.g. regarding risk, tasks to be followed up, etc.). Others reported that the amount of information was overwhelming, and that they found it difficult to retain key points. Interestingly, another individual divulged that he found handover incredibly boring, and on reflection recognized that he had been late for work more times since this new system had been in place. It was useful for the team to reflect on their individual perceptions of their experience, allowing for a cohesive recognition that handover was presenting a difficulty, and invited the team to acknowledge that alternative methods should be considered.

In line with a cognitive behavioural formulation approach, we explored what factors either maintained or perpetuated the problem. The change of the handover protocol was initially highlighted. Guided discovery also allowed for other factors to be identified. A number of inexperienced trained staff and health care support workers, for example, expressed feeling high levels of anxiety at the thought of having to 'present' their patients in handover, and reported that they would try and 'get out of having to do it'. This anxiety was fuelled by concerns over what information they should include. Rather than report key issues, these staff reflected that they had a tendency to read out the past 72-hour nursing note entries verbatim, so as not to overlook any important information. This subsequently prolonged the time taken to hand over a particular patient. Another factor highlighted was the tendency to spend lengthy periods discussing problematic patients and their impact on the team. Staff reported that the handover could be used as a cathartic forum, providing opportunity for the team to 'offload'. A further factor identified was the shortage of time available for staff to adequately prepare for the handover. This was attributed to the vast range of tasks expected to be completed by individual nurses. This led to information being inadequately prepared, and at times could also lead to the handover starting late.

This reflective practice session allowed the nursing team to generate solutions to the problem, and could draw on individual nurses' experience of what had worked in other settings in which they had worked. One suggestion that was subsequently implemented was for all patients to have a short summary included in the front page of the nursing notes detailing presenting problems, section status and specific risks to be noted. This has reduced the time-consuming practice of having to 'trawl through notes' to find information, and can guide the nurse when considering what information pertaining to the previous 72 hours should be passed on. The importance of allocating time for nurses to prepare for handover was also identified.

The reflective practice session described is an example of how nursing teams can contemplate and evaluate routine practices, generate solutions to problems, and take ownership of change. The male ward's reflective practice has become ingrained within the ward culture, to the extent that the group occurs irrespective of whether or not I (Dannahy) am available to facilitate the session. The ward has adopted the use of a 'reflective practice book', whereby they can note suggestions made during the session regarding practice and, if appropriate, these suggestions are subsequently discussed during the team meeting.

An interesting pattern in the process of reflective practice on this ward has also been observed. Initially, reflective practice sessions were used to reflect on the functional aspects of work. This may in part have been attributed to the creation of a 'new' team. As the team has developed and become more cohesive, the team more readily use self-reflection and explore how their individual beliefs and values impact on practice. It is possible that this change reflects an increase in trust amongst team members.

Conclusion

There is a drive within the Department of Psychiatry in Southampton to develop a positive therapeutic environment to improve the lives of both patients and staff. The reflective culture is a major ingredient that is necessary to maintain the therapeutic milieu. The work we have started will continue only with the commitment and individual support of all practitioners and managers; without them the culture of reflection and learning will be lost.

Chapter 11

Working with crisis

The role of the clinical psychologist in a psychiatric intensive care unit

Suzanne Sambrook

Introduction

Psychiatric intensive care units (PICUs) specialize in the care of service users who have been detained under the Mental Health Act and who are currently at risk either to themselves or others and cannot be managed on an open ward. Hence the PICU will have increased levels of physical security such as locked doors and limited access. It will also have increased staffing levels to provide the necessary intensive care. The aim of a PICU is to work with the service users to help them in the crisis period so that they can return to a less restrictive environment as quickly as possible. The types of problems usually encountered within the PICU can be psychosis-driven fears leading to aggression, acute manic states, suicidal behaviour and self-harm.

The *Mental Health Policy Implementation Guide: National Minimum Standards for General Adult Services in PICU and Low Secure Environments* (Department of Health 2002c) advocates multidisciplinary working. This means including occupational therapists, social workers and clinical psychologists working alongside the medical team of nurses and doctors. However, these roles are new with little in the way of history to guide them. This chapter aims to look at some of the work done within one particular PICU by clinical psychology as a way of opening the discussion about what could work.

Psychological working

The *Mental Health Policy Implementation Guide* (DH 2002c) suggests that within multidisciplinary working, a range of psychological work should be provided as core interventions. In particular it highlights counselling, therapy (CBT and DBT), psychosocial interventions and psycho education – all standard work that we could argue should be taking place in any inpatient facility. However, when people arrive on a PICU they are in crisis and as such often unable to engage in direct therapeutic interventions. Key needs when a person arrives are to stabilize and provide a protective environment. However, once the person is stabilized they are likely to be transferred back on to an open ward. Hence, the opportunity for traditional psychological one-to-one type interventions is extremely limited. The challenge for a clinical psychologist is how to intervene with and on behalf of someone who is in crisis and in an environment which is heavily influenced by the medical model (i.e. where diagnosis and medication are often the first line of intervention and the time to develop therapeutic relationships to work individually is very limited).

Going back to the *MHPIG*, it provided another set of clues as to how to work. It states: 'Care and treatment offered must be patient centred, multidisciplinary, intensive, comprehensive, collaborative and have an immediacy of response to critical situations' (DH 2002c: 3). Involving other members of the team in therapeutic work extends the possibility and range of psychological work but would require support and supervision. Extending the role of the nursing staff to include some basic psychological strategies might allow an intensity of work that one lone clinical psychologist could not achieve. Providing this sort of consultancy and supervision is a role which allows clinical psychologists to use their psychological skills beyond the traditional provision of direct therapy and is in line with guidelines in the *New Ways of Working for Applied Psychologists* document currently being developed by the British Psychological Society and which itself has been prompted by the Department of Health document *New Ways of Working for Psychiatrists* (2005).

Discussions with staff on the PICU and with the ward managers also highlighted the difficulties of working in what is often a highly charged atmosphere with frequent turnover of staff and consequent use of agency staff. Burnout and cynicism were often cited as the effects of working for any length of time on the PICU. Here was another opportunity for psychological work as the burnout of staff would affect the quality of care for the service users. Supporting the staff and working collaboratively to develop the milieu could have both short-term and long-term benefits. Short-term benefits would be about providing opportunities for reflection and debriefing from the day-to-day tensions which can be found on the ward. The longer term benefits would be about building knowledge and expertise which would enable the staff to feel more confident and hence less likely to feel overwhelmed and demotivated – the first steps towards burnout.

Developing from these ideas, the strategy for working in our PICU comprised three different but overlapping areas:

1   Provision of limited direct work with the service user.
2   Providing consultancy, supervision and joint working with the staff to provide indirect interventions and to inform the care planning process.
3   Working with the environment to develop a therapeutic milieu.

I will outline each approach with reference to two vignettes and will start by introducing the reader to Danny and Lizzie.

Case study: Danny

Danny is a 19-year-old man who was transferred to the PICU after a brief stay on the acute inpatient ward. He was admitted under a Section 3 of the Mental Health Act following an episode of drug-induced psychosis. Whilst on the ward he had frequently absconded and each time had been returned to the ward in a state of intoxication. When he was present on the ward his behaviour was seen as disruptive, upsetting other service users, touching female members of staff inappropriately, shouting and swearing and, on occasion, physically violent. He was non-compliant with all remediation attempts. When he first arrived on the PICU he was quiet and withdrawn but quickly started to show the behaviours that had caused the transfer, including trying to get over the security fence to abscond.

Case study: Lizzie

Lizzie was a young woman of 22. She had been in and out of various inpatient and residential units since she was a teenager. She had been admitted to the acute ward on this occasion after an attempted suicide. Lizzie had taken large quantities of paracetamol and had then gone to Accident and Emergency from where she had been transferred to the ward. Lizzie has a history of severe self-harm and following admission her self-harm had escalated (cutting, burning and ligature tying). After the last incident where she had tied a ligature, it was felt that the secure environment of the PICU would help prevent further episodes of self-harm.

Direct work

For the reasons already stated, direct work is often limited. However, there are opportunities to carry out initial assessments which can lead to the development of a tentative formulation. The aim was to offer service users on the PICU an initial assessment meeting with the psychologist within the first week of arriving. This was not always taken up by the service user. This could be for a range of reasons. Sometimes this was because of suspicion about the reason for the meeting or a general unwillingness to engage. At other times it was because the person was too distressed to be able to engage.

Assessment

Using objective and standardized assessment tools is problematic. This is partly because of their lack of validity when a person is in acute distress, but more often than not because the simple logistics of filling in a self-report questionnaire (the need for a level of concentration and ability to remain focused) made it too difficult. However, as a team outcomes are important and finding a way to measure change is an ongoing issue. The use of observational or semi-structured interview methods can be employed. These could include the Health of the Nation Outcome Scales (HONOS, Wing *et al.* 1994) and the Brief Psychiatric Rating Scale (BPRS, Overall and Gorham 1962). When they were used in our service, the collection of the data was multidisciplinary and preceded by training sessions on their use to ensure consistency and interrater reliability. However, collecting the data in an environment that was often extremely reactive to ongoing crisis was a constant challenge.

Formulation

Interview, observation, talking with staff and reviewing the medical notes were the key methods of assessment. This allowed the gathering of all available data to begin the process of formulation. The process of formulation has been discussed in Chapter 5 by Dr Fiona Kennedy. Developing a formulation that provides an understanding, albeit in a very tentative form, of how that person arrived in this situation at this time – what Kennedy calls a 'coherent narrative' – provides the basis of appropriate care planning which will take account of the needs of that person.

Danny

After the first few days in the PICU, Danny agreed to meet with the psychologist, but was quite hostile during the meeting. He was very suspicious about my motives for seeing him and was at pains to tell me how he was only on the PICU because other people did not like him and picked on him. However, he was also keen to point out that he could cope and did not need anyone; he was 'tough'. From the interview and from background information a basic initial formulation was developed, based on the cognitive formulations of Beck (1995).

Danny's initial formulation

Early experiences

- Broken family.
- Poor attachments.

- Several periods of time in care.
- Excluded from school.
- Few peer friendships.
- No girlfriends.

Beliefs

- 'No one is there for me; other people always leave me.'
- 'I'm not wanted.'
- 'The world is a bad place.'

Compensatory strategies

- Tries to find a group to belong to.
- Admires the 'tough boys'.
- Tries to fit in by 'copying' the tough boys.
- Drug crowd provides a sense of belonging.
- Drugs provide a brief 'feel-good' factor.

Effects

- Vulnerability to exploitation.
- Used by others but no true friends.
- Drug-seeking behaviour.

Other problems

- Very low self-esteem.
- Disinhibition when on drugs.
- Poor social skills.
- Impulsivity.

Although further direct work with Danny proved to be difficult, he would always seek me out when I was on the ward – only to say 'hello' or to try and be jocular; he would not engage on any other level at this time. Hence there was no opportunity to share the formulation with Danny. However, it was shared with his nursing team to develop a more sympathetic understanding of Danny from the one with which he had arrived. Following the sharing of the formulation with the staff, his difficult behaviours were reattributed to maladaptive and self-defeating coping strategies for managing his low self-esteem and fear of the world, rather than 'trying to upset the staff'. This produced a higher level of positive interactions between the staff and Danny and a greater willingness to spend time with him.

From the formulation, new aims were developed for working with Danny. These were about finding opportunities for building his self-esteem, to model good interpersonal behaviour and to help Danny develop an understanding of his triggers and warning signs for aggressive behaviour.

Lizzie

Developing a formulation with Lizzie was very different from the approach taken with Danny. Staff felt sorry for Lizzie but at the same time were anxious about the self-harm. Hence she was constantly on close observations, sometimes with two nurses. This mirrored what had been happening on the open ward with a similar result that the self-harm was not decreasing and Lizzie's ligature tying was actually increasing, despite almost constant observation.

Formulating the context and identifying maintenance cycles between the person and the environment can be a very helpful way of breaking patterns of unhelpful behaviour. Using functional analysis with knowledge of the laws of operant conditioning enables the development of a cross-sectional formulation of the maintaining factors in the environment. Put simply, operant conditioning predicts that behaviours are maintained by their consequences – if the consequences are reinforcing then the behaviour will be repeated. Self-harm can work this way and a positive feedback loop can quickly become established, where the function of the self-harm, e.g. reduction of distress, self-punishment, communication, is met with a corresponding positive – i.e. distress reduced (even if only briefly); feeling relief after the punishment; establishing contact and being looked after. In all cases the result is short term and never changes the situation as next time there is a need for relief, punishment or communication, the same strategy will be applied. Not only do the consequences maintain the behaviour, but the law of diminishing results also applies, so that the more the strategy is used, the less effective it becomes. In the absence of alternative coping strategies, the person relies on the same strategy but simply increases the intensity or frequency.

This was happening with Lizzie. The reason this is not quickly identified is that the reinforcing properties of the self-harm itself are often overlooked or the way the context acts to reinforce the behaviour is ignored. For example, if the function is a need for comfort, putting someone on close observations fulfils that function. Even if the interactions are not inherently comforting, it may be good enough to meet the need – hence reinforcing the behaviour.

To establish the function of Lizzie's self-harm we employed the simple expedient of asking her. No one had ever asked Lizzie about her self-harm, the assumption being that it was a suicide attempt or if only 'minor' then a way of 'getting attention' – a frequent assumption about people who self-harm. Lizzie had a good relationship with one of the nurses and was willing to talk to her. The nurse was keen to learn about self-harm and following a session with the nurse on functions of self-harm and possible questions to ask Lizzie, she was able to establish a good rapport with Lizzie and an ease with regard to talking about the self-harm.

For Lizzie the self-harm fulfilled two functions. One was the alleviation of distress. Whenever she felt overwhelmed she would take an overdose (if she was in the community) as she knew that this would give her some 'time out' from the situation and allow her to cope better when she woke up. She said that she rarely thought of this as a suicide attempt, but just a means of having a break. Cutting also produced a sense of peace which she found helpful when in distress.

The second function was about being cared for. Although Lizzie's family had been intact, her mother was ill from the time that Lizzie was a young girl. At times her mother was in hospital for long periods. Her father struggled to care for Lizzie and her older sister and was at times emotionally unavailable to both. The only times Lizzie could remember being cuddled were when she had fallen over or hurt herself. She had not linked these events with her current self-harm until these conversations with the nurse. A vicious cycle diagram was drawn out with Lizzie to help her understand and remember each of the functions of the self-harm (see Figures 11.1 and 11.2).

Working with staff

Assessment and formulation are only the beginning of the process of working directly with service users. However, in a PICU it may be all that time allows. The next phase would be to develop goals and care plans that can build on the formulation. Ideally these are collaboratively developed but the reality is that they are often written by the primary nurse in isolation from other professionals and the service user.

The aim in our PICU was to develop a more multidisciplinary approach to care planning. We had occupational therapy and psychology available on the ward but in the main each discipline was working independently. The *Creating Capable Teams Approach* (CCTA, Department of Health 2007) discusses the need for the different health professionals to work together. Whyte and Brooker (2001) in their study of working in secure psychiatric environments cite team working as the second most frequently

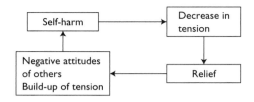

Figure 11.1 Vicious cycle of self-harm (a)

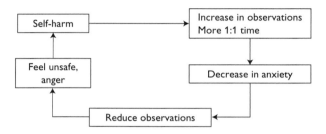

Figure 11.2 Vicious cycle of self-harm (b)

cited source of rewarding work. However, there is little in the way of research to tell you how to develop this approach. Onyett (2004) makes some suggestions, including having shared objectives, enabling participation at all levels and ensuring channels of good communication and support. He suggests that change can and needs to happen from the bottom up, but that the right conditions need to be created by management structures.

In discussions with the ward manager and talking with staff about what they would find helpful from each of the other disciplines, it was clear that communication was key. Having time to meet with each other and to discuss our different perspectives were frequently highlighted. In response to this, two initiatives were set up. The first was to introduce a reflective practice group on the ward, open to everyone who worked there. This was facilitated by the psychologist. The second was the development of care planning meetings and joint working between each of the disciplines. These were set up as needed and usually after the period of assessment when all information could be pooled to help the formulation process.

Reflective practice group

The *New Ways of Working* document specifically highlights the need for opportunities for time to reflect and talk about the work done, if service users are to be best served. However, in a PICU where crisis often dictates the speed of interactions, times for reflection are few and interactions become reactive rather than planned and proactive. Unfortunately, the nature of the reactivity can and frequently works to maintain presenting problems. This was the case with Lizzie as highlighted above, in that the very intervention designed to keep her safe (close observations) was maintaining the problem. Building in weekly reflective practice (RP) group meetings was one way to slow the system and to allow the development of more proactive strategies.

The structure and process of RP has been outlined comprehensively in Chapter 10 of this volume (Cowdrill and Dannahy), and the groups set up in the PICU followed the same guidelines. Staff brought to the group each week particular problems that they were experiencing. Often this would be about care planning or how to overcome difficult interactions with service users, but occasionally it was also about how they, as a team, functioned. Although this group was facilitated by the psychologist, the process of solving the problems and developing answers was a joint process, with an opportunity for all to contribute. The role of the psychologist was to prompt discussion, to use a Socratic questioning style (Padesky 1996) to find out information, and to sum up at the end. Occasionally, where there was a clear need, teaching sessions were requested to ensure that the staff group all had the key skills necessary. These could be facilitated by nursing, medical or psychology staff depending on the topic.

The RP sessions were particularly helpful when there was a disagreement on ways of working. This was the case with Danny. After sharing the formulation, there was an improvement in Danny's behaviour. However, after a week he started to follow one of the female nurses around the ward. Additionally, Danny had become more aggressive. The ward had become quite unsettled, due to the admission of two new service users, both male and both involved in the drug culture. The elder of the two was also extremely verbally hostile to everyone. Danny appeared to be drawn to these two men and indeed had known one of them in the community. He soon started to act in a similar way, shouting, swearing and being very demanding. This had left the female members of staff feeling at risk and reluctant to be on the ward near Danny. The mood towards Danny started to change and there was a split between the staff of those who were still trying to understand Danny and those who were angry with his behaviour. Staff generally spent less time with Danny and he spent correspondingly more time 'hanging around' the two new service users.

Danny was discussed at the RP group. A useful framework for understanding the effects of one person's behaviour either on individuals or on the team is that proposed by Jeremy Safran (1990). His framework provides a way of understanding the relationship between the cognitive (intrapersonal realm) and the interpersonal realm. It helps map out how a person's beliefs can affect how they behave and how in turn the other person reacts in such a way as to maintain the original belief. For example, with Danny we had hypothesized that one of his interpersonal beliefs was that he was not wanted and that people would never be there for him. His compensatory behaviour was to try and get close to people by copying them or following them, a behaviour which at the very best tended to elicit frustration and at the worse would result in people either using him or rejecting him. This had the effect of confirming his original belief about rejection. The behaviour elicited in others (e.g. the frustration and rejection) is named as 'the pull'. Safran suggests that one way of moving the person forward is to deliberately resist the pull, hence disconfirming the original belief and offering alternative ways of interacting.

This framework was adopted within the RP session. Using the formulation to identify the (unconscious) 'pull' that Danny exerted enabled staff to develop alternative actions and to understand the feelings they had towards him.

Joint working

Joint working is a great way for different disciplines to get to know what the others do. It helps overcome unhelpful assumptions about other professions and builds co-operation and respect. Joint assessments between psychology and nursing and between psychology and OT allowed us to develop a more comprehensive approach to care planning. Joint working also meant working with the service user in a collaborative way. The medical model which is paramount in many PICUs tends towards the 'expert' model of care, where the service user is a passive recipient of medical care. With the move towards recovery-oriented services (Repper and Perkins 2003), the role of the service user has become defined as 'expert by experience'. The implication of this is that effective interventions must be collaborative. However, where issues of risk and safety are uppermost, this can become an ideal rather than an actuality.

This was put to the test when working with Lizzie. At that time on the PICU, the policy towards people who used self-harm was one of prevention and protection. Hence the person would be prevented from harming themselves by an increase in observations. The difficulty with this approach was that it was never clear when close observations should be decreased. A time-limited approach was taken on some occasions (i.e. after 24 or 48 hours) but then close observations were quickly re-established if there were any further episodes of self-harm. In addition, the prevailing view of self-harm was that it was either a failed suicide attempt or 'attention seeking'. The former merited sympathy and support, the latter a withdrawal of the attention in the idea that this would 'stop' the behaviour. However, it was unclear which was which, so there would be an inconsistent and somewhat confused response.

As already outlined above, self-harm can have a range of functions, sometimes more than one for any one person. Understanding this is the first step in working effectively with someone who uses self-harm. With Lizzie, our first step was to arrange a series of multidisciplinary meetings to discuss self-harm generally and the function of the self-harm specifically for Lizzie. Drawing on the evidence base for what works with self-harm, I decided to work with all the team using a dialectical behavioural therapy (DBT) framework. DBT is a therapy specifically designed for women who experience frequent suicidal urges and self-harm (Linehan 1993a; see Chapter 14 for a more specific discussion). In this therapy self-harm is seen as a way of coping. The problem is not so much the self-harm itself as the lack of any alternative skills to help manage overwhelming emotions. This understanding leads to an intervention based on offering alternative strategies to help manage these emotions. It also uses ideas from more Eastern traditions about the need for acceptance and validation before people can make changes. There is a comprehensive workbook to support any intervention (Linehan 1993b). Although DBT itself is a structured, multicomponent treatment programme, some of the ideas within it can be adapted to provide both an understanding and some ways of working with self-harm.

Collaborative working is central to DBT. To this end it was agreed that we would encourage Lizzie to write her own care plans with regard to the self-harm. Prior to this much work was carried out ensuring that staff understood the function of the self-harm; that it was not a suicide attempt and that Lizzie was capable of knowing what help she needed. We also worked with Lizzie to understand our model of self-harm, which she agreed with and understood and was willing to work with us in managing. We also looked closely at alternative behaviours – how could Lizzie manage when she felt distressed; what would help when she felt afraid and needed company; what did Lizzie want us to do if she did hurt herself and could she agree to focus on less severe forms of self-harm rather than ligatures?

All of these questions were answered and Lizzie was taught some basic self-management strategies. There was an agreement that if she needed to be close to someone, she could indicate this to staff who would respond by giving her the time. Staff too were taught basic self-harm management strategies so that they could support Lizzie in her attempts to limit the number of times she hurt herself. Key to this was what Linehan calls 'validation': the need for that person to feel understood and for staff to be able to communicate this. We were very clear that we were not going to stop Lizzie from hurting herself unless it was life threatening but we were going to work very hard with her to help her to limit this. This was a hotly debated subject in both joint meetings and RP, but the team agreed to support this approach, as did the consultant psychiatrist and the ward manager. Agreement from all the team was important for success. Lizzie was going to work most closely with her primary nurse, as they had developed a good therapeutic relationship. I supervised and supported the primary nurse. The occupational therapist provided support in terms of a daily programme for Lizzie, which provided distraction and opportunities to build her self-esteem and sense of achievement, and the whole team were involved in understanding and validating Lizzie's progress.

Inevitably there were some slips, but gradually over a period of several weeks Lizzie stopped her self-harm, was able to use a range of strategies to help her with managing her emotions. She was able to talk more effectively with staff, letting them know what she wanted without having to let them know through her behaviour. The team held its nerve over the first few days and did not put her on close observations, in line with Lizzie's request, but were able to engage her in activity in a much more relaxed way. This example of joint working became the template for future management of self-harm in other service users.

Developing a therapeutic milieu

The final strand to developing psychology in the PICU was the milieu. As previously stated, working in a PICU is often stressful, with high levels of risky behaviour from service users, aggression, violence, disrespect and a sense of futility when certain service users re-present themselves at frequent intervals (the so-called 'revolving door syndrome'). This results in high levels of staff turnover, burnout and the growth of cynicism. Couple this with the high usage of agency staff, many of whom have never worked in a PICU before, then the provision of consistent and comprehensive care for the service users can easily get lost, and the whole process can move towards simply containment and over-reliance on medication.

Finding a way to prevent this trend presents a considerable challenge. The *MHPIG* for national minimum standards for PICUs helps to develop the framework, but the process requires support at ground level if the standards are to be implemented. Onyett (2004) suggests that you need to put in place the structures and processes to shape the environment but you also need to attend to the culture if you are to have an effective team working at its maximum potential. Developing a culture which valued and supported staff is essential when developing a therapeutic milieu.

Whyte and Brooker's (2001) survey of staff in secure units found that staff got most job satisfaction from working directly with service users. However, this direct contact can be easily limited by the demands of paperwork or by the very nature of the behaviours on the ward. For example, constant aggressive behaviour, revolving door patients, reactivity, use of restraint and seclusion all militate against feelings of achievement and hence job satisfaction. On the other hand, being able to work consistently with service users, making a difference and seeing people change are all factors which make the job satisfying.

Using the *Ten Essential Shared Capabilities* document (NIMHE 2004d) as a framework for developing the milieu can be very helpful. This includes ideas such as promoting recovery, identifying people's strengths, promoting safety and positive risk taking and personal development and learning. The last point – personal development and learning – was key in working to develop the milieu in our PICU.

The RP groups were the first step in providing support and valuing the views of all the staff. Such groups were also able to highlight the need for further training and development. Specific topics identified included: listening skills, motivational interviewing, behaviour management, working with self-harm, working with voices and delusions, managing aggression and violence. Training packs for all of these were developed and a monthly two-hour teaching slot was established in conjunction with the ward manager and myself. These were generally well attended and inevitably highlighted even more areas for teaching. A culture of developing skills and wanting to learn was established which went a long way towards counteracting the sense of hopelessness that could quite easily slip into the environment.

Additionally, providing opportunities for debriefing and reviewing difficult situations in a non-judgemental way was helpful in enabling staff to feel valued and listened to. The results of these reviews could then help inform future work and interactions with patients. Referring back to Onyett (2004) again, he states that small changes can have big effects and that growth must start from the bottom up. Working with the staff directly to support and empower can help the team to develop and grow so that it can meet the standards set for PICUs and deliver excellence in care.

Difficulties – or what gets in the way

Implementing the types of interventions mentioned above does not go smoothly. I would suggest that perhaps one of the key requirements for psychologists (and other professionals) working on PICUs is the ability to handle setbacks with humour and acceptance. Although small changes can have big effects, they do not always last.

Inevitably there are changes in staff, agency staff who are not sure what they have to do, or times when the environment becomes too unsettled for much therapeutic work to take place. The demands of a few with disruptive behaviour often mean that others are less likely to receive the input they need. Providing consistency for behavioural programmes to be effective is very difficult under these circumstances. However, when you talk to staff about what is most difficult, the answer in many cases is 'communication'. Enabling consistent communication processes between staff working on shifts and who may not overlap for many days is a challenge. Similarly with joint working, the person I am working with may not be on shift for several days, missing opportunities to work with the service user which others may not be able to do. Ensuring robust processes for communication is an essential prerequisite to effective multidisciplinary working.

Risk issues are paramount, of necessity. The need to assess and manage these requires good information and a knowledge of the person's triggers, early warning signs and patterns of behaviour. Although NICE guidelines on risk (NICE 2005c) suggest using positive risk taking to enable the development of new strategies, this can be very difficult in a climate where any risk is seen as unacceptable and where people feel that there is a culture of blame. Trying to prevent all risk often sets up a negative spiral which effectively reinforces the risky behaviour – as in the example with Lizzie above. Finding ways to encourage and support an environment where positive risk taking is accepted and setbacks are seen as opportunities to learn is probably the greatest challenge within the current NHS context.

Perhaps one of the problems facing anyone working on a PICU is being able to identify 'what works'. The day-to-day 'busyness' often means that using systematic evaluations is difficult, and although assistants or researchers are a very scarce commodity, they can be very useful in gathering data. However, the question is – what data? We tried to implement some objective measures as mentioned above with some limited success. An alternative measure of success is discharge back to the open wards, although a better measure of success may be them not returning to the PICU. Our PICU tended to rely on clinical observations and feedback from service users and other staff. This is probably typical of any busy NHS PICU, but we still have only anecdotal evidence for what works. The vignettes in this chapter reflect some of the successes, but also pose questions about the work that we do. For example, how does this type of short-term intervention affect long-term care? How can it be carried on by other teams? We tried to address each of these questions with greater and lesser degrees of success. Creating a forum for discussion between PICUs may help with answering some of these questions and the development of the National Association of Psychiatric Intensive Care Units (NAPICU) has certainly opened up discussion about PICUs on a wider level.

Finally, multidisciplinary working requires a willingness from all professions to work together. From my experience what works seems to be about breaking down the mystique that can attach to different professions, being visible and available, working together and giving the team time.

Chapter 12

Training acute inpatient ward staff to use CBT techniques

Ché Rosebert and Chris Hall

Why training is needed

Setting the context

Cognitive behavioural therapy (CBT) has been developed to treat the wide range of conditions that adult inpatients within acute settings may present with – for example, depression, psychosis and personality disorder. Service users and carers are particularly keen that they are offered talking therapies (Mental Health Foundation 2006) included in a range of biopsychosocial interventions. Earlier chapters in this book have stated the case for providing psychological therapy and CBT in particular to inpatients within acute settings and therefore the rationale for this will not be repeated here. Creating a culture of therapy in the acute inpatient unit is recognized as essential for a well-functioning psychiatric hospital (Clarke, Chapter 1). The case to increase the number of psychological therapists within the NHS has been made (Layard 2004). Developing the workforce to enable inpatient staff to create a culture of therapy is a priority for all mental health NHS trusts.

Inpatient status is not a criterion for exclusion

It is the case that most service users will receive treatment in community settings. Best practice guidelines such as those provided by NICE in relation to schizophrenia, depression and bipolar disorder (NICE 2002, 2004b, 2006) do not however recommend that inpatients should not receive psychological therapies. This particular guide does make some distinctions about the type and length of psychological intervention as well as what other treatments should be combined with psychological therapy dependent on the phase of illness and recovery. Experiencing an acute phase of symptoms does not necessarily mean a service user will become an inpatient, particularly now when crisis resolution and home treatment teams enable potential inpatients to stay at home with extra support, rather than be admitted to acute inpatient wards. However, if a service user becomes an inpatient it is not necessary to create artificial distinctions between community and inpatient care and treatment. Whilst much of the research on the efficacy of CBT is based on community populations, there is evidence that CBT in an acute phase where the service user is an inpatient can reduce symptoms and speed recovery (Drury et al. 1996a, 1996b). Adaptations may be made to the psychological treatment depending on the phase of the illness or which part of the mental health service is providing the treatment, but given that psychological treatments are individually tailored this would be nothing new to the clinician. The onus is on the mental health service to provide a seamless service, including the provision of psychological therapies, regardless of whether the service user happens to reside in the community or not.

Who can provide CBT

Given that CBT should be offered to people with a wide variety of diagnoses, whether or not they happen to be an inpatient, the question of which mental health practitioners should provide this and how they will do so arises. As we have read in earlier chapters, a well-developed strategy for service delivery is required to meet the psychological needs of inpatients (Hanna, Chapter 2). Hanna suggests that this should include the basic training of all staff in cognitive behavioural interventions suited to particular competencies and adjusted for the brief, intensive nature of inpatient care. The Department of Health's New Ways of Working Programme envisages a far greater emphasis on psychological competencies throughout the workforce (Kinderman, Chapter 3). The development of the whole workforce is a critical step towards the successful implementation of the kind of (biopsychosocial) care envisioned in the National Service Framework (Sainsbury Centre for Mental Health 2001).There are just too few clinical psychologists or CBT therapists available to provide CBT to those who would benefit. Therefore it is likely that senior psychological therapy practitioners such as clinical psychologists will work both as trainers and providers of complex interventions that require the skilled use of CBT or the use of more than one therapy modality.

The Health Minister in the UK in 2007, Rosie Winterton, and Chief Nursing Officer Christine Beasley, have published a major review of mental health nursing, *From Values to Action* (Department of Health 2006a). This review recommends key actions needed for nurses to be able to improve the care of people with mental health problems, for example, by providing more psychological therapies within inpatient care. It can be argued that nurses are ideally placed to establish valued therapeutic alliances, because they are the largest discipline providing care on an everyday basis for sustained periods of time (Ironbar and Hooper 1989; Gamble et al. 1994, cited in Cameron et al. 2005). For nursing staff, establishing and maintaining a therapeutic alliance may be a complex and difficult task to achieve. Inpatient mental health nurses have multiple roles and carry out multiple tasks on a daily basis. Sometimes these tasks and roles, such as custodian and therapist, may conflict with each other and affect the therapeutic alliance between nurse and inpatient.

Levels of expertise

In developing the whole workforce to bring about a culture of therapy, it is necessary to consider which staff should deliver what psychological interventions and to what level of expertise. This has resource implications for the training and maintenance of the use of psychological skills. McCann and Bowers (2005) developed a psychosocial interventions for psychosis training package for acute inpatient staff delivered at three staged levels. These were defined as applicator, technician and specialist. The applicator level was delivered to all ward staff, both qualified and unqualified. The technician training was delivered to qualified staff and the specialist training was delivered to a small number of qualified staff who had extra supervision. The applicator level of training amongst other things included an emphasis on the engagement process. As a starting point, an emphasis on engagement at all levels of training is in line with most psychological therapy models which emphasize the therapeutic alliance between staff and service user as essential in supporting change for the service user. A trusting, collaborative relationship is a necessary prerequisite of and arguably as important as any specific treatment (British Psychological Society 2000). In their review of psychosocial intervention training, Brooker and Brabban (2004) found that the training courses they looked at had three levels of training and therefore skills that they conceptualized as Type A, B and C. Briefly, Type A skills could be seen as core values, understanding and skills needed to practice psychosocial interventions. Type B skills equate to the toolbox of manualized or prescribed skills. Type C skills equate to the ability to devise a sophisticated therapeutic intervention based on the sound understanding of a range of relevant therapeutic models. Both McCann and Bowers (2005) and Brooker and Brabban (2004) note that some skills overlap each level of training. Brooker and Brabban (2004) also note that a practitioner may possess one type of skill but not necessarily the others. For example, practitioners with Type C skills may not hold the underlying core values needed to provide psychosocial interventions to people with a psychosis. In addition, each skill type may be held at varying levels of competency.

Summary

This chapter describes our experience of providing training in CBT techniques akin to the applicator level described by McCann and Bowers (2005) and Type A skills described by Brooker and Brabban (2004) to nursing staff on two adult acute inpatient wards. Given the challenges to providing CBT with acute inpatient settings outlined by Clarke in Chapter 1, we considered what skills were the most useful to teach, how we could support nurses to use their skills and how competency could be maintained and developed.

Challenges in training staff in CBT for use with acute inpatient settings

The numerous challenges of providing this training can be divided into the following levels: the individual practitioner, the ward and the wider organization.

Challenges for the individual

Both ward staff and inpatients often observe with regret that nursing therapeutic contact tends to be minimal. In addition, the interaction may not be theoretically informed (Martin 1992; Gijbels 1995; Tyson, Lambert and Beattie 1995; Robinson 1996a, 1996b; Whittington and McLaughlin 2000, all cited in Cameron et al. 2005). On a typical inner city adult acute inpatient ward a lot of nursing time is taken up by administration and bed management (Robinson 1996a, 1996b, cited in Cameron et al. 2005). As well as nursing staff being very busy with multiple tasks, Bowers et al. (2005) found that psychiatric staff view the tasks of acute inpatient care as follows: keeping patients safe; assessing their problems; treating their mental illness; meeting their basic care needs; providing physical health care. These tasks are completed by the processes of containment, 24-hour staffing provision, providing medical treatment, and complex organization and management. In their study, Bowers et al. (2005) found that there was no mention of treating emotional needs. Therefore the link that therapeutic relationships may provide containment in its own right may not be made.

Staff may not think of themselves as the appropriate resource to do therapeutic work. When Bowers et al. (2005) asked different professions involved in inpatient care about the functions of wards, psychotherapeutic approaches were mentioned, but it appeared only as something used by non-medical staff. This implies that therapeutic interactions, particularly with the aim of meeting psychological needs, may be at the bottom of a very long list of things for the ward nurse to do, or that this is seen as a task for community services. Therefore, a challenge for the trainer may be that they are working with staff that either do not recognize the importance of, or do not prioritize, therapeutic time.

Wards contain a mixed staffing group of qualified and unqualified staff. A further challenge for the trainer is that they will often be training staff who have a starting point of different skill sets, experience and motivation to develop their roles. Therefore skills training for one group of staff may not be appropriate for another. Offering tiered training is one way of dealing with this difference, although it is often found that unqualified staff may be more enthusiastic and committed to training programmes. It would be a waste of valuable resource not to develop this part of the workforce. On the other hand, developing their skills might have implications for their pay and grading.

All too often staff do not use their training. This may be for individual reasons such as lack of confidence. Staff may not see training, keeping up to date with training, or developing new roles as a priority, due to excessive demands, stressful environment, and burnout. If one accepts Hinshelwood and Skogstad's (2000) assertion that ward staff unconsciously set up processes and systems within the ward culture that protect them from experiencing the anxiety and distress of the patient, then asking staff to spend therapeutic time with distressed patients breaks down this defence mechanism. For this reason, it is essential that ward staff have other adaptive ways of coping with patients' distress, for example, clinical supervision.

Developing skills is not enough. Staff need to demonstrate any new-found competencies when they return to their original work context. Otherwise, they may not implement newly learned skills or may not implement them properly, when they return to their workplace (Magliano *et al.* 2005). Numerous competing agendas get in the way of inpatient nursing staff developing their practice (Carradice and Round 2004). Davis and Taylor-Vaisey (1997, cited in Hoge *et al.* 2005) state that newly learned skills tend not to be routinely displayed when the learner returns to the workplace if the behaviour is not rewarded or sanctioned or runs counter to prevailing practices. Davis and Taylor-Vaissey (1997, cited in Hoge *et al.* 2005) state that lectures, workshops and conferences tend not to change a health provider's practice, nor do they improve outcomes for consumers.

Challenges for the ward

It may be that inpatient wards are often not functioning to their best capacity. Factors from the Bowers and McCann study (2003) that hindered training included problems within the wards themselves: for example, unstable or inadequate staffing and unpredictable crises on wards coupled with high staff anxiety. In particular high staff turnover and use of agency or bank staff can affect the therapeutic culture of a ward as well as the continuity of specific interventions with specific inpatients and their families.

Crises with bed management with high numbers of inpatients being transferred regularly between wards which may not be on the same physical site, or prematurely sent on leave or discharged due to pressure on beds, also affects the continuity of psychological work. In some wards the use of agency or bank staff is very transient and temporary. In other wards agency and bank staff work regularly, sometimes for years on a ward. This latter scenario can lead to a dilemma for ward managers in terms of how much they encourage the integration of that member of staff into the therapeutic culture, how much of an often limited training budget they may use for them or how much clinical supervision to provide. This can lead to a vicious cycle of a staff group being inadequately resourced with permanent trained staff, leading to providing a service that lurches from dealing with one crisis to the next (as agency or bank staff may be seen as temporary and therefore not be encouraged to intervene proactively), leading to low staff morale, high staff turnover and then high use of agency or bank staff.

In addition to potentially 'chaotic' staff groups, chaotic environments prevent clear planning of shift work and arrangements to meet one to one with inpatients are often rearranged due to the competing demands on the ward staff at the time and emphasis on reducing risk and harm minimization. Traditionally, psychological therapies are delivered within consistent, regular, reliable, negotiated times. This is seen as essential in engaging a patient into therapy and maintaining a successful therapeutic alliance. It is not uncommon for the wards we work with to have periods where they appear to be staffed more by agency staff, who may not know all the relevant protocols or patient group, than by a core stable staff group. The challenge for acute inpatient services is how to develop and sustain working relationships and alliances when the ward is understaffed, overstretched and/ or confronted by inflexible working systems (Gamble and Hart 2003).

Challenges for the wider organization

The organization surrounding the inpatient ward, as well as the ward itself, may not support the development of new competencies. Hoge *et al.* (2005) argue that 'if an organization does not understand, value, supervise or reward competency, then any employee is unlikely to display competency on an ongoing basis'. They draw on ideas from business models on developing competency and argue that an organization needs to support employee competency through information, environment, tools, and motivational enhancements. In a study of offering cognitive therapy training to seven wards, Bowers and McCann (2003) found that only two wards continued with the work beyond the project input. They identified several factors that hindered training. Two key ones were the presence of weak/absent ward management and weak middle management. At both a ward and organizational level, if there are no tangible systems in place that support and expect the individual practitioner to practise their skills, in other words feedback loops, then it is unlikely that new learning will be sustained and used. A wider challenge for primary care trusts and the Department of Health is to ensure that inpatient wards are adequately resourced with an appropriate number of staff with the appropriate level of skills needed.

Overcoming challenges to training

If challenges to training involve individual, ward and organizational factors, it follows that trainers need to take this into account and intervene at all these levels of the organization to give a training opportunity the best chance to be effective, maintained and developed.

Overcoming individual level challenges to training

Given that we know that people often do not practise what they learn, it is important to look at what approaches increase the chances that people will use their new skills. To change clinical behaviour, guidelines have to be specific. The more precisely behaviours are specified, the more they are likely to be carried out (Michie and Johnston 2004). Hoge *et al.* (2005) suggest several strategies from their review of increasing competence in business. They argue that competency will be improved by ensuring that knowledge taught is relevant to work that people do. They argue that it helps to focus on core competencies, rather than all competencies. They argue for teaching students to be self-directed learners and problem solvers.

Bowers and McCann (2003) recommend engaging with staff through working with them on the ward and delivering training onsite and then providing follow-up. Hoge *et al.* (2005) make the point that it can help to identify exemplary performers. Identifying what makes these people exemplary can be applied to help other employees improve their practice. One could argue that a critical mass, that is a significant percentage of the staff team, should be trained in order to change the culture of the team and increase the likelihood of the training being used (Clarke 2004).

Overcoming ward level challenges to training

It is likely that several elements of the ward need to be working well before new developments can be considered. Bowers and McCann (2003) have suggested areas to look at. There needs to be effective leadership and management (Bowers and McCann 2003; McCann and Bowers 2005). There needs to be stable staffing and adequate staffing levels (McCann and Bowers 2005). You need to have the support of the managers and tailor the training to the different skill mixes on the ward (Bowers and McCann 2003) and prior teaching in listening skills. In addition we have found that regular individual and peer supervision needs to be taking place.

Overcoming wider organizational level challenges to training

It is in the Mental Health NHS Trust's best interests to support the provision and use of education and training. It is recognized that providing education and training improves recruitment and retention of staff and that innovative training and education programmes should be developed specific to acute inpatient care (Clarke 2004). NIMHE go on to say that values and attitudes need to be realigned with a specific emphasis on service user and carer participation, structured engagement, purposeful evidence-based interventions and whole system care co-ordination. CBT is an evidence-based therapy model that places engagement and collaboration with the service user as essential to its success.

The *Health Care Commission Core Standards* (Department of Health 2004b) rate health care organizations on their ability to ensure that clinicians continuously update skills and techniques relevant to their clinical work. In addition, clinicians from all disciplines are expected to have access to maintain these standards. The practitioner in acute inpatient care will need to develop their experience in the ability to implement strategies which facilitate adherence to treatment including negotiation skills, early warning signs monitoring and psycho education (Sainsbury Centre for Mental Health 2001) – all of which are skills and techniques used by cognitive behaviour therapists. This makes it in the organization's best interest to provide training that develops its workforce to deliver essential interventions.

Clearly it is important that the organization is able to support new developments. Bowers and McCann (2003) make several recommendations for this, including negotiating with senior managers and seeking support of ward managers. Hoge *et al.* (2005) argue that competency will be improved by shaping the organization to provide culture and supports to foster competent behaviour.

How we implemented training on the ward

In planning and implementing a staff training programme in our acute inpatient setting, there were a number of supports either in place or instituted by ourselves that facilitated the training and the use of the skills learnt. These can be conceptualized in terms of individual support, ward support, and organizational support. However, some of these overlap. We wanted the training to be specific and relevant and supported by the ward and service manager. To maximize attendance we offered the training on the ward. We also wanted to maintain the skills learnt and did this through facilitating a weekly reflective practice group (Shepherd and Rosebert 2007). For a fuller discussion of the benefits of reflective practice groups see Cowdrill and Dannahy, Chapter 10.

Interventions at the individual level

Management and ward staff introduced protected therapeutic engagement time (Kent 2005). This meant that for a daily set period the ward is shut to external visitors; the ward clerk screens all telephone calls; there is no paperwork or meetings at this time, and ward staff spend time with patients either in one-to-one sessions or facilitating groups. This meant that there was supported, predictable time for staff to use the skills they had learnt in our training. The trainers were well known to the ward staff and a good working relationship had been developed. In effect there had been a long period of engagement between the trainers and the ward staff as the trainers had been offering formal and informal supervision and consultation.

Interventions at the ward level

We had run groups, worked with individual patients and their families, attended ward rounds and offered staff support over a number of years. A recent intervention was the introduction of a reflective practice group that we facilitated. We took the opportunity to use concepts discussed within the training in the reflective practice group. All these interventions meant that as psychologists we had a well-established presence as members of the ward team. Time was spent encouraging the ward manager and deputies to identify the skills they thought the ward staff needed, guided by what we thought we could usefully offer, rather than imposing our own ideas. This meant that training would meet the current needs of the ward, as opposed to being imposed by the trainers. For example, basic counselling skills for health care assistants was identified as a training need we could provide. In addition, the ward staff asked for training in the use of CBT techniques for depression and psychosis.

As a consequence of the ward manager identifying skills needed within the staff, some of the training was aimed at different levels for both qualified and unqualified staff. Qualified staff were encouraged to sit in with the unqualified staff training as a way of helping them refresh their knowledge as well as to help mentor the unqualified staff. The ward manager spent time making sure that rotas were arranged so that staff were able to attend training sessions without the danger of them being called out in an emergency. Training was carried out on the ward. Ideas from all the training were then able to be discussed within the reflective practice group.

Interventions at the wider organizational level

At the time this training was developed, the Trust already supported clinical psychologists to provide interventions to the ward in addition to individual work. A clinical governance target of the community mental health team (CMHT) clinical psychologists spending 10 per cent of their time on ward work had already been established. The organization did support development of competency within the wards. There was a ward managers' practice development forum. The Trust supported clinical psychologists to promote the use of psychological models and interventions by other professionals involved in support and treatment of acute inpatient services. A consultant nurse encouraged the ward manager and deputy to visit other wards in other Trusts, which fits with the idea of identifying exemplary performers. In addition, the training was discussed at management meetings with service managers and within the psychologists' own management meetings with the service manager.

Description of training given and rationale for techniques taught

There are many principles and aims of CBT that can benefit the service user during an inpatient stay. CBT can help to instil hope; raise consciousness and promote reflection – necessary in order to take thoughtful action; promote insight and advance stages of change (Prochaska *et al.* 1994). The therapeutic process requires formulating difficulties collaboratively and promotes alternative understanding of (sometimes unusual) experiences that have less distressing consequences. As noted by Kennedy in Chapter 5, shared formulation is an intervention in itself. The therapeutic relationship can make the therapy a time and place where conflicts can be resolved. The therapeutic time can be used to encourage healthy lifestyle choices, reduce risk of self-harm and provide information about follow-up care and local opportunities. As a result the therapy promotes successful discharge.

CBT has been shown to work for those taking part in comprehensive inpatient programmes. Studies have shown that psychosocial interventions can reduce recovery time in those admitted with relapse of schizophrenia. Drury *et al.* (1996b) found that cognitive behaviour therapy with inpatients who had a diagnosis of schizophrenia resulted in people showing less residual symptoms at nine months than those who had informal support with recreation therapy.

Using CBT can help staff feel better about their role and enable them to be more empathic. For example, training in CBT for hallucinations and delusions led staff to have more empathy towards the experiences and to have increases in feelings of adequacy, legitimacy, employment-related self-esteem and expectations of work satisfaction (McLeod *et al.* 2002).

The British Psychological Society (2000) published a clinical practice document, *Recent Advances in Understanding Mental Illness and Psychotic Experiences*, which evaluated and summarized the use of CBT with psychosis. This publication recommended that voice hearers could benefit from using CBT to identify where voices were coming from, reducing stress and levels of arousal and addressing beliefs about the voices. In relation to delusions, it suggests that people who hold unusual distressing beliefs can use CBT to explore their unusual beliefs and to challenge the evidence supporting the belief (not the belief itself).

As well as what to teach, we considered the underpinning values and philosophies that we were trying to promote. When teaching acute mental health staff Clarke (2004) recommends that training provision integrates the following points:

- values
- meaningful service user and carer participation
- thorough evaluation
- capacity building
- integration of skills into practice
- barriers to collaboration, e.g. confidentiality arrangements
- cultural competence
- leadership.

In addition, Clarke (2004) recommends that trainers have a whole team approach that:

- focused on developing skills and attitudes and promoted behaviour change
- trained a critical mass of practitioners
- focused on interventions that had credibility, and were useable and meaningful to practitioners in acute inpatient care
- were open to both professional and non-aligned staff.

Given that an inpatient may or may not have had access to any psychological therapy or may be engaged in such a therapy, we considered which techniques core to a cognitive behaviour therapy are the most useful to teach inpatient staff; which are most likely to be used well and supervised. In devising the training programme, our main struggle was that in reducing a whole therapy model to a set of techniques, how many of those techniques have to be used and how should they be used to be effective? With this in mind, our training aimed to:

- facilitate the transfer of learning across acute inpatient and community teams
- promote the delivery of evidence-based interventions
- bring changes to practice through work-based learning
- encourage structured engagement with inpatients and the use of evidence-based techniques
- develop collaborative understanding and formulation of difficulties – whilst encouraging interactive engagement, partnership and joint problem solving
- provide a means of screening inpatients for referral to clinical psychology
- aid in assessment and the care planning process.

Outline of content

The overall strategy

We asked the ward manager and deputies to identify what they would like workshops to be about. We identified a variety of workshops, some of which were to be run by ward staff. We offered three workshops to be developed and facilitated by ourselves. We hoped this would keep the staff engaged in the training process and to feel they had some ownership of it. We also wanted staff to feel and know that the workshop content would be relevant to them.

We offered workshops that were essentially an introduction to CBT. These were divided into: an introduction to clinical skills; an introduction to CBT for depression; an introduction to CBT for psychosis. We wanted to offer skills and knowledge according to the people's competencies and resources. We did not want people to feel they could offer CBT without the necessary resources. For example, there was a lack of CBT supervision for follow-up and a lack of staff time to take it up if it had been available. In essence we were teaching a set of techniques rather than training staff to provide a complete therapy. In addition, we wanted staff to be able to recognize when referrals to specialists (in CBT) may be appropriate.

We combined different grades of staff, particularly for the introduction to clinical skills. We reasoned that more experienced staff would benefit from refreshing and modelling their own skills to the more junior staff. The workshop teaching style included didactic presentations, case discussion, role play and video material. We hoped this would make the workshops engaging and interesting. In addition, drawing on Kolb's influential Learning Model (1983), we recognized that participants would need a range of different styles, from identifying and reflecting on case studies or actual experience to identifying alternative ideas and trying them out in a safe environment.

Workshop: introduction to clinical skills

We offered teaching on the functional analysis of challenging behaviours. We wanted staff to consider alternative explanations for challenging behaviours displayed in a ward environment. We wanted staff to move away from stereotyped assumptions, e.g. challenging behaviour as 'attention seeking' or 'it's all behavioural' (meaning naughty!). In addition, we wanted staff to consider the effect of different diagnoses on how people may behave.

We offered teaching on engagement skills. We hoped this would allow staff to consider both ways to talk to inpatients and ways to listen to them that were more likely to increase rapport.

We offered teaching on SMART goals, note keeping and avoiding the use of ambiguous language when describing interventions, goals and outcomes. SMART goals stands for goals that are Specific, Measurable, Achievable, Realistic and Time-limited, meaning that they are reviewed at agreed times and not left to drift. This was in part requested by the ward management as a way of making staff note keeping more useful. We also thought that staff needed to be able to set clear goals and targets with inpatients. The emphasis here was on clear communication.

Overall we considered that key skills, before being able to consider applying CBT techniques, were to offer empathic understanding of problem behaviours, to be able to listen, and to think about and record goals and targets in clear, measurable ways.

Workshop: CBT and working with depression

We offered teaching on the basic model of CBT for depression, using Padesky's five-factor model (Greenberger and Padesky 1995). We emphasized the cognitive triad for depression and why it is important to move from the general to the specific when understanding depression. We wanted staff to have a basic understanding of a general CBT model, before considering adapting it to more complex ideas, such as psychosis. Also, we wanted a model that was general enough for staff to be able to apply the ideas to themselves. *Mind Over Mood* (Greenberger and Padesky 1995) as a self-help book is ideal for the task.

We offered teaching on the idea that high arousal can lead to black and white thinking, and that beliefs affect interpretation of events. We hoped staff would start to use the CBT model to understand inpatient behaviours that they were already familiar with.

We offered teaching on the importance of listening skills. Although we had already covered this in the first workshop, we had some different staff in this group and the following group. We consider this so important to a therapeutic approach that we thought it worthwhile repeating. Also, we wanted to highlight the importance of listening skills to the developing therapeutic relationship.

We tried to get staff to identify ways of working that they already used to see if they linked with the CBT model. We wanted staff to frame current skills within the CBT model if possible as a way of highlighting what they were already doing well. It is easier to build on what people already have, rather than trying to develop something from scratch. Also, we recognize that staff already have a wealth of skills and we did not want to be in the position of belittling them. Finally, we wanted staff to consider CBT as a model or philosophy, rather than just a checklist of techniques to run through.

Workshop: CBT and working with psychosis

We offered teaching on the symptoms of psychosis and applying the CBT model to psychosis symptoms. We wanted staff to be clear on what was meant by the term psychosis. Also, we wanted to emphasize that psychosis symptoms can be meaningful. Finally, we wanted to build on the ideas of the previous workshop and use the five-factor model from Padesky, rather than trying to introduce new ideas.

We offered teaching on the way delusional beliefs can affect attention and how delusional beliefs can be maintained. We also emphasized how delusional beliefs can be seen on a continuum with more normal or accepted beliefs. One aim was to help staff consider that there can be ways to discuss delusional ideas with people that help engagement. This was made easier if people thought of delusional beliefs as being on a continuum with more acceptable beliefs. Also, we wanted to get staff to apply these ideas to how to talk to inpatients with delusions on a daily basis and to move away from the idea of trying to challenge delusional beliefs, but rather assist the inpatient to build new or revisit older beliefs that had less distressing consequences for the individual and/or those around them.

We offered teaching on practical strategies for coping with hallucinations and how to build on a sufferer's own coping strategies for hallucinations, i.e. Coping Strategy Enhancement (Tarrier 2002). We wanted staff to be able to offer some basic strategies to those in distress who did not appear to have anything. Also, we wanted staff to help people look for the strategies that they may already have that are useful as it is always easier to build upon what people already know.

Evaluation of the training

We used feedback forms at the end of each workshop. These involved Likert scales, rating areas such as usefulness of workshop, and whether aims were met. These are a routine way of getting a quick measure of staff reactions to the workshop and helped us to get direct feedback, so that we could adjust future workshops accordingly and to consider if the current workshop would be useful to run for other staff on the ward. In addition, this approach fits with Clarke's (2004) recommendations for evaluating training (see Table 12.1).

Staff feedback has been positive. One implication of this is that the training had face validity for staff in terms of being practical and useful for the ward environment. Further, maintaining the use of skills had been achieved by the reflective practice group, discussion within clinical and management supervision as well as individual supervision and consultation – both formal and informal – with the ward clinical psychologists.

Table 12.1 Clarke's four levels of evaluation

Level 1	Trainees' reactions to training. This may include whether or not learning outcomes have been met.
Level 2	Modification of attitudes or perceptions. Acquisition of knowledge or skills. This may include levels of academic attainment.
Level 3	Changes in trainees' behaviours. This may include how skills are further developed.
Level 4	Changes in organizational practice. Benefits to service users from changes in practice. This may include integration of skills in routine practice.

The four levels of evaluation are recommended by Clarke (2004) in order to evaluate the effectiveness of the training.

Further recommendations for evaluation

It can be useful to consider impact in terms of short, medium and longer term changes. Our feedback forms obviously covered short-term changes. For the medium term, we would consider a more systematic assessment of attitudes, perceptions and behaviours in line with Clarke's (2004) recommendations for Levels 2 and 3 (see Table 12.1). Much of this can be noted informally through other means, such as reflective practice groups and supervision, but information gathered this way would be open to subjective bias.

For longer term changes, we would consider the changes in organizational practice. By this we mean application of skills by staff as routine. We would expect it to take time for skills to become more integrated in this way. One could consider involving service user groups to assess the presence or absence of skills shown on the wards.

Summary

There is an increasing awareness of the need for inpatient staff to be skilled in understanding and delivering CBT interventions. We can see the impetus for such changes coming from the Department of Health (2006a) and voluntary organizations (Mental Health Foundation 2006). Also we can see the advantage of the nursing group being involved in offering CBT interventions due to the quantity of time spent with inpatients.

There are ongoing challenges in offering CBT interventions and training to inpatient wards. As outlined earlier, individuals, wards and organizations can help or hinder the process. Individuals may not display new skills when returning to the ward. Wards can be chaotic environments for organizing training. The overall organization may not support the development of new competencies. In spite of the challenges, we believe that training is still possible. We have detailed our own initiative to offer training and teaching to inpatient wards, albeit with limitations.

Conclusions

If training is to succeed in these environments, trainers need to be aware of the challenges to training at the individual, ward and organizational levels. Trainers may need to target initial interventions at the ward and organization before attempting to develop training. In a constantly changing NHS, this is likely to be an ongoing process of negotiation.

Part IV

CBT group work

The 'Making Friends with Yourself' and the 'What Is Real and What Is Not' groups

Graham Hill, Isabel Clarke and Hannah Wilson

Introduction

Groups in hospital

Psychotherapeutic group work in the inpatient setting provides opportunities, along with the familiar challenges. This approach has an honourable history in the therapeutic community initiatives of the 1950s and 1960s (e.g. Bloor *et al.* 1988; Haigh 1998). This philosophy of inpatient care utilized the therapeutic potential of a number of people necessarily thrown together away from normal life by using the group medium to forge a community out of this circumstance. This entailed group meetings involving both staff and patients and focused primarily on their common life in the moment, following the group analytic tradition of treating the group as a reflection of how the individual operates in their life in general. There is a vestige of this approach in the community meetings that continue on wards to this day. The value of these has been recognized, and so they are encouraged by initiatives such as the Star Wards project (Bright 2006).

The same tradition gives us a legacy of explicitly psychotherapeutic group work in the inpatient setting. This predominates in specialist inpatient settings for the treatment of addictions, in the work of private hospitals such as the Priory group, and elsewhere. Where approaches such as DBT and mentalization-based therapy are used in either day hospital or inpatient settings, the group work integral to these approaches occurs in this setting (Bateman and Fonagy 2004).

In the 'ordinary' acute inpatient unit, the activity programme in general is the province of the occupational therapy department. The importance of structured activity, and activity that moves the person back towards normal life in the community, is well recognized as an essential element in the path to recovery. Conversely, boredom and having nothing to do are seen as major anti-therapeutic elements in the inpatient experience. OT-organized group work ranges from the practical and physical – cooking, gym and information technology (IT) skills, for instance – to the more psychotherapeutic and cognitive – concentration groups, for instance, and programmes targeted at stress management, depression and addictions.

Where does the trained cognitive therapist fit into this picture? Do they have a role? Can the potential community aspect of a group of people thrown together, even for a short time and in crisis, be utilized to deepen and widen the impact of the CBT resource within the hospital? Part IV argues that it can, and that there are reasons why this method of therapy delivery can have a wider impact on the institution as a whole than the availability of individual work.

The case for CBT group work

We are here talking about CBT group work. The evidence base for this mode of service delivery has been well established (e.g. Shaffer et al. 1981; Brown and Lewinsohn 1984). There is some controversy about comparative efficacy and cost effectiveness of group as opposed to individual therapy delivery within CBT. (For recent discussion and survey of these issues, see Morrison 2001; Tucker and Oei 2007.) Possible savings from multiple delivery and the added value from group therapeutic factors is set against the practicalities of assembling participants and facilitators together at one time in one place, and the inevitable dilution of the therapy. Within the acute hospital there is an additional problem over length of programme. Because many admissions are short, it is necessary to minimize the length of the programmes, with possible prejudice to their effectiveness, or risk the programme being left half completed. Inviting participants to return to the hospital to complete is offered for the groups described below, but is not practical or acceptable for all. However, within the institution there are other factors recommending CBT group work:

- Running a group is an obvious opportunity for co-working with other staff groups.
- This provides staff development opportunities and spreads CBT knowledge and skills among the staff group.
- Establishing group programmes creates greater visibility for CBT than simply offering therapy to individuals.
- Such programmes can either complement individual therapy for those receiving it, or provide access to CBT for a wider group among the patient body.
- The net result is greater awareness within the institution of the scope and potential of CBT approaches.
- This is particularly relevant for psychosis groups where people who would benefit from a CBT approach are frequently not referred because of lack of awareness of the potential for therapy for people with this diagnosis. Starting a group is an opportunity for a proactive

approach to seeking referrals. Seeing their clients benefit from the group can help to educate other members of the team, leading to more referrals in the future.

Nursing staff working alongside the CBT specialist as group facilitators

Within Woodhaven, the Senior Nurse saw the potential of a CBT group programme for staff development and for involving the nursing staff group in psychotherapeutic work. Previously, attempts to involve nursing and mental health practitioner staff in the delivery of groups had proved difficult because of the inflexibility of nursing rotas and the priority given to crises and staff shortages on the ward. This challenge was met as follows.

The stress and anxiety management programme was produced in the form of two manuals – one for the client and one for the facilitators. The clinical psychologist delivered training to nursing, medical and OT staff, so that a wide variety of staff could facilitate this two-session programme in group format, or use the content to inform their individual approach.

The anxiety and stress management programme was suitable for this level of delegation as it is primarily psycho-educational with the addition of skills teaching in relaxation breathing. The other programmes required more of the facilitators in terms of engaging the group participants therapeutically. Chapter 14 gives an account of the delivery of the emotional coping skills programme. Nursing staff are involved in the co-facilitation of the self-esteem and psychosis programmes that are described in the rest of this chapter in the following manner. Staff are invited to sign up for a group work development programme. Participants are put on the rota additional to the shift to work a nine-to-five day, on a specified day of the week, for a seven-week period. During this day they assist with OT programmes and co-facilitate first the three-week self-esteem group, and then the four-week psychosis group, with the psychologist. A description of these programmes follows.

Example 1: the 'Making Friends with Yourself' group – a self-esteem programme

There are many psychological approaches to improving self-esteem and the associated problems of self-criticism and shame in inpatient populations. Cognitive behavioural therapy (CBT) is one of few group-based psycho-therapeutic interventions which have shown effectiveness in comparison to control (Munro *et al.* 2005). Over the past seven years, four studies examining the effectiveness of CBT for inpatients with psychosis in acute care have been conducted including a total of 460 inpatients, 178 of whom received CBT. Each of the studies conducted used different methodologies and different models of CBT, which inevitably makes comparison difficult. However, this research indicated that CBT can be an effective treatment and is seen as an acceptable intervention by most inpatients (Munro *et al.* 2005). On a very basic level, CBT looks at how people can develop more adaptive coping strategies by making sense of the synergistic interaction between their thoughts, feelings and behaviours. In collaboration with the therapist, the client engages in regular 'behavioural experiments' and through a process of trial and error the client (hopefully) develops new ways of 'making sense' of their problems, and more adaptive coping strategies to deal with them.

Fennell (1997) holds that all forms of CBT and indeed all psychological therapy may first need to address deeply entrenched automatic reactions (negative self-evaluations) in order to reduce the rigidity of core beliefs in people with psychiatric disorders, and problems such as high self-criticism and low self-esteem (LSE). On the other hand, Teasdale and Cox (2001) suggest that high self-critics may be resistant and do less well with standard CBT. This suggests that self-esteem is an important target for group work within the inpatient setting, both as a vital adjunct to other CBT and as an intervention in its own right. The self-esteem programme described below is based on a compassionate mind training rationale.

Compassionate mind training

Compassionate mind training (CMT, Gilbert and Proctor 2006) – a CBT and dialectical behaviour therapy (DBT) based approach incorporating mindfulness, evolved from working with people with shame, self-criticism and LSE (Gilbert 1992, 1997, 2000; Gilbert and Irons 2005) – adopts a different approach to standard CBT and has shown some promising preliminary results. Unlike standard forms of CBT, CMT does not target specific core beliefs and automatic reactions (e.g. Fennell 1997) or schemas (Young 1990), but seeks to alter a person's whole 'orientation' to self and relationships. In contrast to standard CBT, CMT views 'thought' as an affect-related inner conversation. It seeks to help people with high self-criticism and shame to accept their automatic reactions without being self-critical and facilitate them to develop a 'metacognitive awareness' of their difficulties.

Metacognitive awareness is the acceptance of the idea that thoughts, assumptions and beliefs are mental events and processes rather than reflections of objective truth (Fennell 2004). Put another way, automatic reactions are not people's fault or are not easily controlled, but arise as a result of evolved defences, genes, learning and conditioning (Gilbert and Proctor 2006). This 'orientation to self and others' can help reduce people's beliefs that they should be able to control their automatic reactions and that they are wrong or shameful or that there is something wrong with them if they are unable to control them (Leahy 2002, 2005, cited in Gilbert and Proctor 2006: 359). When, high self-critics experience a setback, failure or conflict, they rapidly access internal schema of others as hostile/rejecting (Baldwin 2005) with 'well practised' self-focused attacking. CMT seeks to change this internalized dominant self-critical (attacking) style, which activates a submissive defensive response when dealing with setbacks, failures and conflict, and to replace it with a caring, compassionate way of being with one's distress. The goal of CMT is therefore to give a compassionate and caring approach to self, a retrieval advantage (Gilbert and Proctor 2006). Similar to CMT a number of therapies have shifted emphasis and are now focusing on the importance of helping people with psychiatric problems to develop inner compassion and self-soothing abilities, for example, DBT (Linehan 1993a, 1993b; Lynch *et al.* 2006).

In CMT people are asked to give a self-created 'compassionate image' with the qualities of wisdom, strength, warmth non-judgement or acceptance and to think of their image of having a compassionate focused mind. There is good evidence that such directed imagining and recall affects neurophysiological systems and that mindfulness and compassion-related imagery has a positive affect on immunity. Anger-related imagery on the other hand has a negative affect. Furthermore, imagery may have various recall advantages and be more affect-related than logical thinking alone (Lee 2005 as cited in Gilbert and Proctor 2006).

In summary, CMT involves the elements of a specific psycho-educational focus on the qualities of self-compassion, locating self-criticism as forms of safety strategies/behaviour, recognizing the fears behind it, developing empathy for one's own distress and safety strategies, and refocusing on compassionate images (a person or a place) thoughts, feelings and behaviours, with warmth (Gilbert and Proctor 2006).

'Making Friends with Yourself' – a group-based self-esteem programme for inpatients with LSE and high self-criticism

'Making Friends with Yourself' was adapted from the CMT approach by Isabel Clarke. 'Making Friends with Yourself' makes several generalized assumptions about inpatients in crisis who have low self-esteem and are highly self-critical. These are as follows. They need lots of support and encouragement to recover and tend to be very self-critical. Such people are often very competent at looking after others but not very competent at looking after themselves. 'Making Friends with Yourself' is designed to do something about this situation by looking at practical ways in which they can use their skill at looking after others in order to 'make friends with themselves'. The rationale is that this would help people feel better about themselves and make them feel better able to meet the challenges that life offers. An overview of the aims of the three sessions in the 'Making Friends with Yourself' programme is given below.

The CBT rationale is introduced as follows:

- How you think affects what you do and how you feel.
- How someone thinks about themselves will affect how they feel about themselves.
- How people think about themselves (their core beliefs) are often very resistant to revision.
- The group aims to introduce a new way for the person to think about themselves.
- There is an emphasis on practising this, with support from other group members.
- There is emphasis on trying it out in practical ways, to effect behaviour change.

The idea of the internal dialogue is then introduced, and the effect of living with a critical internal dialogue is compared to the effect of sharing a household with a critical individual. These ideas are discussed. The idea of developing a friendly internal dialogue, by using the approach you would take with a friend (as self-critical people are usually much harder on themselves than on others) is then introduced, and tried out in pairs, with the other person taking the part of the friend. The participants are encouraged to practise this between sessions and note down useful 'friendly' phrases.

The subsequent two sessions explore the approach further, with more pair (or three) work. Obstacles to developing the friendly voice are named and investigated. Practical steps that the new, friendly, approach to the self might make possible are identified and tried. These might entail doing things that had been avoided (e.g. going out in the face of anxiety), not permitted (doing nice things for oneself), or not doing harmful things (taking substances, self-harm, etc.). Group members are encouraged to use the friendly voice to facilitate specific behavioural changes of this sort, to encourage each other to make changes, and to discuss them in the group.

Evaluation

An informal evaluation of several groups was undertaken by a researcher separate from the main facilitators, who reported as follows:

> Group members each contributed to a warm and honest group environment where everyone's opinions and experiences were respected. Sessions were attended volitionally and group members were free to leave at any time should they wish. The content of sessions appeared

salient to all who attended and over the weeks every group member expressed their experiences with their 'critical' and increasingly 'friendly' voices. It appears that despite a wide variety in presenting symptoms and reasons for crisis, the critical voice had been and in many cases continued to be problematic. The concept of the friendly voice, however, was embraced to the extent that group members frequently made note of using it in their previous week's experiences.

Group numbers did decrease somewhat during the course of three weekly sessions owing principally to hospital discharge. Of the 17 patients attending the initial session, 11 completed all three. Of these, seven improved markedly, one remained at a stable score, and three reported lower scores than at session onset (one of these probably misunderstood the questionnaire on first administration from her replies). Measures were taken from comparisons between self-assessment on a brief self-esteem scale, taken at the beginning and end session of each group. Going on individual feedback, nearly all patients showed, and in many cases expressed, increased positivity in their demeanour and approach to using the friendly voice.

Particularly heartening are the reports of behavioural change that people bring to the final group, and the support that they give to each other during their time on the ward in working on the programme of the group.

Example 2: the 'What Is Real and What Is Not' group – a CBT for psychosis group programme

Introduction

The practice of delivering CBT for psychosis in a group format has already been well established, particularly with a focus on auditory hallucinations (see Chadwick *et al.* 2000). The influence of Romme and Escher (1989) and the Hearing Voices movement has been decisive here. Professor Romme appealed for voice hearers to contact him and attend conferences in Holland in 1987. This initiative revealed a surprisingly high incidence of voice hearers in the population, many of whom had never been in touch with the psychiatric services. By comparing the way in which different people made sense of and coped with their voices, he initiated a whole normalizing approach to the phenomenon.

His example led to the setting up of the Hearing Voices Network in England – the first group was held in Manchester. These were self-help groups for people to meet with others in a supportive environment, talk about their experiences and get information. Meeting people with similar problems has many benefits for voice hearers, such as gaining control of their voices and increased self-esteem (Corren and Lucas 2004). The example has been followed for people receiving mental health services. It has been natural for CBT practitioners, with their collaborative stance and openness to coping strategies developed by service users, to adopt this approach.

A separate strand in CBT group work for psychosis uses mindfulness to help people cope with their voices. This has been developed and evaluated by Chadwick and his collaborators (2005), and this approach is particularly relevant for us as it broadens the evidence base for the application of mindfulness, already wide in its scope, to psychosis and psychosis groups.

In Woodhaven, we chose to open the group to a wider range of psychotic symptoms than auditory hallucinations, and to follow on from the development of the approach outlined in Chapter 8, 'Making Sense of Psychosis in Crisis'. We called the resulting group, the 'What Is Real and What Is Not' group. This group was designed for those clients who are having or have had in the past unusual perceptual experiences (e.g. hearing voices or visual/sensory hallucinations) or recurrent strongly held beliefs, unshared by others. It is referred to among the staff group in the unit as the 'psychosis' group, although it takes a normalizing and non-labelling view of such experiences. It was designed in order to be accessible to clients whilst still inpatients and therefore designed to begin the process of making sense of their experiences as well as to feel validated.

The group was designed to run over four one-hour sessions. It was decided to have this as a closed group due to the sensitive nature of the material covered. Individuals were assessed for the group in an initial one-to-one session. It was considered important for the overall success of the group that participants should be willing to participate and open to exploring new ideas in a group format. The group dynamics with this client group needed careful assessment and consideration. The facilitators also offered additional one-to-one time after each group session for any questions or concerns that may have arisen during the group.

Group content

Session one: Introduction

In session one the group rules are established. This was seen as an essential first step in ensuring a sense of safety for the participants. The group rules of respect, responsibility, confidentiality and time keeping are always included, as well as any other specific issues identified by the group. It is also stressed to the group that each member decide for themselves how much they share in the group – if they do not want to talk about something, they do not have to.

Second, we establish the aims of the group and what expectations individual participants have for the group. Being able to learn from others' experiences, share coping techniques and strategies as well as explore alternative opinions about 'psychosis' are either cited by the facilitators as possibilities or offered by the group. We have found that at this point participants are usually curious about the name of the group and this often sparks an interesting discussion about 'reality'. This leads nicely into the following short teaching session.

A short teaching element then follows in which some ways of being able to understand our unshared or unusual experiences are covered. Normalizing auditory and visual hallucinations as part of the normal range, continuum or repertoire of human experiences is introduced. We then review the now famous study of Romme and Escher (1989). The following ideas are then discussed: that these experiences are more common than we usually think; that they are part of being human; and that having a sense of greater control over such experiences and more openness about them leads to better coping.

We then introduce the idea of monitoring the experiences as a way to understand them better. Participants are encouraged to keep a very simple monitoring tick chart of when their experiences occur, or are most troublesome, in preparation for the next session.

Session two: Triggers and coping styles

In session two we explore further this idea of reality. The idea of a continuum between 'shared' experiences at one end and 'non-shared' at the other is introduced. Participants are encouraged to note the advantages and disadvantages to both. The group often come to the conclusion that both have their advantages and disadvantages and both are real to the person experiencing them. However, in order to function in day-to-day life, we need to be able to recognize and operate in the shared reality with others. This does not need to invalidate the reality of the other mode of experiencing for the individual.

We then explore how participants got on with the homework – the monitoring chart. We look at when unshared or unusual experiences are more likely to happen and what sort of situations triggered them. Clients often bring times when they were either highly dysregulated (stressed) or when they were doing nothing; about to fall asleep/watching television, as times they notice they are more likely to experience their psychotic symptoms. We then draw out the level of arousal graph (see Figure 13.1) as a way of illustrating these times of greater vulnerability.

The group then discuss strategies that help achieve a more 'middle ground' arousal level. Avoidance of too much stress or high arousal are usually covered well – staying away from alcohol and drugs, having breaks, relaxation and breathing techniques to reduce stress, etc. are all usually mentioned at some point. Having some structure to each day, making achievable plans as well as rediscovering new and old hobbies are also

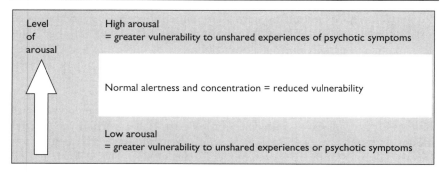

Figure 13.1 Level of arousal and vulnerability to psychotic symptoms

discussed as ways of ensuring there is sufficient demand on the individual as well, so as to avoid boredom and disengagement. The group are then asked to continue with the monitoring chart during the following week before the next session, but this time adding in the coping strategy they used.

Session three: Other ways of coping

We start session three with reviewing the homework exercise, introducing a discussion about what the group noticed: were they able to try anything different and what happened if they did? We introduce our next topic of avoidance and blocking, by getting people to brainstorm what it is like to always distract or push away unpleasant thoughts, feelings or usual experiences. We also recognize and discuss the considerable fear that these experiences can bring with them, which makes the desire to block them all too understandable.

We then consider the role of avoidance and the impact this can have on such experiences. The aim is to convey the message that continued avoidance of distressing and upsetting emotions or experiences ultimately leaves us more afraid and upset. We look at the classic avoidance cycle and how this often sets up subtle (or more often not very subtle but loud!) messages that the individual is not coping and a failure, as he or she is left having not learnt they can face that situation, feeling or experience. At the same time, they have been reinforced for avoidance by the sense of relief it brings, and in this way become locked into the cycle.

The facilitators then introduce the research undertaken by Gillian Haddock (Haddock *et al.* 1998) comparing the efficacy of the different coping strategies of distraction and focusing for the management of auditory hallucinations. This study is a useful illustration as it has a nice simple design, comparing the two interventions, and the results are interesting. Both coping strategies were found to be equally helpful in reducing the impact of the hallucinations. However, a measure of self-esteem produced a superior result for focusing. This finding leads naturally into a discussion of the advantages of feeling in control for self-efficacy, and so helps to persuade those for whom focusing on the symptoms appears overwhelmingly frightening.

We then introduce focusing in a practical way, pointing out that where participants have been completing their monitoring charts, they have been practising focusing already. Where they have been reluctant to do so, it is often because attending to symptoms can be anxiety provoking. We look at what it might be like to focus on our experience or emotion; to watch it, observe it in a mindful way rather than distract ourselves or push it away. A short mindfulness exercise is introduced along the lines of DBT, introducing the key skills of observation, description, and participation in a non-judgemental way. We then ask them to try a short mindfulness exercise each day as part of their homework.

Session four: Making sense of our experiences

In session four we focus on how people make sense of their experiences. After reviewing the homework, we introduce the core CBT concept that different ways of making sense of our experiences will impact on how we feel in different ways, and so impact differently on how we end up reacting. Various ways of making sense are brainstormed by the group. Examples of variety in making sense of the experiences are: differences in how powerful the voice is felt to be; whether or not it is acceptable to feel distressed; what it means to be worried and what that anxiety is about, and whether or not it is 'okay' or 'normal' to have unshared experiences.

We introduce the idea that the thoughts people have about their unique experiences, and in some cases the features of the experiences, may be related to things that were happening in their lives when the experiences first started. We discuss with the group how particular ways of thinking can get stuck, especially at times of great stress. Such ideas and styles of thinking can fade into the background when life returns to normal, only to be retriggered when life events plunge the person into a similarly stressed state. This normalizes the phenomenon of relapse.

We also review how some people are more vulnerable to these types of experience, especially when under stress, or following taking street drugs such as cannabis and amphetamines. Some people are more emotionally thin skinned. Being aware of this vulnerability can lead to the individual being prepared to accept that the way they see things at such times might not be 'reality' for others. Checking out with others what is happening is one way of finding out and helping them to stay 'real'.

We then introduce the idea that mindfulness can also be used as a way to step out of misleading thinking – a way of being able to get a wider perspective on what is happening.

Towards the end of this session we also ask the group to review what aspects they have found useful and what parts of the group were less useful. We set aside some time for further questions and to clarify any points that people are left unsure about.

Reflections on running the group

Our experiences have been interesting to say the least. Getting the right dynamic in the group has been a key factor. We have found that sometimes in a one-to-one session someone is able to reflect on their experiences and start to consider an alternative position, but in a group, where perhaps their arousal is elevated, this ability to be more flexible in their thinking is lost. On occasion this has meant the safety of the environment for everyone to express their feelings and thoughts is lost, as strong beliefs are held on to vehemently. Careful consideration of who comes to the group and their readiness to both face a group situation and be able to participate in it is required. Skilled facilitation and experience of dealing with these sorts of situations is a must for anyone thinking of running these types of groups. We recommend that there are always at least two facilitators, and that one of these has training and experience in running therapeutic groups. However, where the CBT-trained practitioner can co-facilitate the group with other members of staff, it is a very useful way of spreading a normalizing philosophy of psychosis throughout the unit.

On the positive side, when the group dynamic is positive and supportive, some very useful discussions have arisen. Our experiences have been that participants really feel validated that their experiences are real to them and that they are 'normal' in the context of the breadth and depth of human experience. They find it refreshing to explore ways of talking about and making sense of their experiences rather than a push to get rid of them or deny them in some way. This normalization can then increase their willingness to recognize their vulnerability; to accept that other interventions offered by the whole team such as medication can have an important role to play in helping them to lead full lives despite this vulnerability. In this way, offering a very different perspective on experiences usually labelled as psychosis, can lead to a smoother therapeutic alliance with the medically driven mental health services, and can engage people who were initially resistant to a more straightforward 'psycho-educational' approach.

Chapter 14

Running an emotional coping skills group based on dialectical behaviour therapy

Amanda Rendle and Hannah Wilson

Introduction

Dialectical behaviour therapy (DBT) has been developed and extensively researched by Marsha Linehan and her team as a linked group and individual therapy approach for people with self-harming behaviour and a diagnosis of borderline personality disorder (Linehan 1993a). The programme was originally developed as a community outpatient approach, but has been adapted for use in specialist inpatient units (Bohus *et al.* 2000; Swenson *et al.* 2001; Kröger *et al.* 2006).

This chapter will outline an adaptation of this approach to the conditions of an acute inpatient environment where people present with the spectrum of diagnoses and stay for (at times very) brief periods. The result has been the emotional coping skills (ECS) group programme described here. Offering this programme across diagnostic groups is grounded in the conception of psychopathology that sees emotional dysregulation as central (see Clarke 1999 and Chapter 6, which outlines this theoretical position). Further discussion will focus upon the challenges encountered in running a group within the acute hospital environment. Group planning, delivery strategies and evaluation data will also be included, giving the reader an overview of this modified DBT-based group programme.

The biosocial theory that underpins DBT puts forward the hypothesis that individuals with borderline personality disorder (BPD) have difficulties regulating their emotions or have an 'emotionally thin skin' (Linehan 1993a). Despite extensive literature in the psychotherapeutic treatment of BPD, few of these approaches are supported by research (Charles *et al.* 2002). Therefore promoting the delivery of the ECS group within this environment is important, as this chapter demonstrates how such a programme can assist individuals by equipping them with lifelong skills. Hopefully this will ultimately reduce the number of readmissions to hospital, as this client group is well represented in the 'revolving door' clientele (Bohus *et al.* 2000). It is additionally hypothesized that emotion regulation skills are relevant to a wider group than those with a diagnosis of BPD.

Opening the group across diagnoses also makes it easier to deliver in the mixed setting of an acute unit. Establishing an ECS group of this type in an inpatient environment has required ongoing debate, training and continuous evaluation of its structure and delivery within a multidisciplinary approach.

First steps taken to design and establish the group

Establishing the Woodhaven DBT consult team was the initial step in developing the emotional coping skills group and provided a multidisciplinary approach. The consult group consisted of two clinical psychologists, a consultant psychiatrist, three staff nurses and an occupational therapist. As a consult team we completed a two-week intensive training programme, with a period for service development between the two weeks. During the training period the consult team would meet weekly for two-hour periods, completing training exercises, supervision and exploration of 'dialectical dilemmas'. On completion of the first week's training, the consult team utilized part of the meeting to discuss the DBT service and in particular adapting the group mode of the therapy. The result of these discussions was the ECS group. Completing skills modules provided in Linehan's (1993b) training manual during the training period enabled the consult team to understand what we would be asking of our clients and how we may adapt some of the modules to suit the needs of the inpatient environment. Therefore some consideration and debate were required to determine how we would reduce a 12-month group therapy programme into a six-week ECS group for the current setting.

Three members of the consult group, an occupational therapist and two staff nurses took responsibility for taking the lead in the ECS set-up project, putting together group plans for a six-week rolling programme. In setting up the group programme, we took into consideration the participant criteria, module content, duration of session, location, lead facilitators, co-facilitators, equipment required and evaluation.

Having a multidisciplinary approach brought together varying experiences which enhanced the way the ECS group was developed. Weekly progress reports were fed back to the consult team. Regular liaison with the clinical psychologists and the consultant psychiatrist promoted debate and discussion on the team's vision for the ECS group. As a team we established group plans, evaluation tools and outcome measures, some of which will be discussed later in this chapter.

Establishing the group

The programme itself was initially established as a six-week rolling open programme. Clients would access the group during their inpatient stay and join at any time in the six-week rotation. We also agreed that clients would be able to complete the full set of sessions even if they had been discharged from hospital, by returning as outpatients to complete the six-week course. This agreement was discussed and agreed with the hospital and ward managers at the time.

Members of the consult team would meet with clients initially on a one-to-one basis to share information about the group, provide the booklet that detailed session outlines and content as well as review the individual's commitment to signing up to the group itself. The importance of cultivating an attitude of willingness, as opposed to resistant willfulness, was encouraged. Clients were also asked to sign up to the group rules, of which there were two copies, one to adhere to as an inpatient and one to adhere to as an outpatient. Part of the group rules also highlighted that homework was an integral part of the programme, completion of which would be expected. It was stressed that the group was about being taught and learning skills rather than a more typical 'therapy' group. It was explained that individuals would not be expected to talk about their own issues in the group but the facilitators would focus on teaching the emotional coping skills. The group sessions were very much designed with this in mind so the content was full and, some may consider, rather ambitious.

The initial one-to-one session also allowed the DBT therapists to introduce clients to the idea of mindfulness, a core skill that runs throughout the six group sessions. It was here that clients also completed audit tool questionnaires to identify any changes that may occur throughout the group process and skills acquisitions.

An open group allowed the team to accept referrals on a weekly basis and invite people to join at any point in the six-week rotation of the group. Individuals were encouraged to complete all modules. If repetition and revision were required for the individual, they were invited to continue with modules to ensure a good understanding of all the skills. The ECS group was made available to individuals with a broad range of diagnoses, not just for those individuals with a diagnosis of borderline personality disorder. The consult team felt that it would be beneficial for those individuals who experienced problems with expressing or experiencing their feelings and emotions. As noted by Linehan (1993a), emotions can get in the way of everyday life, becoming unbearable, so people often avoid them and look for ways to escape. The ECS group enabled individuals to explore and understand their feelings better, and learn about other ways of coping with them.

When a client had completed six sessions of the group, a further one-to-one session was arranged to review what had been useful, what skills had been learnt and how they had been effective in engineering any change in the client's problem behaviours. This also ensured an opportunity to complete the end of group audit tools as well as fine tune any skills coaching.

Clients were also asked to complete a satisfaction questionnaire and offer any suggestions about how the programme could be improved.

When establishing the group we also considered who would be the facilitators and how many we would need per group. Having multi-disciplinary facilitation was considered important. We tried to have at least two facilitators present from two different professional groups with a third member as observer. This third facilitator proved to be crucial at times to help manage the group run smoothly by helping clients who wanted to leave to exit gracefully. We tried to keep the lead facilitator constant for a six-week rotation. We acknowledged how fortunate we were to have a wide representation of professionals interested and available to run the groups. This was definitely seen as a real asset as we complemented each other's skill and knowledge base.

ECS group content

Skills modules were identified, using Linehan's (1993b) training manual for guidance. Clients explored the following skills:

- mindfulness
- emotional regulation
- distress tolerance
- interpersonal effectiveness.

These skills were delivered across the six sessions as follows: Session 1 – Mindfulness; Sessions 2 and 3 – Emotional regulation; Sessions 4 and 5 – Distress tolerance; Session 6, Interpersonal effectiveness. A detailed break-down of the six sessions now follows:

The first group focused on mindfulness. This skill is at the core of the DBT philosophy, and in the limited time available was the skill around which the rest of the programme was organized. The group content involved defining mindfulness and introducing them to the states of mind concept (Linehan 1993b: 109). The DBT approach to mindfulness was stressed as a means to be able to access 'wise mind'. It was explained that mindfulness was a sort of meditation. Our minds are often very busy and distracted. When they are busy and distracted it is often difficult to make effective or useful decisions. Mindfulness was recommended as a way of being able to still the mind so more useful or helpful ways of responding to situations can be found. Mindfulness was further presented as a way of being able to be in touch with our emotions at the same time as being able to think about them. It was explained that mindfulness simply means paying attention to one thing in the moment without judging it as good or bad, right or wrong.

Examples of being in the various states of minds (i.e. 'reasonable', 'emotion' and 'wise') were used as a basis for group discussion. For example, when our car breaks down, if we are in 'reasonable mind' we are more likely to think, 'Oh well, it is a mechanical object and therefore will be subject to malfunction and "wear and tear" at times. I will need to get it fixed.' However, if 'emotion mind' is dominating we may be more likely to think, 'Oh no, why me! This is so unfair! I cannot tolerate this. Things like this only ever happen to me and especially when I am in a rush.' The 'wise mind' response is explained as the middle ground, searching for the truth in both and coming to the best fit, most effective response (e.g. 'It is annoying my car has broken down but these things happen. Never mind. I'll make some plans to get this sorted. I can only do my best and my best is good enough.'). The group would then be encouraged to think of their own examples in other scenarios such as sitting an exam, going for an interview, meeting someone who you really like or dislike. Normalizing all three states of mind was introduced. None were 'better' than the other; however, 'wise mind' usually facilitates better decision making.

This group session then explored different types of mindfulness and gave the group a chance to experience a mindfulness exercise (e.g. observing and describing a plant, some flowers or a painting mindfully). The group facilitators would then encourage further discussion about the participants' experiences of the exercise. The session would end with setting of homework to try at least once a day to complete an activity mindfully or use a mindfulness exercise if stuck in 'emotion' or 'reasonable' mind. Each subsequent session was then started with a short mindfulness exercise and the theme of mindfulness maintained throughout the following five sessions.

The next two groups concentrated on the ideas of emotion regulation. It was explained that emotions are often complex and can be, at times, confusing. Our feelings are valid and communicate important information to us. Learning how to react to our emotions in a useful way is an important life skill. Sometimes the way we react to our behaviour in response to our emotions is unhelpful, leading to prolonged emotional suffering. Therefore the following skills are taught: letting go of emotional suffering; evaluating our thoughts, interpretations and assumptions of situations; looking after oneself – reducing emotional vulnerability to negative emotions and building steps for increasing positive experiences.

The group was also introduced to the CBT idea that our thoughts and interpretations of a situation impact upon emotions and behaviours through a version of the Padesky 'hot cross bun' (Greenberger and Padesky 1995) which we call an Emotion Circle. The group is encouraged to have a go at thinking 'What else might be going on here?' The homework was then set as practising these skills and completing at least one 'hot cross bun' over the next week on an incident that triggered strong emotion.

In the third session, two further emotional regulation skills of looking after physical health needs and building positive experiences into daily life are taught. Homework for this third session involved clients drawing up their own list of pleasant events and trying to engage in at least one over the following week.

Sessions four and five introduced the ideas of tolerating distress; accepting difficult feelings and finding means of distraction and alternative focus to get through the worst times.

Session six concentrated on interpersonal skills, balancing assertiveness with maintaining and developing healthy relationships.

Location and room set-up

The location of the ECS group was also important. The consult team agreed that emulating a classroom environment with tables and chairs would be more conducive for the skills group, rather than the more typical layout of a therapy group session. This provided for a better learning environment, with the sense of an 'education class' rather than a therapy group. The group was provided with the relevant materials they needed for the class and assigned homework at the end of each session, which was then reviewed at the beginning of subsequent sessions.

The group remained as practical as possible, addressing issues in the present. This meant that the lead facilitators and co-facilitators had to be as creative as possible with various exercises. This proved to be an enjoyable task, thinking up new ideas and gaining inspiration from some of the clients' homework feedback. Individuals, facilitators and clients alike learnt new skills and new ways of looking at things. Clients were encouraged to participate in sessions. However, if they did not want to share issues then they did not have to. Participants were able to complete sessions that would equip them with a set of life skills that they could practise in a safe environment, moving toward utilizing these skills on return to the community.

Challenges

One of the difficulties of running the skills group within a hospital setting is that this can feel like an 'alien' environment to most individuals and generalizing these skills outside the ward can be difficult. Therefore links with the local community mental health teams were crucial. Regular contact via telephone or joint meetings allowed further discussion of ongoing skills training and the possibility of referring suitable individuals for the community 12-month DBT training programme. Continued meetings with the community DBT consult team on a quarterly basis enabled both consult teams to gather updates on both services, discuss possible referrals and maintain links. Continuing to meet with both teams was invaluable, enabling the teams to consistently review their DBT services and groups.

Training

As a small inpatient consult team, we were able to provide some ECS training in-house to our colleagues who had shown an interest in wanting to explore DBT further. Therefore members of the consult group took skills training modules to the wards, providing staff with their own skills training package, so that they could support clients through skills coaching on the ward. This sparked further interest, and with ongoing reflective practice (see Chapter 10) further Trust-wide training was sought, increasing the consult team numbers and promoting DBT as a model of practice. The ECS group seemed to act as a platform for initiating further interest in DBT practice and improving staff confidence in providing skills coaching to individuals on the wards. Clients not only utilized the ECS group but also gained further benefits from receiving one-to-one skills coaching from staff, equipping them with the skills necessary for a more successful discharge as well as addressing the all-important issue of skill generalization.

Evaluation of the group over the first 18 months

This section of the chapter will report the audit data collected over the first 18 months of running the Woodhaven ECS group. During this time nine sets of groups were completed.

Participant attendance

During an 18-month period the group was completed a total of nine times. A total of 57 clients attended at least one session: 34 (59.6 per cent) of which attended three or less sessions, and 23 (40.04 per cent) completed four or more sessions.

Outcome measures

As the group was designed to teach skills for managing emotions, the evaluation tools were chosen to reflect this. It was thought that the group should improve people's confidence in being able to manage their emotions so measures that would reflect this change were used. Three audit tools were used in total: The Mental Health Confidence Scale (MHCS, Carpinello *et al.* 2000) and the Living With Emotions questionnaire (LWE, Durrant *et al.* 2007) were used before and after completion of at least four sessions of the group (see Chapter 15 for a full description of these measures). The third tool was a specifically designed group satisfaction questionnaire that encouraged honest feedback about how the group and service could be improved.

Collection of outcome measures was attempted for all those completing at least four sessions. However, only 16 sets of completed questions were

Table 14.1 Before and after scores on the evaluation measures

	Before group mean scores	After group mean scores
MHCS	45.6	69.0
LWE	8.0	14.0

obtained as people were discharged before completing the group or failed to return the questionnaires. Table 14.1 reports before and after group mean scores for the MHCS and the LWE. Higher post-group scores suggest increased confidence and ability to live with emotions after attending the group. Simple repeated t test analyses indicate that there is significant improvement in clients' scores on the before and after group MHCS and LWE scores (t = 3.35, p < 0.005 and t = 3.11, p < 0.01 respectively).

Satisfaction questionnaire

Clients who completed four or more sessions of the group were also asked to complete a satisfaction questionnaire after their last group session. The satisfaction questionnaire simply asks the client to rate how satisfied they were with the group, the skills taught and teaching quality on a seven-point scale. Open questions were also included: what was liked best and least about the group as well as an invitation to make recommendations about how the group could be improved. The results indicated that on the whole participants felt satisfied that the group was run effectively and the skills taught relevant. Of those who have completed these questionnaires, 75 per cent reported feeling the quality of the service was either excellent or good. Some of the clients' comments suggest that the clients found the skills taught useful and gained benefit from attending the group. Mindfulness was mentioned specifically as being most beneficial. Some of the comments also suggested that the group could be improved by taking more time to cover the material and a greater awareness that sometimes clients may feel that these skills are 'unobtainable'. Feeling rushed and trying to cram too much material into the six sessions was the main area for suggested improvement.

Summary and conclusions

The ECS group at Woodhaven has been a huge success on a number of levels. First, it has helped staff become more familiar with important therapeutic skills that are relevant to their daily work: not only in terms of being able to help clients better, but also to manage our own hectic lives. As the staff became more proficient at teaching and coaching these skills, the knock-on effect on the wards for the nurses became apparent. Subsequently, a further four nurses have shown interest in DBT and have now been trained in the approach. Second, the results themselves indicate how beneficial the group has been in imparting skills and helping individuals to become more confident in managing emotions. Running groups on the ward has been a valuable experience for both facilitator and participant alike.

The comments from clients have been considered by the consult group and changes made to the programme. In addition the local community teams are now developing their own ECS groups as a response to the popularity of the group on the inpatient unit. Plans are also afoot to open the group to the newly formed crisis resolution and home treatment team.

Part V

The challenge of evaluating this service

Chapter 15

Evaluating short-term CBT in an acute adult inpatient unit

Caroline Durrant and Abigail Tolland

The need for evidence

NICE guidelines for the provision of psychological services have been introduced during the past few years in order to inform best practice within our profession. These guidelines are based upon best available evidence at the time of writing. It is therefore the responsibility of practitioners to provide the evidence that their interventions are effective and so should be funded by the NHS.

Currently, NICE guidelines define their gold standard of evidence as the randomized control trial (RCT) and many recommendations are based on these studies. An RCT uses participants who have simple, relatively clear-cut diagnoses and who are willing to take part in therapy (thereby producing a positive bias). The trials involve delivering a psychological intervention standardized in terms of technique and number of sessions. These cases and interventions do not reflect the complex pattern of co-morbidity, diagnostic uncertainty and ambivalence typically encountered in a clinical setting. Neither do they reflect the dynamic and flexible approach taken by therapists. Therefore, within areas of psychological practice where RCT research is not suited there has been a movement towards practice-based evidence. Woodhaven Adult Mental Health Unit is an acute adult mental health unit where the service users and psychology service do not reflect the conditions tested in an RCT. In order to provide the necessary evidence for the psychological interventions provided at Woodhaven, however, a practice-based evidence approach is far more valid than RCT trials.

The approach used at Woodhaven is based on cognitive behavioural therapy which has a considerable evidence base suggesting that it is an effective therapy for a large variety of disorders. This evidence base suggests it is a good foundation for a therapeutic approach to be applied in an acute setting. The challenge at Woodhaven was to provide evidence that CBT could be tailored to suit the short admissions, uncertain or dual diagnosis and high levels of distress that characterize an acute setting. This evidence could then be used to generate interest in order to fully develop and provide an evidence-based psychological intervention for acute inpatient services. The results of this evaluation have been published in Durrant *et al.* (2007). This chapter gives a fuller account of considerations behind the project and how the problems of evaluating brief therapy in an inpatient setting were identified and overcome.

What to measure?

The psychological therapy provided at Woodhaven (as described in Chapters 6, 7 and 8) encompasses the recovery approach. The recovery approach was developed in the 1990s and is largely based on service users' perspectives. The approach encourages professionals to take a more holistic approach to treatment by placing an emphasis on the person rather than the illness. Anthony (1993) explains that the approach brought about the realization that as professionals we need to have broader targets than symptom relief. The approach emphasizes the importance of restoring social and emotional functioning, and learning to cope with symptoms that cannot be medically controlled. Recovery is described as an attitude (Deegan 1996) that needs to be adopted for life in order to maintain an outlook that promotes psychological well-being. This attitude is one of hope and optimism that one can lead a fulfilling life with mental illness. Central to this optimistic attitude is a feeling of control and confidence in one's ability to achieve this goal.

At Woodhaven, admissions are predominantly short and the ward ethos tends to be dominated by the medical model. The recovery approach adopted by the psychology department provides balance for this ethos and has been adapted to fit short admissions. Within this chapter, a small part of the recovery approach has been focused upon as it is most relevant to the service users encountered at Woodhaven. For further discussion of the entire recovery approach, please see Allott *et al.*'s (2002) review. At Woodhaven, the short admissions mean that a full recovery pathway cannot be developed and so psychological interventions focus upon the crucial part referred to as the 'turning point' (Davidson and Strauss 1992). The 'turning point' is described as the time when a person discovers that they can be an active agent in their own recovery. It is a time when someone rediscovers their strengths and begins to believe that these strengths can help them successfully manage their mental illness. The sense of self-efficacy and mastery that marks the 'turning point' is seen as the first step on the road to recovery. In keeping with this, outcome measures in recovery research focus on these central themes of empowerment and self-determination.

With the recovery approach in mind, observation of the consultant clinical psychologist during individual therapy sessions was used to narrow down the choice of variables. I will not discuss the approach used in detail here, but would refer the reader to Chapter 6 of this book for information.

During the observation of sessions it came to light that the approach used focused on providing service users with the skills they needed to cope with their emotions and other experiences of mental illness. The approach was very person centred in that it was flexible and aimed to make changes meaningful to the service user themselves. Overall the approach appeared to empower service users by increasing feelings of mastery in relation to their symptoms of mental illness. This led to narrowing the choice of variables to be measured to self-efficacy, self-esteem, locus of control and emotional well-being. To fit with this person-centred approach it would also be useful to look at individual goal setting in addition to these psychological variables.

The next step was to discuss the results of observations with the consultant clinical psychologist. It was considered that an increase in self-esteem was a secondary effect that would occur as a result of increased confidence in coping with the symptoms of mental illness. In addition to this, changes in self-esteem during such a short admission were likely to be too small to be measured using questionnaire data. Therefore, it was decided not to include a measure of self-esteem as part of the study. The remaining variables of self-efficacy, locus of control and goal setting were retained, as it was agreed that these were the aims of psychological therapy and they also reflected the concepts contained within the 'turning point' discussed in the recovery approach.

When discussing the inclusion of a measure of emotional well-being it was decided that this variable needed specifying further. Literature on the skills taught within sessions such as mindfulness, relaxation and breathing techniques suggests that these skills aim to help people cope with their emotions so that they do not become overwhelmed by them. It appeared that the emotional well-being component of the therapeutic process was also aimed at creating a sense of mastery and increased coping ability. Therefore, emotional well-being was redefined as emotional coping or self-efficacy in relation to managing emotions.

How to measure the selected variables?

Once the challenge of choosing variables had been overcome, it was necessary to choose appropriate measures for each of them. There were several issues that needed to be considered when choosing the measures to be used. The service users at Woodhaven were admitted during times of acute mental distress. Any assessments carried out would need to place as few demands on the service user as possible. This meant trying to minimize the number of questions, providing scales so that coherent responses need not be generated and keeping the measures simple. In light of this, it was decided that questionnaire data would be most appropriate. Questionnaires allow for ease of responding, independence to reduce evaluation apprehension and can reduce the demands placed on the service user at any one time by allowing one or two questionnaires to be completed in a session if the full battery cannot be managed. The measures would be completed both prior to therapy and after the final therapy session to assess changes that had occurred during the intervention.

When choosing measures for each variable it seemed necessary to follow Rosenberg's argument (Rosenberg et al. 1995) that when measuring a concept such as self-esteem it is preferable to use a measure that applies to the specific circumstances in which self-esteem is needed as opposed to using a global measure. This is because a person who has high self-esteem in one area does not necessarily have high self-esteem in another. It logically follows that this argument should apply to self-efficacy and locus of control. A service user may feel confident they can manage to ride a bike but this does not mean they feel confident in their ability to manage their emotions. Therefore, measures were sought that looked at locus of control and self-efficacy specifically in relation to mental illness and emotional coping.

A literature search revealed two suitable measures that looked at self-efficacy and locus of control in relation to mental health. The Mental Health Confidence Scale (MHCS) was designed by Carpinello et al. (2000) to measure self-efficacy in relation to mental health. The scale consists of 16 items that tap into three underlying factors: optimism, coping and advocacy. The authors of the scale report high levels of construct validity and low error variance, suggesting it is a reliable measure. The Locus of Control of Behaviour (LCB) Scale (Craig et al. 1984) looks at perceived sense of control, in terms of internal or external control, over mental health problems. The measure has been used with clinical samples and found to be a reliable and valid measure. The specific focus of the two scales on mental health problems made them ideal measures for the audit.

Having chosen the MHCS and LCB scales it appeared necessary to generate a measure specific to a person's confidence in their ability to manage their emotions and the utility of the skills taught by the psychologist at Woodhaven (for full review see Chapters 6, 7 and 8). The literature on emotion regulation revealed that such a specific measure had not yet been developed (see Austenfield and Stanton 2004) and there is a paucity of research in this area. For these reasons, a measure of emotional coping was developed and based mainly on the techniques used by the consultant clinical psychologist rather than literature. A review of the consultant clinical psychologists interacting cognitive subsystems approach (Clarke 1999) and an informal interview concerning the aims of therapeutic input specific to managing emotions supplemented the information already gathered from observation of therapy sessions.

The argument for developing the measure using this method is that it was designed specifically for this audit and so it is logical that the underlying theory and therapy delivered at Woodhaven guided question development. The information gathered was amalgamated to find overriding themes that could be used to guide question formation. The themes that emerged were those of facing emotions, expressing emotions and letting go of emotions. Due to the need to keep measures short and simple, one question was allocated to each theme. A fourth question was added to aid the development of the psychological approach at Woodhaven. Participants were asked which skills they found most helpful for managing their emotions. This question was looking at the subjective utility of skills for distress tolerance in order to guide future skills teaching and so further develop the approach used at Woodhaven. Although it is recognized that this measure is idiosyncratic, there is potential to develop it so that it can be generalized to other acute settings. Reliability testing for the Living with Emotions scale revealed high reliability co-efficient (0.84) and good internal consistency (0.51) that suggest this measure could be used as a foundation for a more generalizable measure for acute settings. Some suggestions for this have been included at the end of this chapter.

In keeping with the person centred, recovery approach, a goal-setting form was created for the purposes of this study. The recovery approach advocates the use of self-generated goals as this increases sense of ownership of one's own path to recovery and so such goals should be regarded as an important theme in therapy. The goal-setting forms followed a standard format of asking participants to identify two to three goals of therapy. It was emphasized that this was the participant's chance to identify and reflect on what they hoped to gain, not what people around them told them needed to change. In this way it was hoped that this measure itself would empower clients and aid the person-centred component of therapeutic process. A different form was presented for follow-up assessments where participants were asked to mark how far they felt they had progressed (or regressed) in the achievement of their set goals. Participants were presented with their first goal-setting sheet as a memory aid and a visual analogue scale was used to measure progress. The use of a visual analogue scale is argued to be less demanding and more accurate. The absence of a numbered scale with definitions for the numbers means that the researcher is not directing the participant in any way as to how to respond. It was necessary to add letters representing no change, goal attainment or feeling further away from personal goals in order to clarify the scale, but apart from this participants' responses were not influenced by the researcher.

The Clinical Outcomes in Routine Evaluation (CORE) was developed by Evans et al. (2000) to provide a global measure of psychological distress. The measure consists of 34 items that make up four subscales: Problems/Symptoms, Life functioning, Subjective well-being and Risk. These subscales are then combined to form a measure of global distress. The subscales or the global score can then be used as clinically reliable measure of change.

The CORE has been found to be a useful and suitable measure for clinical audit where the auditors are looking at outcomes that include levels of distress (e.g. see Barkham *et al.* 2005). Despite its length and relatively difficult questions, the CORE was included in order to place the audit within a nationally recognized system of classifying levels of distress. This can help the reader identify the level of psychological distress of participants in order to appreciate the population for whom the therapeutic approach may be effective.

This pilot study was conducted from January 2005 to April 2005 at Woodhaven Acute Mental Health inpatient unit. The sample definition was all service users referred to the psychological services between January and April 2005. Complete data sets were collected for 14 service users, with equal numbers of men and women. Major problems with collecting post-therapy data, which are explored below, meant that this number only represents a proportion of those receiving input from the psychological therapies service over this period. There was only a slight variation in the age range between the two genders: male age range 21–60 years old (mean age 43 years old); female age range 26–50 years old (mean age 42 years old). Table 15.1 shows the participants' diagnoses and Table 15.2 shows the breakdown of the number of sessions that each participant received.

Once the service user had been accepted for psychological therapy, one of the assistants went to the ward to complete the pre-therapy assessment. Prior to completing the assessment, the study was explained and consent obtained. Obtaining consent presented the first challenge, as the participants were experiencing acute distress and frequently did not want to answer questions that explored and highlighted their levels of distress. However, all the service users who were approached agreed to complete the measure, which reflects their courage. The pre-therapy psychometric assessment produced many varied challenges for the assistants: forming a working alliance, lack of trust, difficulty understanding the forms (including illiteracy), problems with concentration and motivation, and high levels of expressed emotion.

Challenges forming a working alliance

Initially, the main aim for the assistant psychologists was to form a collaborative, safe working alliance. This was viewed as vital for gaining accurate reporting of symptoms, both pre and post therapy. If the alliance was weak then participants may be less likely to disclose the true level of their symptoms, or be able to establish realistic goals for therapy.

Initially, the participants were often suspicious of our motives for collecting the data. The main concerns were around how the data would be used and whether it would impact on their care, either positively or negatively. These concerns were addressed using reassurance and re-explaining

Table 15.1 Service users' diagnoses

Diagnosis	Number of participants
Mood disorders	
Depression	1
Depressive disorder and anxiety	2
Bipolar	1
Substance-related disorders	
Alcohol dependency	1
Paranoia brought on by drugs and alcohol	1
Schizophrenia and other psychotic disorders	
Paranoid schizophrenia	2
Paranoia, Severe Depression, Anxiety	1
Paranoid schizophrenia, Anxiety	1
Cluster B – personality disorders	
Borderline Personality Disorder, Depression	1
Diagnosis unknown	3

Table 15.2 Number of sessions that service users received

Number of therapy sessions	Number of participants
1	2
2	3
3	4
4	0
5	3
6	0
7	0
8	1
Unknown	1

the nature of the study. The participants were also reminded that they did not have to join the study in order to receive the therapy, and that they would still receive the therapy, whether or not they filled in the forms. Once an alliance had been formed between the participant and assistant psychologist these concerns usually dissipated.

A further barrier was that the participants sometimes felt that they were not getting anything from the study. This was often reflected in poor motivation; either participants did not want to leave what they were doing or would answer the questions very quickly without appearing to give the items any thought. When this occurred, the assistants might comment on it to the participant and look at the barriers. It usually only required listening to the concerns and further explanation of the study and possible benefits for the participant and future service users (such as a clear picture of how their symptoms had improved and an added awareness of new skills they had learnt).

Challenges completing the psychometric assessment

The pre-therapy psychometric assessment comprised five measures, including three that were scored on either a five-point (the CORE) or six-point (Mental Health Confidence Scale and Locus of Control) Likert scale. These scales proved difficult for some service users to complete because of poor reading ability, cognitive ability and decreased levels of concentration.

The reading ability of the participants was mixed: some participants had a low reading ability, or could not read at all. In these cases, the assistants would read the questions and possible answers to the participant who would select the appropriate answer. This method of data collection could be hard for participants because it did not offer the same level of privacy as independent completion. In answering the questions, some participants expressed concerns about what the assistant might think of them when they gave their answers. When this arose, reassurance was given until the person was able to carry on. Furthermore, if a participant had a low reading ability, they often had problems understanding the language used in the scales. In these cases, rather than rephrasing the question which may have led to inaccurate responses, the keywords were explained to enable understanding.

The participants who were able to read and write could still have difficulty completing MHCS, LCB and CORE because of the Likert scales. A lot of participants found it difficult to differentiate between the points on the Likert scale and could become frustrated. In some cases the scale was drawn out so that the patient could have a visual display. Although this could be viewed as a crude measure, it did help participants distinguish between the different points. Arguably, simpler language might help resolve the issue of difficulty in understanding for the other scales used but this has not been attempted at Woodhaven as it can be a time-consuming process.

Finally, the symptoms of their illnesses meant that most participants had difficulty concentrating on the task. For some participants this meant that the task took only slightly longer, but for others they required more than one session to complete the pre-therapy psychometric assessment. This could be tricky because they were often seen by the psychologist very quickly and this did not give much time to complete the measurements. Ethically it was not possible to delay the therapy session solely for the purpose of audit and because admissions were often short.

The participants' difficulties in reading and processing the information contributed to the design of the Living With My Emotions Scale. During the initial assessment, the participants appeared to find this scale easier to complete. This was confirmed in the data analysis as all participants in this study completed the scale both pre and post therapy. It seems that it was the concrete nature of these scales that makes them easier to complete. Participants seemed to find it especially helpful in the post-therapy assessment when they were able to reflect on their improvement. This sometimes led to an exploration of how they felt that they had achieved this improvement. For some participants this seemed to be quite empowering and reassuring for them. The above findings support the continuing research into the reliability and validity of the Living With My Emotions Scale which is continuing at Woodhaven.

Overall, the pre-therapy psychometric assessment was quite cognitively demanding for some participants and this meant that the data collection could be very time consuming. On a few occasions, it was difficult to get the pre-therapy assessment completed before the first therapy session. This highlights the need for short simple measures to be used.

The participants in this study were experiencing high levels of negative emotions, which prior to therapy many felt unable to cope with. In order to ascertain the levels of pre- and post-therapy distress, the psychometric assessments included items about negative emotions, thoughts and suicidal ideation. Some of the participants were distressed by these questions and did not answer them. This was a potential problem because if the person left so many questions blank per scale then the scale was invalid. There is no easy answer to this because one can only encourage a participant so much, as one must also respect their decision not to answer the questions.

Another scale that could cause distress was the goal-setting scale. A minority of participants found it difficult to identify goals because they felt so overwhelmed by their emotions.

Post-therapy psychometric assessment

The main challenge for the post-therapy psychometric assessment was getting the forms completed. Woodhaven is an acute mental health hospital so individual service users all have very different needs and severity of symptoms. Thus, discharge points vary greatly between individuals and this poses a significant challenge with data collection as one never knows the likely length of hospital stay in advance. This meant that the study team were sometimes unable to get the post-therapy assessment completed while the participant was an inpatient. The situation of the psychological therapies service within the hospital compounded this problem. Communication between disciplines takes place most reliably within ward rounds. However, attendance at these is extremely time consuming, and there was no way that the department could both deliver a service and attend all the ward rounds. Consequently, the psychological therapies department was not always aware of discharge time scales. Bed management pressures result in decisions to discharge being taken outside of any formal communication channels. Moreover, some participants were admitted from outside the catchment area and so could be discharged quickly when a bed became available within their locality. This meant that on some occasions the forms would be sent to the participant by post, perhaps lessening the chance of their being completed, or that contact details were insufficient to allow the assistants to follow up. These challenges help explain the low rate of completed post-therapy assessments. However, data collection is continuing at Woodhaven and the approach is being refined and developed.

Table 15.2 illustrates the variation in the number of sessions that participants received. This should be taken in to account when analysing the data. For instance, the therapeutic alliance and treatment outcomes of a participant who has had one session are likely to be different when compared to a participant who has had eight sessions.

Results summary

This section offers a brief summary of the findings from the study (Durrant *et al.* 2007). The results show that participants significantly increased in self-efficacy, especially coping style, pre to post therapy. Moreover, the participants reported a significant increase in internal locus of control post therapy when compared to pre therapy. Additionally, participants reported a greater ability to express their emotions and more coping strategies for managing their emotions. Finally, the participants set themselves goals to be met while in therapy. At least half of the participants felt that they had met at least one of their goals. Although a reasonable proportion felt that they had met none of their goals, participants generally felt they were closer to meeting their goals post therapy. There are many factors that may influence this finding but perhaps one of the most important was the number of therapy sessions that the participants had received. Some of the participants had only one or two therapy sessions and it would be unrealistic to expect them to have made significant progress towards their goals within this time frame.

Confounding factors

The service users in this study were all receiving additional routine treatment (medication, occupational therapy, etc.) so it is not possible to state that these results were all due to psychological therapy. This is a common problem in clinical research as it is not usually possible to stop all other forms of treatment. One possible solution might be to use a waiting list control and compare the differences between the two groups. This method would be valuable because it is likely that the waiting list is receiving the same standard treatment. However, in an acute inpatient setting this may be difficult as admission times are generally short and therefore it may be difficult to get these two groups. A further possibility may be a randomized controlled trial with treatment as usual and different psychological treatments. While this may provide the data to show the benefits of psychological therapy in an acute inpatient setting, it is difficult to set up such a project.

Conclusion

The pilot study covered a four-month period and comprised 14 clients. Results, especially for those who had multiple therapy sessions, were encouraging and illustrate that even with limited time, meaningful improvements can be made.

Future directions

The issues encountered during this study suggest future research needs to focus on simplifying measurements in order to increase understanding and participation while reducing frustration and cognitive demands. The success of the Living With My Emotions Scale suggests that short, concrete measures are more suitable for use in acute settings. Participants' frustrations with Likert scales combined with the relative ease with which they completed the goal-setting visual analogue scale further suggests that visual analogue may be preferable to Likert scales and it is worth investigating whether the Likert scales used in the Living With My Emotions Scale could be replaced with visual analogues. Further research would be needed to fully assess the validity of visual analogue scales in psychological research, but they may well prove to be a useful tool in settings where acute symptoms of mental illness reduce ability to understand numbered scales.

Participants tended to have difficulty with the LCB and MHCS which again reflected the use of Likert scales. There were also difficulties understanding some of the terms used in these measures. Future research may want to explore the possibility of adapting these scales for use in an acute setting. Adaptations may be needed to simplify the language used to make the questions more concrete, attempt to reduce the number of questions in the measure or consider the viability of visual analogue scales.

Future research may question the use of the CORE as part of a battery of assessments to evaluate effectiveness in acute inpatient settings. During the current study, questions regarding symptomatology and risk to self or others could cause some distress to the participants and often the questions remained blank. Ethically the use of this measure needs to be carefully considered in the future. It is also evident that the use of a five-point scale is demanding and could cause frustration. For these reasons I would suggest that the CORE is not used as part of a battery of tests and that it may not even be suitable for use in acute settings where it may add to already high levels of mental distress.

Chapter 16

Conclusion

Isabel Clarke and Hannah Wilson

Putting this book together has been a heartening experience for us. We knew that there was enthusiasm locally for the challenge of bringing CBT into the inpatient unit, and that is what inspired us to get started. We have now learnt that this enthusiasm is nationwide, and that there are pockets of good practice all over. The book certainly does not include them all. Many more inspiring initiatives have come to our notice since we embarked on this enterprise. The process of compiling the book, and of presenting our research at meetings and conferences, has put us in touch with these initiatives. Our hope is that by raising awareness of what is going on and what is possible, more CBT therapists will consider working in the inpatient setting, and more managers and commissioners of services will see the inclusion of a therapist in the skill mix of their unit as essential.

In fact, from our experience in Woodhaven, I would say that the employment of two therapists makes all the difference. It has made it possible for us to develop initiatives on several fronts at once, rather than concentrate on one area at a time: for instance, having to decide whether to prioritize either work with staff or individual work, as opposed to developing both. It has given us the confidence to be bold and provided support when the going gets tough.

What future directions for CBT for inpatients does this book suggest? We hope that our core aim of making the case for developing such a service has been successful. This argument needs to be taken forward. Obviously it needs to be heard where services are commissioned, but the evidence of good and creative practice on the ground needs to be heard too. Above all, the voice of service users such as Marie needs to be taken seriously, and their plea to be supported to make sense of their experiences, and so to be able to take charge of their own future, needs to be honoured.

The difficulties and arguments against such developments have been comprehensively covered in the preceding chapters. From the commissioning point of view, the lack of an evidence base is probably the most cogent. This book makes the plea for the development of a body of practice-based evidence. As the field is new and developing, time will inevitably be needed for a convincing evidence base to build. One of the conclusions of the book is that it is essential to allow for flexibility in the type of evidence that is given credence. The high demands of the setting will not allow for the rigours of the sort of randomized and controlled data collection that is possible in, for instance, institutions with more coherent populations who are detained for fixed periods, such as specialist personality disorder units. Data collection in the fluid world of the inpatient unit must necessarily be more ad hoc and hit and miss. This volume reflects some of the flexibility and creativity needed to measure interventions in this setting. Creativity is needed in order to evaluate important elements of the work of the psychologist or CBT therapist such as reflective practice and formulation of cases for the benefit of the team.

When considering future directions, it is necessary to be clear about what this book leaves out. We are only too aware that the medical perspective is lacking. None of our contributors is a medical doctor (though nurse therapists, occupational therapists and mental health practitioners are represented). The medical model is cited at times as an inhibiting factor for the development of a culture of therapy. We consider that this is a nettle that needs to be grasped. Dialogue needs to be opened. For the good of the milieu in the institution, for the staff group who are otherwise torn uncomfortably in two conflicting directions, a real accommodation needs to be sought. This sort of cultural split is just as harmful to the clients of the service. Any resolution will probably require an enlargement of vision by both parties. Addressing this has been beyond the scope of this volume. Perhaps it is the next challenge, along with further publication of the good work being accomplished in institutions up and down the country.

So, therapy has a place in the inpatient setting. It is not a job for the fainthearted, or for the inflexible practitioner. It is easy to get discouraged. We know that only too well. Imagery and metaphor play a central role in my therapeutic approach, so I offer here a concluding metaphor to reflect on at times of discouragement. I offer you the sandcastle model of working as a therapist in the acute hospital. You do some training, set up reflective practice systems, collaborate with one or two brilliant staff, have the odd success – you build your sandcastle. Then everything changes. There are one or two untoward incidents; a few difficult admissions; the regular staff leave or go off sick, so the ward is staffed by 'agency'; even your allies get new jobs; the psychiatrist gets risk averse – the tide comes in and sweeps it away – so, you start building another sandcastle! The important thing is to avoid getting discouraged and to keep building. The service users do not have the luxury of leaving this particular beach. At least doing research and publishing means that you have a photograph of that special sandcastle. But who knows what the next one will look like – maybe slightly bigger with a drawbridge and flags on the turrets?!

References

Accreditation for Acute Inpatient Mental Health Services (AIMS, 2006) *Standards for Acute Inpatient Wards*, 1st edn, London: Royal College of Psychiatrists' Centre for Quality Improvement.

Allot, P., Logananthan, L. and Fulford, K.W.M. (2002) *Discovering hope for recovery from a British perspective: a review of a selection of recovery literature, implications for practice and systems change*, West Midlands Partnership for Mental Health, Birmingham (www.wmpmh.org.uk).

American Psychiatric Association (APA, 1994) *Diagnostic and Statistical Manual of Mental Disorders*, 4th edn, Washington DC: APA.

Anthony, W.A. (1993) 'Recovery from mental illness: the guiding vision of the mental health service system in the 1990s', *Psychosocial Rehabilitation Journal* 16, 4: 11–23.

Atkins, S. and Murphy, K. (1993) 'Reflection: a review of the literature', *Journal of Advanced Nursing* 8, 39: 50–56.

Austenfield, J. and Stanton, A. (2004) 'Coping through emotional approach: a new look at emotion, coping and health-related outcomes', *Journal of Personality* 72, 6: 1335–1363.

Austin, J.T. and Vancouver, J.B. (1996) 'Goal constructs in psychology: structure, process and content', *Psychological Bulletin* 120, 3: 338–375.

Baldwin, M.W. (2005) *Interpersonal Cognition*, New York: Guilford Press.

Barkham, M., Gilbert, N., Connell, J., Marshall, C. and Twigg, E. (2005) 'Suitability and utility of the CORE-OM and CORE-A for assessing severity of presenting problems in psychological therapy services based in primary and secondary care', *British Journal of Psychiatry* 186: 239–246.

Barkham, M., Mellor-Clark, J., Cornell, J. and Cahill, J. (2006) 'A brief history of the origins and application of the CORE-OM and CORE', *Journal of Counselling and Psychotherapy Research* 2: 357–374.

Barnard, P. (2003) 'Asynchrony, implicational meaning and the experience of self in schizophrenia', in T. Kircher and A. David (eds) *The Self in Neuroscience and Psychiatry* (pp. 121–146), Cambridge: Cambridge University Press.

Barnard, P.J. (2004) 'Bridging between basic theory and clinical practice', *Behaviour Research and Therapy* 42: 977–1000.

Baron, R.M. and Kenny, D.A. (1986) 'The moderator–mediator variable distinction in social psychological research: conceptual, strategic and statistical considerations', *Journal of Personality and Social Psychology* 51, 6: 1173–1182.

Bateman, A. and Fonagy, P. (1999) 'Effectiveness of partial hospitalization in the treatment of borderline personality disorder: a randomized control trial', *American Journal of Psychiatry* 156: 1563–1569.

Bateman, A. and Fonagy, P. (2001) 'Treatment of borderline personality disorder with psychoanalytically oriented partial hospitalization: an 18-month follow-up', *American Journal of Psychiatry* 158: 36–42.

Bateman, A.W. and Fonagy, P. (2004) *Psychotherapy for Borderline Personality Disorder: Mentalization Based Treatment*, Oxford: Oxford University Press.

Bateman, A.W. and Tyrer, P. (2002) *Effective Management of Personality Disorder*. Online. Available HTTP: http://www.dh.gov.uk/assetRoot/04/13/08/43/04130843.pdf (accessed 27 January 2007).

Bateman, A.W. and Tyrer, P. (2004) 'Services for personality disorder: organization for inclusion', *Advances in Psychiatric Treatment* 10: 425–433.

Beck, A.T. (1976) *Cognitive Therapy and the Emotional Disorders*, New York: International Universities Press.

Beck, J.S. (1995) *Cognitive Therapy: Basics and Beyond*, New York: Guilford Press.

Bennett-Levy, J. (2003) 'Reflection: a blind spot in psychology?', *Clinical Psychology* 27: 16–19.

Bentall, R.P. (2003) *Madness Explained: Psychosis and Human Nature*, London: Allen Lane.

Bieling, P.J. and Kuyken, W. (2003) 'Is cognitive case formulation science or science fiction?', *Clinical Psychology: Science and Practice* 10: 52–69.

Blackburn, R. (2006) 'What is personality disorder?', in M.J. Sampson, P.A. McCubbin and P. Tyrer (eds) *Personality Disorder and Community Mental Health Teams: A Practitioner's Guide* (pp. 21–39), Chichester: Wiley.

Bloor, M., McKeganey, N. and Fonkert, D. (1988) *One Foot in Eden. A Sociological Study of the Range of Therapeutic Community Practice*, London: Routledge.

Boardman, J. and Parsonage, M. (2005) *Defining a Good Mental Health Service*, London: Sainsbury Centre for Mental Health.

Bohus, M., Haff, B., Stiglmayr, C., Pohl, U., Bohme, R. and Linehan, M. (2000) 'Evaluation of inpatient DBT for BPD – a prospective study', *Behaviour Research and Therapy* 38: 875–887.

Bomford, R. (1999) *The Symmetry of God*, London: Free Association Books.

Bott, E. (1976) 'Hospital and society', *British Journal of Medical Psychology* 49: 97–140.

Bower, P. and Gilbody, S. (2005) 'Stepped care in psychological therapies: access, effectiveness and efficiency', *British Journal of Psychiatry* 186: 11–17.

Bowers, L. and McCann, E. (2003) 'Rapid recovery from acute psychosis', *Developing Practice Improving Care* 1, 6: 1–4.

Bowers, L., Simpson, A., Alexander, J., Hackney, D., Nijman, H., Grange, A. and Warren, J. (2005) 'The nature and purpose of acute psychiatric wards @ the Tompkins Acute Ward Study', *Journal of Mental Health* 14, 6: 625–635.

Bowles, N., Mackintosh, C. and Tom, A. (2001) 'Nurses' communication skills: an evaluation of the impact of solution focused communication training', *Journal of Advanced Nursing* 36, 3: 347–354.

Bradbury, K.E. and Clarke, I. (2006) 'Cognitive behavioural therapy for anger management: effectiveness in adult mental health services', *Behavioural and Cognitive Psychotherapy* 35: 201–208.

Bright (2006) *Star wards: practical ideas for improving the daily experiences and treatment outcomes of acute mental health inpatients*, London: Bright. Online. Available HTTP: http://www.starwards.org.uk (accessed June 2007).

British Psychological Society (BPS, 2000) *Recent Advances in Understanding Mental Illness and Psychotic Experiences*, Leicester: BPS.

British Psychological Society (BPS, 2002) *Clinical Psychology in Services for People with Severe and Enduring Mental Illness*, Leicester: BPS.

British Psychological Society, Division of Clinical Psychology (2000) *Understanding Mental Illness and Psychotic Experiences: A Report by the British Psychological Society Division of Clinical Psychology*, Leicester: BPS.

British Psychological Society, Division of Clinical Psychology (2004) *Estimating the Applied Psychology Demand in Adult Mental Health*, Leicester: BPS.

British Psychological Society, Division of Clinical Psychology (2007) *Leading Psychological Services*, Leicester: BPS.

Brod, J.H. (1997) 'Creativity and schizotypy', in G.A. Claridge (ed.) *Schizotypy: Implications for Illness and Health*, Oxford: Oxford University Press.

Brooker, C. and Brabban, A. (2004) *Measured Success: A Scoping Review of Evaluated Psychosocial Intervention Training for Work with People with Serious Mental Health Problems*, London: NIMHE/Trent Workforce Development Confederation.

Brown, R.A. and Lewinsohn, P.M. (1984) 'A psycho-educational approach to the treatment of depression: comparison of group, individual and minimal contact procedures', *Journal of Consulting and Clinical Psychology* 52: 774–783.

Bruch, M. and Bond, F.W. (eds) (1998) *Beyond Diagnosis: Case Formulation Approaches in CBT*, Chichester: Wiley.

Butler, G. (2006) 'The value of formulation: a question for debate', *Clinical Psychology Forum* 160: 9–12.

Cameron, D., Kapur, R. and Campbell, P. (2005) 'Releasing the therapeutic potential of the psychiatric nurse: a human relations perspective of the nurse–patient relationship', *Journal of Psychiatric and Mental Health Nursing* 12: 64–74.

Campling, P. and Haigh, R. (eds) (1999) *Therapeutic Communities. Past, Present and Future*, London: Jessica Kingsley Publishers.

Carper, B. (1978) 'Fundamental patterns of knowing', *Advanced Nursing Science* 1: 13–23.

Carpinello, S.E., Knight, E.L., Markowitz, F.E. and Pease, E.L. (2000) 'The development of the mental health confidence scale: a measure of self-efficacy in individuals diagnosed with mental disorders', *Psychiatric Rehabilitation Journal* 23: 236–243.

Carradice, A. and Round, D. (2004) 'The reality of practice development for nurses working in the inpatient service for people with severe and enduring mental health problems', *Journal of Psychiatric and Mental Health Nursing* 11: 731–737.

Castillo, H. (2003) *Personality Disorder: Temperament or Trauma?*, London: Jessica Kingsley Publishers.

Centre for Economic Performance (2006) *The Depression Report: A New Deal for Depression and Anxiety Disorders*, London: London School of Economics.

Chadwick, P.D.J. (2006) *Person-Based Cognitive Therapy for Distressing Psychosis*, Chichester: Wiley.

Chadwick, P.D.J., Newman-Taylor, K. and Abba, N. (2005) 'Mindfulness groups for people with distressing psychosis', *Behavioural and Cognitive Psychotherapy* 33, 3: 351–360.

Chadwick, P., Sambrook, S., Rasch, S. and Davies, E. (2000) 'Challenging the omnipotence of voices: group cognitive behaviour therapy for voices', *Behaviour Research and Therapy* 38, 10: 993–1003.

Chadwick, P., Williams, C. and MacKenzie, J. (2003) 'The impact of case formulation in cognitive therapy for psychosis', *Behaviour Research and Therapy* 41: 671–680.

Charles, R., Swenson, M.D., William, C., Torrey, M.D. and Korerner, H. (2002) 'Implementing dialectical behaviour therapy', *Psychiatric Services* 53, 2: 171–177.

Chiesa, M., Fonagy, P., Holmes, J., Drahorad, C. and Harrison-Hall, A. (2002) 'Health service use costs by personality disorder following specialist and non-specialist treatment: a comparative study', *Journal of Personality Disorders* 16: 162–173.

Claridge, G.A. (1997) *Schizotypy: Implications for Illness and Health*, Oxford: Oxford University Press.

Clarke, B., James, C. and Kelly, J. (1996) 'Reflective practice: reviewing the issues and refocusing the debate', *International Journal of Nursing Studies* 33, 2: 171–180.

Clarke, I. (1999) 'Cognitive therapy and serious mental illness. An interacting cognitive subsystems approach', *Clinical Psychology and Psychotherapy* 6: 375–383.

Clarke, I. (2001) 'Psychosis and spirituality: the discontinuity model', in I. Clarke (ed.) *Psychosis and Spirituality: Exploring the New Frontier*, London: Whurr.

Clarke, I. (2002a) 'Introducing further developments towards an ICS formulation of psychosis: a comment on Gumley *et al.* (1999). An interacting cognitive subsystems model of relapse and the course of psychosis', *Clinical Psychology and Psychotherapy* 9: 47–50.

Clarke, I. (2002b) 'Case experience from a rehabilitation service', in D. Kingdon and D. Turkington (eds) *The Case Study Guide to Cognitive Behaviour Therapy of Psychosis*, Chichester: Wiley.

Clarke, S. (2004) *Acute Inpatient Mental Health Care: Education, Training and Continuing Professional Development for All*, London: NIMHE/SCMH.

Clouder, L. (2000) 'Reflective practice in physiotherapy', *Studies in Higher Education* 25, 2: 211–223.

Cooke, A., Harper, D. and Kinderman, P. (2001) 'Government proposals for reforming the Mental Health Act: implications for clinical psychologists', *Clinical Psychology* 1: 48–52.

Corren, D. and Lucas, D. (2004) 'Hearing voices: and proud of it', *Mental Health Practice* 7: 16–17.

Craig, A.R., Franklin, J.A. and Andrews, G. (1984) 'A scale to measure locus of control of behaviour', *British Journal of Medical Psychology* 57: 173–180.

Cullen, C. (1983) 'Implications of functional analysis', *British Journal of Clinical Psychology* 22: 137–138.

Davidson, L. and Strauss, J.S. (1992) 'Sense of self in recovery from severe mental illness', *British Journal of Medical Psychology* 65: 131–145.

Davis, D. and Taylor-Vaisey, A. (1997) 'Translating guidelines into practice: a systematic review of theoretic concepts, practical experience, and research evidence in the adoption of clinical practice guidelines', *Canadian Medical Association Journal* 157: 408–416.

Deegan, P. (1996) 'Recovery as a journey of the heart', *Psychosocial Rehabilitation Journal* 19, 3: 91–97.

Department of Health (DH, 1996) *NHS Psychotherapy Services in England: Review of Strategic Policy*, London: DH.

Department of Health (DH, 1999a) *National Service Framework for Mental Health: Modern Standards and Service Models*, London: DH.

Department of Health (DH, 1999b) *Press Release issued on behalf of the Mental Health Act Commission, ref 1999/0479*, London: DH.

Department of Health (DH, 2000) *The National Plan for the NHS*, London: DH.

Department of Health (DH, 2001a) *The Mental Health Policy Implementation Guide: Crisis Resolution/Home Treatment Teams*, London: DH.

Department of Health (DH, 2001b) *Treatment Choice in Psychological Therapies and Counselling. Evidence Based Practice Guidelines*, London: DH.

Department of Health (DH 2002a) *Community Mental Health Teams Mental Health Policy Implementation Guide*, London: DH.

Department of Health (DH, 2002b) *Mental Health Policy Implementation Guide: Adult Acute Inpatient Care Provision*, London: DH.

Department of Health (DH, 2002c) *Mental Health Policy Implementation Guide: National Minimum Standards for General Adult Services in PICU and Low Secure Environments*, London: DH.

Department of Health (DH, 2002d) *Improvement, Expansion and Reform: The Next Three Years' Priorities and Planning Framework 2003–2006*, London: DH.

Department of Health (DH, 2004a) *Organising and Delivering Psychological Therapies*, London: DH.

Department of Health (DH, 2004b) *Standards for Better Health – Health Care Commission Core Standards*, London: DH.

Department of Health (DH, 2004c) *The National Service Framework for Mental Health – Five Years On*, London: DH.

Department of Health (DH, 2005) *New Ways of Working for Psychiatrists*, London: DH.

Department of Health (DH, 2006a) *From Values to Action: The Chief Nursing Officer's Review of Mental Health Nursing*. London: DH.

Department of Health (DH, 2006b) *Our Health, Our Care, Our Say: A New Direction for Community Services: White Paper*, London: DH.

Department of Health (2006c) *Press release*. Online. Available HTTP: http://www.dh.gov.uk/PublicationsAndStatistics/PressReleases/PressReleasesNotices/fs/e.

Department of Health (DH, 2007) *Creating Capable Teams Approach (CCTA): Best Practice Guidance to Supporting the Implementation of New Ways of Working (NWW) and New Roles*, London: DH.

Department of Work and Pensions, Department of Health and the Health and Safety Executive (2006) *Health, Work and Well-being – Caring for our Future. A Strategy for the Health and Well-being of Working Age People*, London:

Department of Work and Pensions, Department of Health and the Health and Safety Executive.

Derogatis, L.R. (1992) *The Brief Symptom Inventory: Administration, Scoring and Procedures Manual*, Baltimore: Clinical Psychometric Research.

Dewey, J. (1933) *How We Think*, Boston: D.C. Health.

Dietrich, A.J., Oxman, T.E., Williams, J.W. Jnr., Schulberg, H.C., Bruce, M.L., Lee, P.W. *et al.* (2004) *Modelling Stepped Care in Mental Health Care Provision. Draft working paper – no. 797*, London: Clinical Operational Research Unit at University College London.

Driscoll, J. (1994) 'Reflective practice for practise – a framework for structured reflection for clinical areas', *Senior Nurse* 14, 1: 47–50.

Driscoll, J. (2000) *Practicing Clinical Supervision: A Reflective Approach*, London: Baillière-Tindall.

Driscoll, J. and Teh, B. (2001) 'The potential of reflective practice to develop individual orthopaedic nurse practitioners and their practice', *Journal of Orthopaedic Nursing* 5: 95–103.

Drury, V., Birchwood, M. and Cochrane, R. (1996a) 'Cognitive therapy and recovery from acute psychosis: a controlled trial. I: Impact on psychotic symptoms', *British Journal of Psychiatry* 169: 593–601.

Drury, V., Birchwood, M., Cochrane, R. and McMillan, M. (1996b) 'Cognitive therapy and recovery from acute psychosis: a controlled trial. II: Impact on recovery time', *British Journal of Psychiatry* 169:, 602–607.

Durrant, C., Clarke, I., Tolland, A. and Wilson, H. (2007) 'Designing a CBT service for an acute in-patient setting: a pilot evaluation study', *Clinical Psychology and Psychotherapy* 14: 117–125.

Engel G.L. (1980) 'The clinical application of the biopsychosocial model', *American Journal of Psychiatry* 137: 535–544.

Evans, C., Mellor-Clark, J., Margison, F., Barkham, M., Audin, A., Connell, J. and McGrath, G. (2000) 'CORE: Clinical Outcomes in Routine Evaluation', *Journal of Mental Health* 9, 3: 247–255.

Fagin, L. (2004) 'Management of personality disorders in acute in-patient settings. Part 1: Borderline personality disorder', *Advances in Psychiatric Treatment* 10: 93–99.

Fennell, M.J. (1997) 'Low self-esteem: a cognitive perspective', *Behavioural and Cognitive Psychotherapy* 25: 1–25.

Fennell, M.J. (2004) 'Depression, low self-esteem and mindfulness', *Behaviour, Research and Therapy* 9: 1053–1056.

Fowler, D.G. (2000) 'Psychological formulation of early psychosis: a cognitive model', in M. Birchwood, D. Fowler and C. Jackson (eds) *Early Intervention in Psychosis: A Guide to Concepts. Evidence and Interventions*, Chichester: Wiley.

Frese, F.J., Stanley, J., Kress, K. and Vogel-Scibilia, S. (2001) 'Integrating evidence-based practices and the recovery model', *Psychiatric Services* 52: 1462–1468.

Frith, C.D. (1992) *The Cognitive Neuropsychology of Schizophrenia*, Hove, UK: Lawrence Erlbaum Associates Ltd.

Gabbard, G., Coyne, L., Allen, J., Spohn, H., Colson, D.B. and Vary, M. (2000) 'Evaluation of intensive in-patient treatment of patients with severe personality disorders', *Psychiatric Services* 51: 893–898.

Gamble, C. and Hart, C. (2003) 'The use of psychosocial interventions', *Nursing Times* 99, 9: 46–47.

Gamble, C., Midence, K. and Leff, J. (1994) 'The effects of family work training on mental health nurses' attitude to and knowledge of schizophrenia: a replication', *Journal of Advanced Nursing* 19:, 893–896.

Garety, P.A., Kuipers, E., Fowler, D., Freeman, D. and Bebbington, P.E. (2001) 'A cognitive model of the positive symptoms of psychosis', *Psychological Medicine* 31: 189–195.

Ghaye, T. and Lillyman, S. (1997) *Learning Journals and Critical Incidents: Reflective Practice for Healthcare Professionals*, London: Mark Allen Publishing.

Gijbels, H. (1995) 'Mental health nursing skills in an acute admission environment: perceptions of mental health nurses and other mental health professionals', *Journal of Advanced Nursing* 21: 460–465.

Gilbert, P. (1992) *Depression. The Evolution of Powerlessness*, Hove, UK: Lawrence Erlbaum Associates Ltd.

Gilbert, P (1997) 'The evolution of social attractiveness and its role in shame, humiliation, guilt and therapy', *British Journal of Medical Psychology* 70: 113–147.

Gilbert, P. (2000) 'Social mentalities: internal "social" conflicts and the role of inner warmth and compassion in cognitive therapy', in P. Gilbert and K.G. Bailey (eds) *Genes on the Couch: Explorations in Evolutionary Psychotherapy* (pp. 118–150), Hove: Brunner Routledge.

Gilbert, P. (2005) *Compassion: Conceptualizations, Research and the Use in Psychotherapy*, London: Routledge.

Gilbert, P., Birchwood, J., Gilbert, J., Trower, J., Hay, B., Murray, A. *et al.* (2001) 'An exploration of evolved mental mechanism for dominant and subordinate behaviour in schizophrenia and critical thoughts in depression', *Psychological Medicine* 31: 1117–1127.

Gilbert, P. and Irons, C. (2005) 'Focused therapies and compassionate mind training for shame and self attacking', in P. Gilbert (ed.) *Compassion: Conceptualizations, Research and the Use in Psychotherapy* (pp. 263–325), London: Routledge.

Gilbert, P. and Proctor, S. (2006) 'Compassionate mind training for people with high shame and self-criticism: overview and pilot study of a group therapy approach', *Clinical Psychology and Psychotherapy* 13, 6: 353–379.

Gray, J.A., Feldon, J., Rawlins, J.N.P., Hemsley, D.R. and Smith, A.D. (1991) 'The neuropsychology of schizophrenia', *Behavioural and Brain Sciences* 14: 1–20.

Greenberger, D. and Padesky, C.A. (1995) *Mind over Mood. Change How You Feel by Changing the Way You Think*, New York: Guilford Press.

Gumley, A. and Schwannauer, M. (2006) *Staying Well After Psychosis: A Cognitive Interpersonal Approach to Recovery and Relapse Prevention*, Chichester: Wiley.

Gutheil, T.G. (1985) 'The therapeutic milieu: changing themes and theories', *Hospital Community Psychiatry* 36: 1279–1285.

Haddock, G., Slade, P.D., Bentall, R.P., Reid, D. and Faragher, E.B. (1998) 'A comparison of the long-term effectiveness of distraction and focusing in the treatment of auditory hallucinations', *British Journal of Medical Psychology* 71: 339–349.

Haigh, R. (1998) 'The quintessence of a therapeutic environment', in J. Cox, P.

Campling and R. Haigh (eds) *Therapeutic Communities: Past, Present and Future*, London: Jessica Kingsley Publishers.

Haigh, R. (2002) *Services for People with Personality Disorder: The Thoughts of Service Users*. Online. Available HTTP: http://www.dh.gov.uk/assetRoot/04/13/08/44/04130844.pdf (accessed 27 January 2007).

Haigh, R. (2006) 'People's experiences of having a diagnosis of personality disorder', in M.J. Sampson, P.A. McCubbin and P. Tyrer (eds) *Personality Disorder and Community Mental Health Teams: A Practitioner's Guide* (pp. 161–177), Chichester: Wiley.

Hanna, J. (2006a) 'Psychology on the wards', in Bright (2006) *Star Wards: Practical Ideas for Improving the Daily Experiences and Treatment Outcomes of Acute Mental Health Inpatients*, London: Bright.

Hanna, J. (2006b) 'The evidence base', in M. Janner (ed.) *Star Wards: Practical Ideas for Improving the Daily Experiences and Treatment Outcomes of Acute Mental Health In-patients* (pp. 26–29). Online. Available HTTP: http://www.brightplace.org.uk/pdfs/starwards.pdf (accessed 25 January 2007).

Harder, S. (2006) 'Self image and outcome in first-episode psychosis', *Clinical Psychology and Psychotherapy* 13: 285–296.

Hastings, R. and Remington, R. (1994) 'Rules of engagement: toward an analysis of staff responses to challenging behaviour', *Research in Developmental Disabilities* 14: 279–298.

Hayes, S., Strosahl, K.D. and Wilson, K.G. (1999) *Acceptance and Commitment Therapy*, New York: Guilford Press.

Hayward, M., Slade, M. and Moran, P.A. (2006) 'Personality disorders and unmet needs among psychiatric inpatients', *Psychiatric Services* 57: 538–543.

Hemsley, D.R. (1993) 'A simple (or simplistic?) cognitive model for schizophrenia', *Behaviour Research and Therapy* 31: 633–645.

Hinshelwood, R.D. (2002) 'The psychosocial process', in R.D. Hinshelwood and M. Chiesa (eds) *Organisations, Anxieties and Defences: Towards a Psychoanalytic Social Psychology*, London: Whurr.

Hinshelwood, R.D. and Chiesa, M. (2001) *Organisations, Anxieties and Defense: Towards a Psychoanalytic Social Psychology*, London: Whurr.

Hinshelwood, R.D. and Skogstad, W. (2000) 'The dynamics of healthcare institutions', in R.D. Hinshelwood and W. Skogstad (eds) *Observing Organisations: Anxiety, Defence and Culture in Health Care*, Hove, UK: Brunner Routledge.

Hoge, M.A., Tondora, J. and Marrelli, A.F. (2005) 'The fundamentals of workforce competency: implications for behavioural health', *Administration and Policy in Mental Health and Mental Health Services Research* 32: 509–531.

Holmes, J. (2002) 'Acute wards: problems and solutions. Creating a therapeutic culture in acute psychiatric wards', *Psychiatric Bulletin* 26: 383–385.

Hull, J.W., Yeomans, F., Clarkin, J., Li, C. and Goodman, G. (1996) 'Factors associated with multiple hospitalizations of patients with borderline personality disorder', *Psychiatric Services* 47: 638–641.

Ironbar, N. and Hooper, A. (1989) *Self Instruction in Mental Health Nursing*, London: Ballière-Tindall.

Jackson, M.C. (1997) 'Benign schizotypy? The case of spiritual experience', in G.S. Claridge (ed.) *Schizotypy. Relations to Illness and Health*, Oxford: Oxford University Press.

Jackson, M.C. (2001) 'Psychotic and spiritual experience: a case study comparison', in I. Clarke (ed.) *Psychosis and Spirituality: Exploring the New Frontier*, London: Whurr.

Jacobson, N. and Greenley, D. (2001) 'What is recovery? A conceptual model and explication', *Psychiatric Services* 2: 482–485.

Johns, C. (1995) 'Framing learning through reflection within Carper's fundamental ways of knowing in nursing', *Journal of Advanced Nursing* 22: 226–234.

Johns, C. (1996) 'Visualizing and realizing caring in practice through guided reflection', *Journal of Advanced Nursing* 22: 226–234.

Katz, D. and Khan, R.L. (1966) *The Social Psychology of Organisations*, New York: Wiley.

Kennedy, F.C., Smalley, M. and Harris, T. (2003) 'Developing inpatient clinical psychology services, an account and audit', *Clinical Psychology* 30: 29–35.

Kent, M. (2005) 'Protected therapeutic engagement time', *Mental Health Practice* 8: 8–22.

Kinderman, P. (2005a) 'A psychological model of mental disorder', *Harvard Review of Psychiatry* 13: 206–217.

Kinderman, P. (2005b) 'Delivering psychological therapies in acute inpatient settings', in P. Campling, S. Davies and G. Farquharson (eds) *From Toxic Institutions to Therapeutic Environments: Residential Settings in Mental Health Services*, London: Gaskell.

Kinderman, P. (2007) 'Reforms to the Mental Health Act and implications for psychologists', *Issues in Forensic Psychology* 6: 86–91.

Kinderman, P. and Tai, S. (2006) 'Clinical implications of a psychological model of mental disorder', *Behavioural and Cognitive Psychotherapy* 35: 1–14.

Kinderman, P., Sellwood W. and Tai, S. (in press) 'Service implications of a psychological model of mental disorder', *Journal of Mental Health*.

Kingdon, D., Siddle, R. and Rathod, S. (2001) 'Spirituality, psychosis and the development of normalizing rationales', in I. Clarke (ed.) *Psychosis and Spirituality: Exploring the New Frontier*, London: Whurr.

Kolb, D. (1983) *Experiential Learning: Experience as the Source of Learning and Development*, London: FT Press.

Krawitz, R. and Batcheler, M. (2006) 'Borderline personality disorder: a pilot survey about clinician views on defensive practice', *Australasian Psychiatry* 14: 320–322.

Kröger, C., Schweiger, U., Sipos, V., Arnold, R., Kahl, K.G., Schunert, T., *et al.* (2006) 'Effectiveness of dialectical behaviour therapy for borderline personality disorder in an inpatient setting', *Behaviour Research and Therapy* 44: 1211–1217.

Labour Party (2005) *Britain Forward not Back: The Labour Party Manifesto 2005*, London: The Labour Party.

Lavender, T. (2003) 'Redressing the balance: the place, history and future of reflective practice in clinical training', *Clinical Psychology* 27: 11–15.

Lavender, T. and Paxton, R. (2004) *Estimating the Applied Psychology Demand in Adult Mental Health*, Leicester: British Psychological Society.

Layard, R. (2004) *Mental Health: Britain's Biggest Social Problem?*, London: Cabinet Office Strategy Unit. Online. Available on HTTP: http://www.strategy. gov.uk/downloads/files/mh_layard.pdf (accessed December 2004).

Layard, R. (2005) *Sainsbury Centre Lecture: Therapy for All on the NHS*, London: SCMH.

Layard, R. (2006) 'The case for psychological treatment centres', *British Medical Journal* 33: 1030–1032.

Leahy, R. (2005) 'A social-cognitive model of validation', in P. Gilbert (ed.) *Compassion: Conceptualizations, Research and the Use in Psychotherapy*, London: Routledge.

Leichsenring, F. and Leibing, E. (2003) 'The effectiveness of psychodynamic and cognitive behaviour therapy in the treatment of personality disorders: a meta-analysis', *American Journal of Psychiatry* 160: 1223–1232.

Linehan, M. (1993a) *Cognitive Behavioural Treatment of Borderline Personality Disorder*, New York: Guilford Press.

Linehan, M. (1993b) *Skills Training Manual for Treating Borderline Personality Disorder*, New York: Guilford Press.

Lynch, T.R., Chapman, A.L., Rosentahl, M.Z., Kuo, J.R. and Linehan, M. (2006) 'Mechanisms of change in dialectical behaviour therapy: theoretical and empirical observations', *Journal of Clinical Psychology* 62: 459–480.

McCann, E. and Bowers, L. (2005) 'Training in cognitive behavioural interventions on acute psychiatric inpatient wards', *Journal of Psychiatric and Mental Health Nursing* 12: 215–222.

McGowan, J. (2007) 'Acute psychiatric wards: a good place for research?', conference presentation, Fifth World Congress of Behaviour and Cognitive Therapies, Barcelona.

McLeod, H., Deane, F.P. and Hogbin, B. (2002) 'Changing staff attitudes and empathy for working with people with psychosis', *Behavioural and Cognitive Psychotherapy* 30: 459–470.

Magliano, L., Fiorillo, A., Fadden, G., Gair, F., Economou, M., Kallert, T. *et al.* (2005) 'Effectiveness of a psychoeducational intervention for families of patients with schizophrenia: preliminary results of a study funded by the European Commission', *World Psychiatry* 4, 1: 45–49.

Manpower Advisory Service (MAS, 1989) *Review of Clinical Psychology Services*, Cheltenham: MAS.

Martin, T. (1992) 'Psychiatric nurses' use of working time', *Nursing Standards* 6: 34–36.

Mental Health Foundation, Mind, Sainsbury Centre for Mental Health, Rethink and Young Minds (2006) *We Need to Talk*, London: Mind.

Meyer, V. and Turkat, I.D. (1979) 'Behavioural analysis of clinical cases', *Journal of Behavioural Assessment* 1: 259–270.

Michie, S. and Johnston, M. (2004) 'Changing clinical behaviour by making guidelines specific', *British Medical Journal* 328: 343–345.

Miller, W.R. and Rollnick, S. (1991) *Motivational Interviewing*, London: Guilford Press.

Millon, T. (1997) *Millon Clinical Multiaxial Inventory – III Manual*, 2nd edn, Minneapolis: National Computer Systems.

Mind (2004) *Ward Watch: Mind's Campaign to Improve Hospital Conditions for Mental Health Patients*, London: Mind.

Moorey, J., Davidson, K., Evans, M. and Feigenbaum, J. (2006) 'Psychological theories regarding the development of personality disorders', in M.J. Sampson,

P.A. McCubbin and P. Tyrer (eds) *Personality Disorder and Community Mental Health Teams: A Practitioner's Guide* (pp. 91–123), Chichester: Wiley.

Moran, P. (2002) *The Epidemiology of Personality Disorder*. Online. Available HTTP: http://www.dh.gov.uk/assetRoot/04/13/08/45/04130845.pdf (accessed 27 January 2007).

Morrison, A.P. (1998) 'A cognitive analysis of the maintenance of auditory hallucinations: are voices to schizophrenia what bodily sensations are to panic?', *Behavioural and Cognitive Psychotherapy* 26: 289–303.

Morrison, A.P. (2001) 'The interpretation of intrusions in psychosis: an integrative cognitive approach to hallucinations and delusions', *Behavioural and Cognitive Psychotherapy* 29: 257–277.

Morrison, A.P., Renton, J.C., Dunn, H., Williams, S. and Bentall, R.P. (2004) *Cognitive Therapy for Psychosis: A Formulation Based Approach*, Hove, UK: Brunner-Routledge.

Morrison, N. (2001) 'Group cognitive therapy: treatment of choice or sub-optimal option?', *Behavioural and Cognitive Psychotherapy* 29: 311–332.

Munro, S.L., Baker, J.A. and Playle, J. (2005) 'Cognitive behaviour therapy within acute mental health care: A critical appraisal', *International Journal of Mental Health Nursing* 14, 2: 96–102. Online. Available HTTP: http://www.blackwell-synergy.com/doi/full/10.1111/j.1440-0979.2005.00365.x.

Myin-Germeys, I., Delespaul, P.A.E.G. and deVries, M.W. (2000) 'Schizophrenia patients are more "emotionally active" than is assumed based on their behaviour', *Schizophrenia Bulletin* 26, 4: 847–878.

National Institute for Clinical Excellence (NICE, 2002) *Schizophrenia: Core Interventions in the Treatment and Management of Schizophrenia in Primary and Secondary Care*, London: NICE.

National Institute for Clinical Excellence (NICE, 2004a) *Anxiety: Management of Anxiety in Adults in Primary, Secondary and Community Care*, London: NICE.

National Institute for Clinical Excellence (NICE, 2004b) *Depression: Management of Depression in Primary and Secondary Care*, London: NICE.

National Institute for Clinical Excellence (NICE, 2004c) *Eating Disorders: Core Interventions in the Treatment and Management of Anorexia Nervosa, Bulimia Nervosa and Related Eating Disorders*, London: NICE.

National Institute for Clinical Excellence (NICE, 2004d) *Self-Harm: The Short-term Physical and Psychological Management and Secondary Prevention of Self-harm in Primary and Secondary Care*, London: NICE.

National Institute for Clinical Excellence (NICE, 2005a) *Anxiety: Management of Post-traumatic Stress Disorder in Adults in Primary, Secondary and Community Care*, London: NICE.

National Institute for Clinical Excellence (NICE, 2005b) *Obsessive Compulsive Disorder: Core Interventions in the Treatment of Obsessive Compulsive Disorder and Body Dysmorphic Disorder*, London: NICE.

National Institute for Clinical Excellence (NICE, 2005c) *Short-term Management of Disturbed/Violent Behaviour*, London: NICE.

National Institute for Clinical Excellence (NICE, 2006) *The Management of Bipolar Disorder in Adults, Children and Adolescents in Primary and Secondary Care*, London: NICE.

National Institute for Mental Health in England (NIMHE, 2003a) *Personality Disorder: No Longer a Diagnosis of Exclusion*, London: NIMHE.

National Institute for Mental Health in England (NIMHE, 2003b) *Breaking the Cycle of Rejection: The Personality Disorder Capabilities Framework*, London: NIMHE.

National Institute for Mental Health in England (NIMHE, 2004a) *Acute Inpatient Mental Health Care*, London: NIMHE.

National Institute for Mental Health in England (NIMHE, 2004b) *Education and Training of Inpatient Staff*, London: NIMHE.

National Institute for Mental Health in England (NIMHE, 2004c) *Emerging Best Practices in Mental Health Recovery*, London: NIMHE.

National Institute for Mental Health in England (NIMHE, 2004d) *The Ten Essential Shared Capabilities: A Framework for the Whole of the Mental Health Workforce*, London: NIMHE.

National Institute for Mental Health in England (NIMHE, 2005a) *Guidance on New Ways of Working for Psychiatrists in a Multi-disciplinary and Multi-agency Context*, London: NIMHE.

National Institute for Mental Health in England (NIMHE, 2005b) *NIMHE Guiding Statement on Recovery*, London: NIMHE.

Nicholson, J.M. and Carradice, A. (2002) 'Clinical psychology provision for inpatient settings: a challenge in team working?', *Clinical Psychology* 18: 25–30.

O'Brien, L. and Flote, J. (1997) 'Providing nursing care for a patient with borderline personality disorder on an acute inpatient unit: a phenomenological study', *Australia and New Zealand Journal of Mental Health Nursing* 6: 137–147.

Ogden, T.H. (1983) 'The concept of internal object relations', *International Journal of Psychoanalysis* 64: 227–241.

Onyett, S. (2004) 'The joy of wading: leadership and team working in swampy conditions', *Mental Health Review* 9, 3: 35–41.

Overall, J. and Gorham, D. (1962) 'The Brief Psychiatric Rating Scale', *Psychological Reports* 10: 799–812.

Owens, R.G. and Ashcroft, J.B. (1982) 'Functional analysis in applied psychology', *British Journal of Clinical Psychology* 21: 181–189.

Padesky, C. (1996) 'Developing cognitive therapist competency: teaching and supervision models', in P. Salkovskis (ed.) *Frontiers of Cognitive Therapy*, New York: Guilford Press.

Paget, T. (2001) 'Reflective practice and clinical outcomes: practitioners' views on how reflective practice has influenced their clinical practice', *Journal of Clinical Nursing* 10: 204–214.

Paris, J. (2004) 'Is hospitalization useful for suicidal patients with borderline personality disorder', *Journal of Personality Disorders* 18: 240–247.

Pearson, D., Burrow, A. FitzGerald, C., Green, K., Lee, G. and Wise, N. (2001) 'Auditory hallucinations in normal child populations', *Personality and Individual Differences* 31: 401–407.

Persons, J.B. (1989) *Cognitive Therapy in Practice: A Case Formulation Approach*, New York: Norton.

Persons, J.B. and Bertognolli, A. (1999) 'Inter-rater reliability of cognitive-behavioural case formulations of depression: a replication', *Cognitive Therapy and Research* 23: 271–283.

Pidd, H. (2006) 'A little more conversation', *The Guardian*. Online. Available on HTTP: http://www.guardian.co.uk/g2/story/0,,1809389,00.html (accessed 30 June 2006).

Pilgrim, D. (2002) 'The biopsychosocial model in Anglo-American psychiatry: past, present and future?', *Journal of Mental Health* 11: 585–594.

Prochaska, J.O., Norcross, J.C. and DiClemente, C.C. (1994) *Changing for Good*, New York: Avalon.

Rachlin, S. (1984) 'Double jeopardy: suicide and malpractice', *General Hospital Psychiatry* 6: 249–257.

Rathbone, G. and Campling, P. (2005) 'Psychotherapeutic approaches on acute wards', *Psychiatry* 4: 14–18.

Read, J. (2005) 'The bio-bio-bio model of madness', *The Psychologist* 18: 596–597.

Repper, J. and Perkins, R. (2003) *Social Inclusion and Recovery: A Model for Mental Health Practice*, London: Baillière-Tindall.

Robbins, C.J. and Chapman, A.L. (2004) 'Dialectical behaviour therapy: current status, recent developments, and future directions', *Journal of Personality Disorders* 18: 73–89.

Robinson, D. (1996a) 'Measuring psychiatric nursing interventions: how much care is individualized?', *Nursing Times Research* 1: 13–21.

Robinson, D. (1996b) 'Observing and describing nursing interactions', *Nursing Standard* 13: 34–38.

Romme, M. and Escher, S. (1989) *Accepting Voices*, London: Mind Publications.

Rosenberg, M., Schooler, C., Schoenbach, C. and Rosenberg, F. (1995) 'Global self-esteem and specific self-esteem: different concepts, different outcomes', *American Sociological Review* 60, 1: 141–156.

Ross, D. (1990) 'Programmatic structures for the preparation of the reflective practitioner', in R.T. Cliff, W.R. Houston and M.C. Pugach (eds) *Encouraging Reflective Practice in Education*, New York: Teachers College Press.

Ryle, A. (1995) *Cognitive Analytic Therapy*, Chichester: Wiley.

Ryle, A. (1997) *Cognitive Analytic Therapy and Borderline Personality Disorder: The Model and the Method*, Chichester: Wiley.

Ryle, A. (2004) 'The contribution of cognitive analytic therapy to the treatment of borderline personality disorders', *Journal of Personality Disorders* 18: 3–35.

Safran, J. (1990) 'Towards a refinement of cognitive therapy in light of interpersonal theory', *Clinical Psychology Review* 10: 87–121.

Sainsbury Centre for Mental Health (SCMH, 1997) *A One-day Visit to 309 Acute Psychiatric Wards by the Mental Health Act Commission in collaboration with The Sainsbury Centre for Mental Health*, London: SCMH.

Sainsbury Centre for Mental Health (SCMH, 1998) *Acute Problems: A Survey of the Quality of Care in Acute Psychiatric Wards*, London: SCMH.

Sainsbury Centre for Mental Health (SCMH, 2001) *The Capable Practitioner*, London: SCMH.

Sainsbury Centre for Mental Health (SCMH, 2002) *An Executive Briefing on Adult Acute Inpatient Care for People with Mental Health Problems*, London: SCMH.

Sainsbury Centre for Mental Health (SCMH, 2005) *Acute Care 2004: A National Survey of Adult Psychiatric Wards in England*, London: SCMH.

Sainsbury Centre for Mental Health (SCMH, 2006a) *Choice in Mental Health: Briefing Paper 31*, London. SCMH.

Sainsbury Centre for Mental Health (SCMH, 2006b) *The Search for Acute Solutions: Improving the Quality of Care in Acute Psychiatric Wards*, London: SCMH.

Salkovskis, P.M. (1985) 'Obsessional-compulsive problems: a cognitive-behavioural analysis', *Behaviour Research and Therapy* 23: 311–313.

Sambrook, S., Abba, N. and Chadwick, P. (2006) 'Evaluation of DBT emotional coping skills groups for people with parasuicidal behaviours', *Behavioural and Cognitive Psychotherapy* 35: 241–244.

Schon, D.A. (1983) *The Reflective Practitioner*, London: Basic Books.

Schon, D.A. (1987) *Educating the Reflective Practitioner*, Oxford: Jossey Bass.

Schon, D.A. (1991) *The Reflective Practitioner*, 2nd edn, San Francisco: Jossey Bass.

Schore, A.N. (1994) *Affect Regulation and the Origins of the Self: The Neurobiology of Emotional Development*, Hillsdale, NJ: Lawrence Erlbaum Associates, Inc.

Schore, A.N. (2001) 'The effects of early relational trauma on right brain development, affect regulation and infant mental health', *Infant Mental Health Journal* 22: 201–269.

Segal, Z.V., Williams, J.M. and Teasdale J.D. (2000) *Mindfulness-Based Cognitive Therapy for Depression: A New Approach to Relapse Prevention*, New York: Guilford Press.

Shaffer, C.S., Shapiro, J., Sank, L.I. and Coghlan, D.J. (1981) 'Positive changes in depression, anxiety and assertion following individual and group cognitive behavioural intervention', *Cognitive Therapy and Research* 5: 149–157.

Shepherd, E. and Rosebert, C. (2007) 'Setting up and evaluating a reflective practice group', *Clinical Psychology Forum* 172: 31–34.

Simon, G.E., Katon, W.J., Von Korff, M., Unutzer, J., Lin, E.H.B., Walker, E.A. *et al.* (2001) 'Cost-effectivenesss of a collaborative care programme for primary care patients with persistent depression', *American Journal of Psychiatry* 158: 1638–1644.

Slade, P. (1982) 'Towards a functional analysis of anorexia nervosa and bulimia nervosa', *British Journal of Clinical Psychology* 21: 167–179.

Sullivan, P. (1994) 'Recovery from schizophrenia: what we can learn from the developing nations', *Innovations and Research in Clinical Services, Community Support, and Rehabilitation* 3, 2: 7–15.

Swenson, C., Sanderson, C., Dulit, R. and Linehan, M. (2001) 'The application of dialectical behaviour therapy for clients with borderline personality disorder on inpatient units', *Psychiatric Quarterly* 72: 307–324.

Tarrier, N. (2002) 'The use of coping strategies and self-regulation in the treatment of psychosis', in A. Morrison (ed.) *A Casebook of Cognitive Therapy for Psychosis*, Hove, UK: Brunner-Routledge.

Tarrier, N. and Calam, R. (2002) 'New developments in cognitive-behavioural case formulation. Epidemiological, systemic and social context: an integrative approach', *Behavioural and Cognitive Psychotherapy* 30: 311–328.

Teasdale, J.D. and Barnard, P.J. (1993) *Affect, Cognition and Change: Remodelling Depressive Thought*, Hove, UK: Lawrence Erlbaum Associates Ltd.

Teasdale, J.D. and Cox, S.G. (2001) 'Dysphoria: self de-valuative and affective components in recovered depressed and never depressed controls', *Psychological Medicine* 31: 1311–1316.

Tucker, M. and Oei, T.P.S. (2007) 'Is group more cost effective than individual cognitive behaviour therapy? The evidence is not solid yet', *Behavioural and Cognitive Psychotherapy* 35: 77–91.

Turpin, T., Hope, R., Duffy, R., Fossey, M. and Seward, J. (2006) 'Improving access to psychological therapies: implications for the mental health workforce', *Journal of Mental Health Workforce Development* 1, 2: 7–15.

Tyson, G.A., Lambert, W.G. and Beattie, L. (1995) 'The quality of psychiatric nurses' interactions with patients: an observational study', *International Journal of Nursing Studies* 32: 49–58.

Van Manen, M. (1991) *The Tact of Teaching*, New York: State of University of New York Press.

Vaslamatzis, G., Coccossis, M., Zervis, C., Panagiotopoulou, V. and Chatziandreou, M. (2004) *Bulletin of the Menninger Clinic* 68: 337–349.

Watkins, J. (1996) *Living with Schizophrenia. An Holistic Approach to Understanding, Preventing and Recovering from Negative Symptoms*, Melbourne: Hill of Content.

Wells, A. (1997) *Cognitive Therapy of Anxiety Disorders: A Practice Manual and Conceptual Guide*, Chichester: Wiley.

Wheeler, M.A., Stuss, D.T. and Tulving, E. (1997) 'Towards a theory of episodic memory: the frontal lobes and autonoetic consciousness', *Psychological Bulletin* 121: 331–354.

Whittington, D. and McLaughlin, C. (2000) 'Finding time for patients: an exploration of nurses' time allocation in an acute psychiatric setting', *Journal of Psychiatric and Mental Health Nursing* 7: 259–268.

Whyte, L. and Brooker, C. (2001) 'Working with multidisciplinary teams in secure psychiatric environments', *Journal of Psychosocial Nursing and Mental Health Services* 39, 9: 26–34.

Wilkinson, J. (1999) 'Implementing reflective practice', *Nursing Standard* 10, 13: 36–39.

Williams, L. (1998) 'Personal accounts: a "classic" case of borderline personality disorder', *Psychiatric Services* 49: 173–174.

Wing, J., Curtis, R. and Beavor, A. (1994) 'Measuring mental health outcomes', *Psychiatric Bulletin* 18: 680–691.

World Health Organization (WHO, 1953) *Expert Committee on Mental Health: 3rd Report*, Geneva: WHO.

World Health Organization (WHO, 1992) *International Classification of Mental and Behavioural Disorders (ICD-10)*, Geneva: WHO.

Yalom, I.D. (1983) *Inpatient Group Psychotherapy*, New York: Basic Books.

Young, J.E. (1990) *Cognitive Therapy for Personality Disorders: A Schema-Focused Approach*, Sarasota FL: Professional Resource Press.

Young, J.E. (1994) *Cognitive Therapy for Personality Disorders: A Schema Focused Approach*, rev. edn, Sarasota FL: Professional Resource Press.

Index

Note: page numbers in **bold** refer to figures and tables.

wise mind 68, 72, 73, 79, 86, 176–7
withdrawal 69, 87
women: and reflective practice groups
    122; *see also* female patients; female
    wards
Woodhaven Adult Mental Health Unit
    66, 70–1, 163, 168, 174, 179–80,
    185–90, 192–4, 197
Workforce Development Consortium 5
working alliance 190–2

workshops (training) 154–6; CBT and
    working with depression 154, 155;
    CBT and working with psychosis
    154, 156; introduction to clinical
    skills 154–5
World Health Organization (WHO) 116
world views 56, 89, 91

Yalom, I.D. 103
Young, J.E. 49